TOURO COLLEGE LIBRARY
Kings Hwy

WITHDRAWN

Vouchers within Reason

Vouchers within Reason

A CHILD-CENTERED APPROACH
TO EDUCATION REFORM

JAMES G. DWYER

TOURO COLLEGE LIBRARY
Kings Hwy

Cornell University Press

Ithaca and London

KH

To my wife

Copyright © 2002 by Cornell University

All rights reserved. Except for brief quotations in a review, this book, or
parts thereof, must not be reproduced in any form without permission in
writing from the publisher. For information, address Cornell University
Press, Sage House, 512 East State Street, Ithaca, New York 14850.

First published 2002 by Cornell University Press

Printed in the United States of America

Library of Congress Cataloging-in-Publication Data
Dwyer, James G., 1961–
    Vouchers within reason : a child-centered approach to education
reform / James G. Dwyer.
        p.   cm.
    Includes bibliographical references and index.
    ISBN 0-8014-3948-5 (alk. paper)
    1. Educational vouchers—Law and legislation—United States.
2. Educational vouchers—United States.   3. School choice—United
States.   I. Title.
    KF4137 .D98 2002
    379.1′11′0973—dc21   2001002973

Cornell University Press strives to use environmentally responsible
suppliers and materials to the fullest extent possible in the publishing
of its books. Such materials include vegetable-based, low-VOC inks
and acid-free papers that are recycled, totally chlorine-free, or partly
composed of nonwood fibers. For further information, visit our website
at www.cornellpress.cornell.edu.

Cloth printing   10 9 8 7 6 5 4 3 2 1

FSC FSC Trademark © 1996 Forest Stewardship Council A.C.
        SW-COC-098   ® GCU

10/25/04

Contents

Acknowledgments

I began writing this work while at the University of Wyoming College of Law, with financial support from the law school's George William Hopper Faculty Research Fund. I am grateful to Dean Jerry Parkinson and to all my former colleagues at Wyoming for their support, encouragement, and camaraderie. Thanks also to Robert Hoban for his excellent research assistance.

I completed the book at the Marshall-Wythe School of Law at the College of William and Mary. Many thanks to Dean Taylor Reveley for his provision of generous research funding, and to all my new colleagues for their interest in and insights into this work. Special thanks to Dave Douglas for inviting me to give a presentation on this topic at a William and Mary Bill of Rights Institute conference. Thanks also to Natalie Collins for her excellent research assistance.

I received very helpful comments on drafts of portions of this book from Peter Alces, Brian Bix, Harry Brighouse, Neil Devins, Brian Feldman, Alan Meese, Catherine Ross, Joel Selig, and Cynthia Ward.

Much of Chapter 2 is adapted from "Changing the Conversation about Children's Education," which appeared in *NOMOS XLIII: Moral and Political Education*, eds. Stephen Macedo and Yael Tamir (2001) and is reprinted with the permission of New York University Press.

Introduction

In American political and legal discourse today, the prevailing perspectives regarding state involvement in child rearing are adult-centered—that is, they look to the interests of adults first to determine whether particular policies are good or bad, and they look to the interests of children only secondarily or not at all. Politicians, academics, and the general public, despite their recurrent preoccupation with children's education, manifest little genuine concern for the welfare of the individual children whose lives are at stake. If they take any interest in the kind of upbringing children other than their own receive, it is because of the ways children's upbringing might affect particular groups of adults—in particular, parents—or affect society as a whole. Are children receiving the kind of upbringing their parents want them to receive? Will today's schools create the right kind of citizens and laborers for our society and our economy, and minimize the number of people who become sociopaths or social burdens? Does education policy comport with the right of taxpayers not to support particular forms of schooling? The well-being of the individual children immediately affected by education policy seldom captures serious attention; at best it is cited to add rhetorical force to arguments for positions motivated by other concerns. Nowhere is this more evident than in the current debate about school vouchers.

Political momentum for school vouchers today is huge. There are still few voucher programs in place, but proposals for new voucher programs have been on the legislative agenda in every state and in the federal government. Vouchers were a major issue in the 2000 presidential election, and voucher supporters at the state and national levels rejoiced at the victory of George W. Bush, a strong supporter of vouchers and a president likely to select Supreme Court

[1]

justices who would uphold voucher programs against constitutional attack. Voucher programs and other strategies for directing public funds to private schools are therefore likely to proliferate. Vouchers have become the cure of the day for what ails our education system, eclipsing in the public imagination other innovations such as magnet schools and charter schools.

School vouchers are revolutionary both conceptually and in their potential impact. They represent the first major government education reform that entails looking elsewhere than the public school system to deliver elementary and secondary education. If adopted universally, voucher programs could transform the basic structure of our educational system, moving us toward a regime in which private schools educate as many children as do public schools, and perhaps even toward a regime in which the state no longer operates schools of its own. Unsurprisingly, then, vouchers have been enormously contentious. Debate over the policy and legal issues they raise has been extensive and heated. Unfortunately, the welfare of the children whose lives would be directly affected does not appear foremost in the minds of those participating in this debate, both those for and those against vouchers. As explained below, the most common arguments for and against vouchers—even those that emphasize the plight of children in poor urban areas—are adult-centered ones, motivated principally by concern for the interests of adults. As a result, there is little reason to expect the outcome of the debate will be one that is good for children, and much reason for concern that it will be bad for children.

The adult-centered nature of reasoning about child rearing is evident in discussion of many other topics of popular interest as well. For example, why is it that people get so worked up about prayer in public schools? Is it really out of concern for the welfare of children? Is there any reason to believe excluding *or* including prayer at the beginning of the school day is inherently harmful to children? Has any individual, after being educated in the public schools, complained that his life went awry because he did not have the experience of group prayer at the beginning of each school day? On the other hand, while it is certainly true that prayer done in a certain way can make children of adherents to minority faiths uncomfortable, and that in an overall climate of religious bigotry organized prayer can contribute to a child's experience of oppression and exclusion, is school prayer in and of itself harmful? Opponents of prayer in public schools object, as a matter of principle, to prayer under any circumstances and no matter how it is done. This is largely because prayer might constitute an influence on children's religious belief that competes with parents' influence. There is also simply a fair amount of hostility in our society toward the particular religious groups—most commonly Fundamentalist Christians—that push for school prayer. Opponents of prayer in public schools speak of coercion of belief by the majority or by the state, yet clearly they do not object to coercion of children's religious beliefs as a general matter, because they typically support parents' rights to indoctrinate their own children, at home or in private schools. Prayer in public schools is seen as bad principally because it might undermine the ability of Jewish parents to ensure that their children become Jewish and the ability of Catholic parents to ensure that their children become Catholic. The debate over school prayer is thus much more a battle for adult control of children' minds than a difference of opinion concerning the developmental needs of children.

The same is true of controversies over "liberal programs" such as values curricula and condom distribution in public schools. The impetus in favor of these programs does not arise principally, if at all, from a concern that individual children in school today will live unfulfilling, because unexamined, lives, or that some will never realize their human potential because saddled with the burdens of child rearing. Rather, the arguments advanced in support of these programs suggest a concern principally that the rest of us will suffer from higher crime rates and higher taxes if the next generation lacks proper values and swells the welfare rolls. On the other side, objections to having such programs in public schools rest primarily on parents' rights to govern their children's lives, rather than on evidence that children are harmed by critical examination of their values or by the availability of contraceptives. Certainly some parents fear for their own children's welfare if the children come to question the parents' values or somehow get the message that extramarital sex is acceptable. But for those who oppose these programs in public debates, it is irrelevant as a legal and public policy matter whether those parents' views are correct. What is really at stake is parents' exclusive dominion over matters of morality, and that, they contend, is a God-given right, not susceptible to government override on the grounds that parents' views rest on false empirical assumptions or illogical reasoning.

The adult-centered nature of thinking about child rearing is hardly confined to schooling issues. It is pervasive, infecting public deliberation about almost every aspect of child rearing. Consider the recent court battle over the power of the Boy Scouts of America (BSA) to exclude homosexuals from the scoutmaster ranks, in contravention of a state statute prohibiting discrimination on the basis of sexual orientation in employment.[1] The legal issue was framed as one pitting an organization's right to freedom of "expressive association" against an individual's right to equal employment opportunity. Never mind that scouting is a child-rearing activity, and that BSA's policies concerning scoutmasters might affect the welfare of the boys participating in the organization—for example, by determining the quality of troop leaders, the kind of role models the boys have, and the messages sent to boys (some of whom, undoubtedly, are gay) concerning the worth and dignity of persons. According to the courts, the parties to the litigation, and public commentators, this dispute was solely about the right of the adults who direct the BSA to send a particular message to the

[3]

world and to the boys in the organization, and about the right of an adult individual to pursue an avocation. The fact that BSA's directors never polled the organization's members—that is, the boys—for their views on gay scoutmasters, and the fact that the organization's members are, as a legal and practical matter, not fully autonomous, did not prevent anyone from conceptualizing this as a case about freedom of expressive association. What the boys wanted and what was best for the boys were implicitly deemed irrelevant. The boys were treated as merely instruments for the realization of the competing aims of adults.

Apart from particular controversies, there is a troubling and paradoxical self-centeredness to our general cultural discourse about the way children are raised. We want today's young generation to acquire good values and complain that they appear self-centered, but what motivates our desires and complaints is not care about the well-being of today's children; it is concern for our own well-being. What kinds of people will I have to deal with in the future? Will I have to worry more about crime? Will I have to pay higher taxes because more people will be on welfare? Will the institutions I cherish deteriorate or be defiled? Will my conception of the good continue to govern social institutions? Will I or my children have to deal with bigots or godless individualists? The paradox is that in our very complaints about the self-centeredness and callousness of today's youth, self-centeredness and instrumental treatment of others are precisely what we model. We are dismayed when young people act with seeming disregard for the value of others' lives and experiences, yet that is what we do when we treat children's lives as in the service of our good. If we want the next generation to care about others, we should begin caring about them, and not just our own offspring but all children. If we want today's youth to value service to others, we should put ourselves in service to them and show them how much *we* value service to others, rather than valuing only service given to us. There is no needier group in our society than children, especially the millions of children living in poverty. If we put our own interests above theirs, if we think of our own well-being before we think of theirs, then we cannot reasonably expect them to care about anyone but themselves as they grow into adults.

The first order of business in this book is to demonstrate that we adults need to reform ourselves before we undertake to reform our schools or to make any other important public policy decisions regarding the lives of today's children. We need to recognize and reject adult-centered ways of thinking about child rearing, and to adopt instead a child-centered perspective. A child-centered perspective operates from the fundamental premise that children are persons, distinct from their parents and from any other adults who seek power over their lives, and that as persons children are entitled to have their individual interests receive full consideration in state decision making. This perspective dictates that we first look to see how alternative policy proposals concerning child-rearing practices would affect the well-being of the children upon whom they would operate, because it presumes that children, rather than any group of adults, have the most important interests at stake in connection with their own upbringing. It also presumes, on that same basis, that these children are entitled to have their interests control the outcome of policy deliberations. Thus, anyone who advances a position on any child-rearing policy would have to demonstrate first how that position would affect the lives of individual children. Then, to the extent the position rests on any interests or alleged rights of any group of adults, such as parents, that might conflict with children's welfare, its proponent would be under the burden of demonstrating that the adults' interests are actually more important than the children's interests. Absent such a showing, the interests and rights of adults would be subordinated to those of the children.

In other words, a child-centered approach to government policies concerning child-rearing activities, such as schooling, would accord to children the same respect the legal system now accords to other groups of nonautonomous persons, such as permanently mentally disabled adults. When we establish policies governing the lives of mentally handicapped adults, we insist that their interests and rights receive highest priority. Children likewise deserve to be the focus of moral and legal attention in decision making about their lives. To whom the state will accord authority to make particular decisions in children's behalf, and what criteria the state will establish to evaluate exercise of such authority, should be decided first and foremost on the basis of what is best for children. Doing so would effect a major transformation of public debates about education reform and about other government policies affecting children.

Is it not the case, though, that the voucher debate, whatever its origins and whatever its character in years past, has become one about how best to further the developmental interests of children in poor urban areas? True, there are still objections by secularists who do not want any of their tax money going to religious institutions. True, there is much discussion of parental freedom, parents' entitlement to send their children to a school that will teach the parents' religion, and fairness to parents. But there is also much talk of the plight of children in urban public schools, and in fact voucher supporters have increasingly put forward the aim of saving these children as their reason for seeking to redirect state education funds to private schools. And no doubt many participants in the debate do genuinely care about the welfare of those children and believe something ought to be done for them. There are several reasons, though, why I doubt that the voiced concern for the plight of a group of children really signals a cultural transformation to child-centered thinking about education policy.

First, there is every reason to suspect that the principal advocates for vouchers have an ulterior motive in supporting current programs, which are limited

[5]

to the neediest children. The groups who started the voucher bandwagon rolling—conservative economists, the religious right, and Republican legislators—are ones that have in the past manifested little concern about the gross disparities in funding between poor urban public school districts and more affluent public school districts, and have in fact opposed measures to reduce those disparities. Jonathan Kozol's 1991 book *Savage Inequalities,* which documented the tremendous difference in resources between schools in poor urban areas and schools in nearby suburbs, has been widely and favorably cited among scholars, but has caused little stir in conservative economic, religious, or political circles. Yet the ways in which inadequate funding cripples public schools in poor urban areas are obvious.

Jobs for teachers and administrators in these schools typically pay substantially less than comparable jobs in suburban areas, despite the fact that teachers and administrators in poor urban areas must deal with a host of social ills that interfere with instruction—hunger, homelessness, drugs, violence, disease, teen pregnancy, transience, and so on. To work in these schools, teachers and administrators must either commute long distances or live in the same hellish neighborhoods from which their students come. And they must work in crumbling buildings with outdated and worn-out instructional equipment and inadequate supplies. The entirely predictable result of this situation is that schools in poor urban areas get the least qualified and least motivated teachers and administrators. If you are a good teacher or school administrator and can secure a position in a suburban school district with abundant resources, that is what you do, unless you are among the few extraordinary individuals willing to sacrifice a great deal of their own comfort and that of their families in order to tilt at windmills. With the least able teachers and administrators, the neediest children, and the most meager resources, these schools are doomed from the outset.

Given this reality, it is surprising these schools do not perform even worse than they currently do. And given this reality, it is hard to view as other than cynical arguments for state funding of private schooling coming from groups that never supported, and even opposed, better funding of public schools in these poor areas. It is hard to avoid the conclusion that the reasons many voucher proponents want funding for private schools have little to do with justice for disadvantaged children.[2] In fact, voucher progenitor Milton Friedman makes no secret of the fact that the ultimate aim is a "system of universal vouchers, available to all parents and usable at any school," and that programs for poor children are simply "an entering wedge."[3] Voucher proponents have already pushed for broader programs in several states, even succeeding in getting an initiative for a universal voucher program on the 2000 election ballot in California. Conservatives hope to use smaller existing programs to get favorable judicial precedent before transferring their attention to funding of private schools for wealthier families. My point is not that it would necessarily be a bad thing to expand voucher programs much more broadly, but rather that the real impetus for vouchers is likely not a sudden wave of sympathy for the children we as a society allow—and will continue to allow, irrespective of vouchers—to grow up in horrendous circumstances.[4] Were the courts to decide that vouchers are permissible *only* if limited to the poorest families in our society, we could expect support for vouchers largely to evaporate.

Second, the nature of the programs that voucher proponents support suggests a predominant purpose of supporting parental choice per se, and in particular religiously grounded choice, not children's well-being. The focus is on parental satisfaction rather than doing justice to children or promoting the developmental interests of children. All existing programs and all proposed programs give vouchers to parents who affirmatively seek them out—that is, to parents who have a sufficiently strong desire to transfer their children to private schools. No one even considers a program in which children are placed in superior private schools randomly or because they have the greatest educational need. In fact, the end result of current programs is that the public school students who move to private schools are those who on average one would expect to have the least need to move, at least if one assumes—as voucher supporters do—that when parents act they always do so consistently with their children's educational interests. These are the children whose parents presumably care the most about their education and / or are most capable of acting to effect what they believe to be in their children's educational interests, and who would therefore be more likely to advance the children's intellectual development in a number of other ways throughout the children's lives.[5]

A simple thought experiment demonstrates the truth of this claim that parental choice per se is the paramount aim for most voucher proponents. Imagine the following voucher program were proposed: 20 percent of children in failing public schools will automatically be enrolled in superior private schools at the beginning of the next school year, unless their parents have a strong objection to the transfer (as measured, perhaps, by their willingness to make an oral or written statement to a school superintendent). The 20 percent will be those who are doing the worst academically or those whom teachers determine are most likely to benefit from the transfer. Arguably, such a scheme would be the most just and would create the greatest gain in children's welfare overall. Children would benefit not as the result of the luck of having more concerned or resourceful parents, but as the result of having the greatest need. How much political support would such a program garner? Close to none, I suspect. What objections would current supporters of vouchers have to such a plan? Most likely they would object that some parents who want vouchers would not get them, while other parents who are indifferent get the vouchers. But that is not a child-centered objection. It is an objection grounded in a desire to gratify parents. Add to this hypothetical program a limitation that vouchers could be used only at nonreligious schools, and most current supporters would vehemently oppose the program, no matter how good the available nonreligious private schools were, because advancing parental religious aims and the conservative social and political worldview that many religious schools impart is of greatest importance to many voucher supporters.

A third indication that support for vouchers rests on adult-centered thinking is that few voucher supporters take the view that states should maintain current levels of funding, or even increase funding, of public schools following implementation of a voucher program. In the 2000 Democratic presidential primary campaign, Bill Bradley advanced this view, and a few of the hundreds of voucher proposals state legislatures have considered in recent years have embodied such a view. Otherwise there has been little support for the idea of maintaining or increasing the resources of public schools at the same time that states pay for children to attend private schools. Yet that would surely be best for the children who would remain in the public schools after vouchers are in place, who are likely to far outnumber those who transfer out. With the same total funding and fewer students, public schools could, at a minimum, lower class sizes. Everyone recognizes that reducing class sizes would help urban public schools. With *increased* funding, school districts could do much more. They could attract more and better teachers, not only with smaller classes but also with better compensation. They could repair old school buildings or construct new and better-designed ones. They could modernize equipment in classrooms. They could improve safety. They could hire teacher aides. They could provide universal preschool and after-school programs.

Yet voucher supporters manifest little interest in the fate of children whose parents do not act to move them to private schools. Somehow the concern for children in poor schools gets transmuted into a concern only for those whose parents want to remove them. Of course, hard-nosed critics of public schools will reply that there is no point in throwing good money after bad. Only the most cynical, though, would claim that increased funding for public schools would have no positive effect whatsoever. The lack of support for an approach to vouchers of the sort Bradley recommended thus bolsters the conclusion that the real aim of most voucher supporters is furthering adult interests, rather than doing whatever can be done to give all children in poor urban areas a fighting chance in life. Indeed, for many, *the* reason they support voucher programs has nothing to do with children—rather, they hope that moving children to private schools will lower their taxes. It is unsurprising, therefore, that they do not support an increase in total education spending.

Finally, one of the most disturbing aspects of the voucher debate is that voucher supporters manifest no interest in examining the practices of the private schools to which they would direct state money and to which they would have children transferred. If they were intent on doing right by children, they would urge that voucher programs should include only those private schools able to demonstrate that they provide, or will provide, a good education. Yet voucher proponents are generally opposed to attaching conditions to vouchers, some even to superficial prerequisites such as nondiscriminatory admissions and religious instruction opt-outs, let alone meaningful academic standards. It surely cannot be the case that academic accountability is a foreign concept to them. Today even politicians who know little about how schools operate compete with each other to appear toughest on public school accountability. Why do they never speak of private school accountability?

There is, to be sure, a widespread myth in this country that all private schools equal or outdo public schools academically. Supporters of vouchers are content to cite studies purporting to show equal or superior performance on standardized tests by students in private schools, while ignoring other studies and ignoring criticisms of the studies they cite—not just criticisms of the studies' methodologies, but also criticisms that the tests themselves are meaningless because they bear little or no relation to the cognitive skills children today need to acquire. On the basis of the studies they like, voucher supporters assert—illogically and irresponsibly—that parental choice of a private school necessarily equates to a superior education for a child. Yet it is inconceivable that anyone prominently involved in the voucher debate is unaware that there are many bad private schools in this country, just as there are bad public schools. If ensuring a good education for children were the genuine aim of voucher supporters, they would be intent on ensuring that children are not transferred from a bad public school to a bad private school. In fact, they would be intent on eliminating bad private (and public) schools altogether. But bad private schools are ones parents have chosen, typically for religious reasons, and from an adult-centered perspective that makes it irrelevant whether anyone other than the parents believes those schools are good for children. Misuse of test data thus serves as a smokescreen for conservatives' fundamental aim of increasing parental power over children's lives.

Opposition to vouchers is also beset with adult-centered thinking. I mention here only briefly the kinds of arguments advanced against school vouchers, because I ultimately come out, qualifiedly, in favor of vouchers and spend much of the book responding to antivoucher arguments. Legal challenges to vouchers have primarily rested on Establishment Clause claims by taxpayer groups, whose desire not to subsidize religious entities is clearly not a child-centered concern. Some might believe religious schooling is generally harmful to children, but such a belief is rarely if ever expressed in advocating against vouchers, and they cannot reasonably deny that some religious schools would be better for children than the public schools from which voucher students exit. In public debates, voucher opponents also express concern regarding the fate of public school systems. Sometimes the concern is that children left behind in public schools will suffer from the exodus of better students and from decreased funding for their schools. This concern *is* child centered and deserves serious consideration. Ultimately, I find it insufficient to make the antivoucher case, but it does support the case for a Bradley-type approach to reform through vouchers.

In some quarters, however—in particular, academic departments housing political theorists—concern regarding the fate of public education has more to do with societal aims not directly tied to the well-being of children. Political theorists and some public commentators fear that a retreat from the common school ideal will lead to a decline in "civic education," threaten liberal values such as toleration, and diminish citizen control over how the next generation is reared. As explained in Chapter 2, this concern arises out of a perspective that, just as much as a parents' rights perspective, treats children's lives instrumentally. The civic education perspective asks how children's collective upbringing can be used to secure certain goods for society as a whole, rather than how each child's upbringing enhances his or her chances for living a fulfilling and happy life. As such, it is not child centered.

A child-centered approach to the voucher issue would require a much different kind of analysis than either supporters or opponents now bring to the debate. It would require that any voucher proposal first be evaluated in terms of its costs and benefits for individual children and in terms of all children's rights relating to education. It would require that any proposed program be presumed unacceptable insofar as it would result in net harm to, or violation of the rights of, some children. It would thus require that most of the considerations that have until now dominated the discussion—parental freedom, religious pluralism, taxpayer rights, separation of church and state, and civic education—be subordinated to the interests and rights of the children whose lives vouchers would directly affect.

Such an analysis, this book shows, would generate startling conclusions. I conclude that it is not merely *permissible,* morally and constitutionally, for states to enact voucher programs, but in fact *mandatory.* It is mandatory not because of any supposed rights of parents who send, or want to send, their children to private schools. Nor is it mandatory because of the right of children in failing public schools to a better education. It is mandatory as a right of children who already attend private schools in the absence of vouchers. Children who are in religious and other private schools today, many of which strive to provide a good secular education but are severely hampered in doing so by inadequate resources, are entitled to share in state spending on education. When all is said and done, the analysis of this book shows, *that* is the best argument for school vouchers. Yet these children have remained virtually invisible in debates about vouchers.

This argument for vouchers appears plausible only after shifting the focus of moral attention from adults to children. One fact about religious and other private schools that is of critical importance to a normative assessment of voucher programs, yet is generally ignored, is that children who attend private schools are not responsible for the fact that they are attending those schools rather than a public school. The issue becomes somewhat complicated in the case of adolescents, but surely children first entering school are not making the decision as to which school they will attend. This fact is overlooked because adult-centered ways of thinking about child rearing implicitly treat children as appendages of their parents, morally and conceptually indistinct from parents, presumed to have identical interests and rights. Much scholarly debate and judicial reasoning about the fairness and legality of vouchers have turned on the fact that all parents are free to send their children to public school, so that enrollment of children in private schools is a matter of free choice for the parents. Based on this fact, one side argues that parents cannot expect the state to subsidize their free choice to opt out of the public school system, that it is not unfair to expect them to bear the cost of the choices they freely make. The other side argues that parents should be unconstrained in exercising what the Supreme Court has said is their constitutional right, so that funding only public schools or attaching conditions to funding of private schools wrongfully coerces their choices.

This debate about the implications of free choice, however, becomes impertinent when the primary focus shifts, as it should, to the just claims of children who are in private schools, because these children are generally not doing the choosing and, as a matter of justice, should not suffer for choices the state gives their parents the legal authority to make.[6] The state has an obligation to *all* children to ensure that they receive a good secular education,[7] in addition to whatever religious training and instruction their parents provide them. The state cannot relieve itself of that obligation by pointing to parents' exercise of powers that the state has conferred upon them. The import of this obligation, the early chapters of this book show, is that states should be *required* to support financially provision of secular education in these schools.

Critically, however, states must also ensure that every voucher school is in fact providing a good secular education. A child-centered justification for vouchers turns entirely on whether adequate safeguards are in place to ensure that voucher money is being used for that purpose. This means that states enacting voucher programs *must* exercise sufficient regulatory oversight to ensure that every school receiving vouchers is striving to provide a good secular education, will use the voucher money for that purpose, and is sufficiently successful in accomplishing that purpose. In addition, states must ensure that schools receiving state subsidies do not engage in practices the state deems harmful to children, such as sexist teaching and sexist treatment of students.

Introduction

To those not familiar with private education in this country, it might seem an unremarkable point that states should ensure that aid to religious schools advances children's secular education. Most people assume private schools are already closely regulated to ensure that they provide a good education and do not engage in practices the state deems harmful to children. But it is actually a radical proposal to suggest that states regulate private schools in these ways. If enacted, it would transform private schooling in America, and indeed our culture, as much as would the shift in state spending that vouchers represent. What most people fail to realize, and what voucher supporters choose to ignore, is that private schooling in this country is now virtually unregulated, and many private schools in this country do *not* provide a good secular education. For some schools, this is largely because they *do not wish* to provide a good secular education, and so they would not use state aid for that purpose. Such an education is antithetical to their religious mission. Some religious groups that operate schools reject certain of the values of contemporary liberal culture that inform state education policy, such as intellectual autonomy and gender equality, and do not want their children to acquire knowledge of prevailing views in certain subjects or to pursue careers in mainstream society. Many schools engage in practices that, from the state's perspective, are harmful to children—for example, actively stifling creative and critical thinking and teaching sexist views. All states currently allow private schools to do this.

Voucher programs now in existence demand little or nothing more of recipient schools than the precious little that is otherwise required for them simply to operate. As such, vouchers actually encourage and support educational deprivation and harm to some children—the very opposite of their stated purpose. Some schools that receive money from the state do not use it to advance children's interest in receiving a good secular education; they instead use it to bolster their efforts to provide what, from a secular perspective, is the antithesis of education. Because of this reality, a child-centered assessment of vouchers yields the conclusion that voucher programs in the form they now take are morally and constitutionally impermissible.

To illustrate the problem with a voucher program that does not include robust academic requirements, consider the following news story relating to the Cleveland voucher program. In 1999, a reporter discovered that a Fundamentalist Christian school in Cleveland was receiving vouchers even though it had no teachers and even though it used the state money to purchase Christian videos.[8] Students in this school spent most of the school day in front of a television watching these videos. The videos, to the extent they taught anything other than religious doctrine, taught views in ostensibly secular subjects, such as biology and history, tailored to conform to biblical teaching. In addition, students in that school, assuming the school is like other Fundamentalist Christian schools described in the social scientific literature,[9] would likely be taught that thinking for themselves or questioning what they are taught is sin-ful. They would be discouraged from pursuing a college education in other than a Bible college, or pursuing a college education at all if they are female. They would be instructed not to interact with non-Fundamentalists.

There is, quite simply, no plausible justification for giving public money to such a school. Yet nothing in the rules of the Cleveland program precludes such a school from receiving vouchers! The same is true of the other existing pro-grams that include religious schools, in Milwaukee and Florida. Under those programs as well, schools can be entirely or almost entirely state funded with-out providing any significant secular education and without showing any aca-demic proficiency on the part of their students. It is astounding how little at-tention even opponents of vouchers have given to this problem.

If vouchers survive initial court challenges, states will be forced to grapple with the regulation issue. The first round of litigation has primarily involved "fa-cial challenges" to vouchers—that is, claims that use of state money to pay for education in religious schools is inherently unconstitutional, regardless of the quality of the education religious schools provide. If those legal claims ultimately fail, as is increasingly likely, voucher opponents will shift to a litigation strategy of advancing "as applied" challenges—that is, claims that funding of *particular* schools, such as the one just described, is unconstitutional. As-applied challenges will undoubtedly succeed; it is inconceivable that courts would find constitu-tional state funding of the video school described above. Thus, even though there is no political will today for regulation of religious schools, courts will nec-essarily force states to regulate voucher schools, in order to comply with the strictures of the Establishment Clause, by prohibiting states from including in voucher programs schools that are not using the state money to provide a bet-ter secular education. One purpose of this book is to communicate the funda-mental importance of regulation to the entire voucher question.

The analysis of this book thus demonstrates that the permissibility, morally and constitutionally, of providing vouchers for use at religious schools is not a fixed or inherent characteristic of voucher plans that include religious schools. There is a right way to do vouchers and a wrong way. It does not make sense to debate vouchers in the abstract, as necessarily good or necessarily bad, as is typically done. States can alter the normative status of voucher plans by either (1) enacting voucher plans that limit eligibility to private schools that agree to abide by robust requirements for the quality of education and treatment of stu-dents or (2) changing the larger regulatory environment in which religious schools operate—that is, requiring that *all* nonpublic schools satisfy such re-quirements or be shut down, and making vouchers available to all schools per-mitted to operate.

Either of these approaches would have substantial coercive effects on reli-gious schools, and for that reason would trigger protests from supporters of

[13]

religious schools, and from current supporters of vouchers, who would assert that such effects violate the rights of parents, school operators, and religious groups. A child-centered analysis demonstrates, however, that such coercive effects are not only permissible but in fact mandatory. Indeed, I have argued in a previous book that states owe a duty to children in religious schools, independent of any public funding of such schools, to closely regulate the content and nature of instruction in those schools.[10] The political reality is such, however, that that is simply not going to happen. There is no political will today to regulate religious schools that the state is not funding, precisely because of our adult-centered perspective on such issues. The welfare of the children in those schools is of little or no concern to the rest of society; whether they have equal educational opportunity is their parents' problem or right to determine.

The current book approaches the question of regulation in a different way—namely, by considering what obligations to children the state incurs, and what opportunities arise, by virtue of the state's role as the principal source of funding for children's education and as the result of a decision to expand its spending on education to include religious schools. State funding of religious schools changes the normative analysis and the political reality of regulating religious schools considerably. It makes much clearer that the state has an obligation with respect to what goes on inside religious schools. In addition, it makes the general, taxpaying public believe that they have a greater self-interest at stake in what goes on in those schools.

Because of the effect vouchers can have on the general public's interest in what goes on inside religious schools, anyone who is now concerned about the kind and quality of education that children in religious schools are receiving should, ironically, give qualified support to the concept of state funding for religious schools. Creating a program of substantial financial assistance to religious schools, but conditioning participation on compliance with substantial regulatory strings, may be the only feasible way of accomplishing the ultimate end of ensuring a good secular education for, and otherwise safeguarding the welfare of, those children. In the past, when states have attempted to impose regulations on religious schools, they have met with fierce resistance by parents and religious leaders. The beauty of vouchers is that they create a mechanism for states to induce religious schools voluntarily to comply with academic standards and guidelines for treatment of students. States can use vouchers to influence the private school market, creating a large incentive for parents to choose schools that agree to follow such requirements. Market forces would then eliminate many of the schools that are academically inadequate or that mistreat students. Many religious leaders are ambivalent about vouchers precisely because they fear this will happen. Many supporters of vouchers are quick to assure them that it will not. A child-centered analysis shows that it must.

Now for some preliminary procedural matters: The analysis of school vouchers in this book focuses on religious schools as potential recipients of state funding. There is occasional reference to nonsectarian private schools, but the real aim is to determine the permissibility of allowing vouchers to be used at religious schools. I focus on religious schools in part because they constitute 85 percent of private schools, but primarily because they raise the most difficult moral and legal questions in the voucher debate. If it is permissible for the state to pay for education provided in religious schools, then surely it is permissible for the state to pay for education provided in nonsectarian private schools, subject to the same conditions. The reader should not, however, mistake statements about religious schools as implying anything, favorable or unfavorable, about other private schools. For the most part, what is true of all or some religious schools could also be true of all or some nonsectarian private schools. For the sake of writing economy, though, I often refer simply to religious schools. The reader also should not assume that anything said about religious schools implies the opposite about public schools—in particular, any criticism of the practices of some religious schools does not logically entail the position that no public schools are subject to the same criticism. In some respects, the nature and condition of public schools are relevant to the voucher question, but in many respects they are not.

The structure of the book is as follows: Chapters 1 and 2, after a brief description of existing voucher programs and of recent proposals for new programs, describe how courts and scholars have analyzed voucher programs in adult-centered ways. These chapters show why these adult-centered ways of thinking are untenable and make the case for a child-centered approach. The remaining chapters of the book then undertake a normative assessment of vouchers—that is, whether state aid to religious schools is forbidden, permissible, or mandatory—that gives appropriate weight to the interests and rights of children.

In addition to being child centered, the book's normative analysis is unusual in that, rather than beginning with an assessment of existing programs, it begins by analyzing a somewhat idealized voucher program that differs in critical respects from existing ones. I describe a program that would effectively ensure that the only schools receiving vouchers would be ones that strive to provide the best possible secular education, that succeed sufficiently in doing so, that use voucher money only to improve the secular education they provide, and that endeavor not to engage in practices, such as sexist teaching, that the state deems harmful to children. A voucher program that did this would clearly advance the aim of enhancing the secular education children receive. I begin the normative analysis in this way in part because most commentators and judges appear to assume that existing voucher programs actually do this, either because of requirements built into the programs or because of the background regulatory environment in which all private schools operate. I show that even if this assumption were true, prevailing analyses of vouchers would be wrongheaded because adult centered.

After the initial normative assessment of this idealized voucher program, the later chapters of the book describe what the regulatory environment for religious schools really is, what existing voucher programs actually require of participating schools, and what available evidence shows some religious schools to be truly like. These chapters examine whether and how the facts of the real world alter the outcome of the normative analysis. When the conclusions reached by analyzing the idealized voucher program are contrasted with conclusions reached by analyzing existing programs, the crucial importance of regulation becomes clear.

The normative analysis is also somewhat unusual in adopting several different modes of normative reasoning. I apply two different styles of moral / political reasoning, one utilitarian and one rights-based, and then take two different avenues of legal and specifically constitutional reasoning, one originating in the Establishment Clause and one in the Equal Protection Clause. I approach the voucher issue in these several different ways because each has some currency among the public and among members of the legal and academic communities. In fact, it is probably the case that most people look through each of the four lenses—welfare, rights, church-state separation, and equality—at different times, and perhaps more than one at once. We are accustomed to engaging in decision making by balancing the interests at stake, as well as by articulating rights. And most people are familiar with both antiestablishment restrictions on state action and the mandate of equal protection, each of which is invoked by participants in the voucher debate.

Each of these four approaches supports the same conclusion: The interests and rights of children are the most important at stake in this and other education reform debates, and they should be controlling. The interests and rights of children already attending private schools make it mandatory for states to enact a voucher program properly designed to improve the secular education their schools provide. Moreover, no other persons' rights would pose an obstacle to states' doing so. All four approaches also generate the conclusion that existing programs are morally irresponsible and unconstitutional. States should, and ultimately will be judicially compelled to, add a substantial regulatory overlay to any voucher programs.

In the Conclusion, I consider which of the features of the idealized voucher program that I describe might be essential and which merely desirable. I also consider there (and at other points in the book) some practical obstacles to implementing a well-designed voucher program. I suggest possible solutions but do not purport to prove the viability or superiority of any. Questions of implementation are important and unavoidable, but I assume that persons engaged in creating education policy, writing education laws, administering school districts and schools, and actually teaching children are in the best position to analyze such questions of implementation.

Questions of implementation cannot even arise, however, until we have some idea of what ought to be done, and that depends in large part on a normative analysis that practitioners of education are not uniquely suited to address, and perhaps are not even in the best position to address. Teachers, school administrators, and the faculty of schools of education are well positioned to tell us what it takes to deliver a service to children, how educational aims combine and how classroom activities interrelate, and what effects legal mandates have on schools. But they are not necessarily well positioned to tell us how educational resources should be distributed in a society, how child-development-driven educational aims should be balanced against other societal aims such as securing religious freedom or creating good citizens, and how considerations of justice should be balanced against the practicalities of implementation that they identify. This book is addressed to such normative issues and endeavors to change the basic moral, political, and legal outlook that is brought to bear on education reform issues such as school vouchers.

[1]

Vouchers and Adult-Centered
Legal Reasoning

The school voucher debate serves in this book as the topical focus for an argument that prevailing ways of thinking about child-rearing policies are adult centered, that this is inappropriate, and that child-centered thinking can produce dramatically different outcomes. The reader will therefore want to have a concrete sense of what voucher programs are, where they exist, and how they operate.[1]

Existing Voucher Programs and Recent Proposals

The evolution of Supreme Court Establishment Clause doctrine in recent years toward a position more tolerant of evenhanded aid to religious and non-religious schools has encouraged legislators throughout the country, at the urging of parents and religious groups, to propose new programs of aid for all private schools. Publicly financed voucher programs now exist in five jurisdictions. The most often discussed programs are in Milwaukee, Cleveland, and Florida. These programs are controversial because they enable parents to move their children from neighborhood public schools to private schools, and because they include religious schools among the recipients of vouchers. Vermont and Maine also have voucher programs, but they do not have these two characteristics and so do not receive a great deal of attention. Vermont and Maine authorize school districts that do not operate a public school to pay for children in the district to attend a nonsectarian private school or another district's public schools.

The Milwaukee Program

Among voucher programs that include religious schools, Milwaukee's is the oldest. Initially Milwaukee's program did not include religious schools. The Wisconsin legislature created a program in 1989 that would pay for children from low-income families, defined as families with an income at or less than 175 percent of the poverty level, to attend a nonsectarian private school. Eligibility was limited to students attending a public school prior to enactment. The amount of the voucher was equal to the per pupil state expenditure on public schools and was paid directly to the private schools. The governing law also reduced state funding of the Milwaukee public school system by the amount directed to private schools.

In 1995, after parents of religious school pupils brought a lawsuit challenging exclusion of religious schools from the program, the Wisconsin legislature voluntarily amended the governing statutes to allow participation by religious schools. Under the current program, students in grades K through 3 can enter the voucher program even if they have already been attending a religious school. New entrants in the older grades must have been enrolled in a Milwaukee public school in the preceding year.

The 1995 legislation also changed the payment mechanism, so that checks are now made out to individual parents rather than to schools. However, the checks are still sent to the schools, and parents must endorse them over to the schools. The 1995 legislation also changed how the amount of the vouchers is determined; the amount is now the lesser of the state's per pupil expenditures on public schools ($5,326 in the 2000–01 school year) and the private school's " 'operating and debt service cost per pupil that is related to educational programming.' "[2] Either of these amounts would exceed the tuition charged by a majority of religious schools. A religious school's tuition is typically less than its per pupil costs, because the schools receive contributions from their sponsoring religious organizations' churches, and is also typically less than the amount of per pupil state funding for public schools. In addition, the amount of the vouchers could cover all of a religious school's operating costs, because the governing statute does not exclude religious instruction from the definition of educational programming. In fact, there are no restrictions whatsoever on how religious schools spend the state money. Thus, recipient schools might use state money to pay salaries of catechism teachers, to buy religious books, and even to maintain a church building if that is somehow "related to" educational programming. Schools may not charge voucher students tuition over and above the amount of the voucher.

In the 2000–01 school year, the maximum family income cutoff for a family of four was roughly $31,000. Nearly ten thousand children participated in the program, distributed among 103 participating schools, the vast majority of them in religious schools. State funding of the Milwaukee Public School System was cut by an amount equal to half of the roughly $50 million cost of the voucher program, and state funding for public schools in the rest of the state was also cut by that amount. Separate statutory provisions create a public school choice program, which facilitates transfer to another public school in the Milwaukee area.

The Cleveland Program

In 1995, Ohio initiated a voucher program for the city of Cleveland, whose public school system was also in dire straits.[3] The Cleveland program included religious schools from the start. The authorizing legislation also provided a mechanism whereby students could attend a public school in a neighboring school district. However, no neighboring district has ever permitted children from the Cleveland City School District to attend one of its schools, in large part, no doubt, because under the program a district would receive only $2,250 for each child it accepts—about a third of its per pupil costs. In addition, the program provides tutorial assistance grants, initially in the amount of $500, for students who remain in the city's public schools.

The Cleveland program distributes vouchers by lottery among parents who apply. It accords priority to poorer parents, but any parent in the school district may apply. Private schools that wish to participate must register with the state superintendent. In the 1999–2000 school year, fifty-six schools were registered, at least forty-six of which were religious schools. The precise number of religious schools in any given year is unknown, because state education department officials do not ask participating schools whether they are religious. Ninety-six percent of the 3,761 students receiving vouchers in the 1999–2000 school year attended one of the schools believed to be sectarian. As with the Milwaukee program, under the Cleveland program the state makes out checks to parents of private school pupils but sends the checks to the schools, where the parents must endorse them over to the schools. The amount of the voucher depends on a private school's tuition and on the income level of a student's family, but in no case may exceed 90 percent of a school's tuition or $2,250, whichever is less. Thus, the amount of the state subsidy will exceed the portion of a religious school's budget, on a per pupil basis, devoted to secular education, if that is less than 90 percent of tuition revenue and less than $2,250 per pupil.

The Florida Program

In June 1999, Florida created the first statewide voucher program. It allows students enrolled in the state's worst-performing public schools to transfer to participating private schools, which can include religious schools, with the state paying the cost of tuition through "opportunity scholarships."[4] The program also allows students to transfer to other public schools. The enacting legislation expresses the Florida legislature's finding "that a student should not be compelled, against the wishes of the student's parent or guardian, to remain in a school found by the state to be failing," and the program's purpose "to give parents and guardians the opportunity for their children to attend a public school that is performing satisfactorily or to attend an eligible private school when the parent or guardian chooses." One might infer that the legislature deems it appropriate to compel a child to remain in a failing school if that is what the child's parents want or if the child's parents are indifferent.

Under the Florida program, only students who attended a failing public school in the previous year, or who are entering school for the first time and have been assigned to a failing public school, are eligible for scholarships. Children previously attending private schools thus would not be eligible, even if their schools were academically inadequate, and even if the sole reason for that inadequacy was a lack of resources. By July 1 of the year for which a scholarship is sought, parents must obtain admission for a child at a private school and notify the Department of Education and the school district of their wish to receive a scholarship. Thus, only children whose parents have the wherewithal and motivation to plan for the next school year months in advance and to submit a formal notice of application to public agencies can benefit from the program.

Opportunity scholarships are distributed in the same way as vouchers in the Milwaukee and Cleveland programs. The Florida Department of Education mails an individual check for each parent to the chosen private school. The check is made out to the parent, and the parent must restrictively endorse it over to the school. The state's checks are drawn on an account that would otherwise be used for public schools, and the state did not allocate additional money to that account to pay for the opportunity scholarships, so the program has the effect of reducing spending on public schools. The amount of each check is the lesser of the state's per pupil spending for public schools in the student's school district and the tuition and fees the private school charges. Thus, a religious school whose budget is paid for entirely from tuition and fees could be 100 percent funded by the state.

These descriptions of the three programs reveal a number of important features common to all existing programs. First, all three existing programs target the poorest families or students attending the worst-performing public schools. Second, under all of the programs, students transfer to private schools only if their parents take the initiative to apply for a voucher and to apply for admission to a private school. Students whose parents are unable or insufficiently motivated to take these steps remain in the failing public schools. Third, under all the programs, money directed to private schools is taken out of the school district's budget for public schools. All the programs also allow for transfer to a better public school, and such a transfer would likewise result in money's being taken from the public school left and given to the school chosen. Fourth, under all the programs, the vast majority of participating schools are religious schools, as one would expect given that the vast majority of all private schools are religious schools. Fifth, under each program, the state sends checks directly to the schools, and while the checks are made out to parents, they are worthless unless signed over to the designated private school. Each private school deposits the signed-over checks into its own bank account, and state money is then transferred directly from the state treasury to the private school's bank account. Finally, under all the programs, the amount of the voucher can exceed the per pupil portion of a religious school's budget devoted to secular instruction. Under the Milwaukee and Florida programs, state money can pay for the entirety of a religious school's budget.

Characteristics of Recent Proposals

In 1999 alone, legislators in forty states considered voucher proposals.[5] In addition, numerous statewide voucher ballot initiatives have been put to voters in recent years, and President George W. Bush included a federal voucher plan in his first budget proposal. The state programs proposed would have closely resembled the programs in Milwaukee, Cleveland, and Florida. Most would have limited eligibility to relatively poor families or would have limited eligibility to students in the worst-performing school districts or schools. All would have made affirmative steps by parents necessary to a child's benefiting from the program. Nearly all the proposed programs would have reduced funding of public schools by the amount given to private schools. Nearly all would have included religious schools as well as nonsectarian private schools. Most also would have included some kind of public school choice provision, directing school districts to allow and pay for parents to transfer their children to another public school, within the same district or in another district. A few would have provided, instead of or in addition to public school choice, tutorial assistance grants of the sort the Cleveland program offers, which children in public schools could use to obtain extra help after school. All of the proposed programs that involved vouchers per se, rather than a tax credit or deduction or "tuition reimbursement," would have involved the state's sending checks to private schools, made out to individual parents, and requiring parents to endorse the checks over to the schools. Finally, most plans that have been proposed would have paid the full amount of tuition at private schools, as long as this amount was not greater than a certain percentage of state per pupil spending on public schools, and that percentage has varied in the proposals from 50 percent to 100 percent.

However, some recent voucher proposals have included features that would distinguish them from the existing programs. Some proposals, including a major ballot initiative in California, would not have limited eligibility to parents below a certain income level or to students in the worst-performing schools; all students in the state would have been eligible. A few proposals would have required that new funds be appropriated for the vouchers and that the budgets for public schools not be reduced. A few of the proposals would have excluded religious schools from participation. And a small number of proposed plans would have included home schools as well as all private schools.[6]

How the Legal System Analyzes Vouchers

All the existing voucher programs have been challenged in state and/or lower federal courts, so there are numerous published judicial opinions on the constitutionality of vouchers. In addition, legal scholars and public policy writers have created a voluminous literature on the constitutionality of vouchers. As described below, both courts and commentators focus almost exclusively on the rights and interests of adults, mirroring the ways in which parties to the legal disputes—who typically are all adults—frame the issues. In litigation, parents assert a right to choose what form of schooling their children will receive, often based on their desire to impart their religious faith to their children and to make that choice without cost. Taxpayer groups, on the other hand, claim a right not to be forced to subsidize someone else's religion and assert that the state violates this right by using tax dollars to pay for tuition at religious schools. Judicial and scholarly analysis has primarily addressed the merits of these adult-centered claims.

Another important characteristic of litigation concerning aid to religious schools is that courts typically treat the Establishment Clause as a trump over all other considerations, including other constitutional considerations such as free exercise of religion and equal protection. If they find a program of aid inconsistent with Establishment Clause norms, that is the end of the matter; the program is invalidated. Legal scholars typically accept this absolutist approach to application of the Establishment Clause without question. Yet such an approach is hardly a necessary, or even typical, one in constitutional jurisprudence. When courts analyze state action under many other constitutional provisions, such as the Free Speech Clause, and find a prima facie violation of a constitutional mandate, they typically go on to ask whether the state has a sufficiently strong policy reason for the action that outweighs the infringement of constitutional values in that instance. The courts' treatment of the Establishment Clause is in this respect anomalous.

In voucher cases, as in cases scrutinizing other types of aid to religious institutions, courts continue to apply, even while criticizing, a three-part Establishment Clause test that the Supreme Court established in 1971 in *Lemon v. Kurtzman*.[7] That test requires that a challenged form of state aid (1) have a secular purpose, (2) have as a primary effect neither the advancement nor the inhibition of religion, and (3) not give rise to an excessive entanglement between church and state. The Supreme Court recently demoted excessive entanglement from its status as an independent element to merely one factor in the primary effect analysis, but entanglement remains a significant consideration.[8] If courts find that state aid fails any part of the *Lemon* test, they invalidate the aid program without inquiry into whether the aid serves competing interests or rights that might outweigh the Establishment Clause values or interests at stake under the circumstances of the case. While it might seem that the test itself allows for a balancing, or tolerates some violation of the principle that the state should not advance religion, because the second prong of the test requires only a *primary* secular effect, the courts have actually interpreted the second prong as requiring a *solely* secular effect. Thus, *any* advancement of religion fails the second prong, even if it is dwarfed by salutary secular effects.

The courts have not explained why they elevate the Establishment Clause to this position of lexical priority.[9] They appear simply to assume that avoiding an Establishment Clause violation justifies an infringement of free exercise, free speech, or equal protection rights, or that Establishment Clause strictures define the limits of all other constitutional provisions.[10] They also implicitly assume that Establishment Clause values override in every case any other interests that might be at stake—including children's interest in receiving a good education.

From a child-centered perspective, however, this is very puzzling. It is puzzling to read a judicial analysis of state aid to religious schools that begins by pronouncing that the purpose of the aid is to advance children's educational interests, that this aim is of tremendous importance, and that the aid in fact has that effect, but then concludes that the aid is nevertheless impermissible, simply because it also advances religion in some way. This is particularly puzzling when the way in which the aid might advance religion is comparatively insignificant—for example, by simply creating an impression of church-state coziness in the minds of (perhaps irrational) bystanders. Typically such a pronouncement about the importance of improving education, if it appears in a court's analysis at all, is uttered solely for the purpose of establishing a secular purpose and is the only hint in judicial opinions that children have interests at stake in disputes over state aid to religious schools. And often when courts speak of improved education they are not even thinking about children's interests, but rather about interests of society as a whole—that is, the state's interest in the next generation's being well educated. A few courts have mentioned improved education with an evident concern for the well-being of the children who would benefit from the aid, but no court has considered whether this effect is due children as a matter of right or is important enough to override concerns about advancing religion or about offending nonreligious persons. And most often, courts characterize the purpose of voucher programs as providing a benefit to parents and not a benefit to children at all.

The analysis presented in the remaining chapters of this book does not give antiestablishment principles and interests the sort of trumping character or lexical priority that courts give them. Unless there is some reason to assume that the interests Establishment Clause jurisprudence has developed to protect are in all contexts weightier than any competing interests, it is more appropriate to balance the values or interests underlying competing claims. This is especially true when fundamental interests of children are at stake. Subsequent chapters of this book undertake the sort of balancing of values and interests that the courts have failed to do, to determine the implications of giving children's interests the weight they deserve.

A third important characteristic of judicial analysis of voucher programs is that courts place little or no emphasis on the extent to which religious schools are subject to regulation or on the nature and quality of pedagogy and treatment of students in different types of religious schools. Courts reviewing aid programs do not inquire into whether the state ensures that all recipient schools provide a good secular education. What little discussion of regulation there is relates to either (1) whether anything ensures that state aid will not be used for religious instruction or activities; and (2) ironically, whether there is *too much* regulation, in the sense that it would create an "excessive entanglement" of the state with religious schools. Courts do consider whether schools receiving vouchers are "pervasively sectarian," but as explained in Chapter 5, this consideration, as the courts have interpreted it, reveals little or nothing about the quality of education or about the appropriateness of the way in which children are treated. Accordingly, courts have actually had little or no basis for determining whether aid programs advance the secular educational interests of children in religious schools, even though that is supposed to be the purpose of the programs. As the later chapters of this book show, this is a major deficiency in the courts' analysis of the permissibility of vouchers for religious schools.

The next section of this chapter illustrates the points above by describing the analysis lower courts have brought to bear in voucher litigation. Lower court analysis necessarily takes place against the backdrop of the Supreme Court's general jurisprudence on state aid to religious institutions. However, I reserve to Chapter 5 a description of relevant Supreme Court decisions. In addition, in describing the litigation in lower courts, I largely ignore the courts' substantive

Establishment Clause analysis, because it is of only transitory interest. Ultimately, the United States Supreme Court will decide whether school vouchers are constitutional, and in doing so the justices will not pay much heed to how lower courts have interpreted the Establishment Clause.

Lower Courts' Analysis of Voucher Programs

Litigation in state and federal courts in Maine and Vermont has addressed the constitutionality of excluding religious schools from voucher programs. As noted above, statutes in both those states require school districts that do not operate a public school to pay for children in the district to attend a nonsectarian private school or a public school in another district. Early litigation in Wisconsin also addressed this issue, before the Wisconsin legislature amended the Milwaukee program to include religious schools, and I discuss that litigation below in connection with the Milwaukee program. The most closely followed court battles, however, have involved challenges to voucher programs that include religious schools, as those in Milwaukee, Cleveland, and Florida now do.

MAINE   Under the Maine program, roughly half the state's school districts pay for children in the district to attend a nonsectarian private school or a public school in another district, making payments directly to the schools attended. In both state and federal courts, parents in such districts who wished to send their children to a religious school challenged the exclusion of such schools as a violation of the parents' constitutional rights. In both fora, the children were not made parties to the action and the parents did not assert any rights of the children; the parents claimed rights only for themselves. The parents lost their cases in both federal and state courts, and the United States Supreme Court declined to review either.

The first court decision, in federal district court, rejected the parents' claims summarily, stating simply that while parents have a right to place their children in a private school, they have no right to taxpayer support for their choice of schools.[11] On appeal, the First Circuit Court of Appeals, in *Strout v. Albanese*,[12] addressed each of the legal claims separately and at greater length. Because all the claims were on behalf of parents rather than children and asserted rights of the parents, they necessarily all rested ultimately on the parents' interests rather than on interests of the children whose education was actually at stake. The court therefore never discussed the effect of excluding religious schools on the welfare of children in such schools.

The parents first claimed in federal court that the voucher program violated the Establishment Clause, because it constituted hostility toward religion. The court of appeals rightly saw this as really a free exercise claim, and therefore redundant of the parents' separate claim under the Free Exercise Clause. The role of the Establishment Clause, said the court, is to prevent a *favoring* of religion, while the Free Exercise Clause serves the purpose of preventing *discrimination against* religion. Both claims based on the religion clauses of the First Amendment were therefore about protecting the parents' interest in pursuing their religious aims through control of their children's lives. The court rejected both claims, but not because it believed it inappropriate to focus on the interests of parents rather than children, or to attribute rights to parents rather than children in connection with schooling. Rather, the court concluded that including religious schools in the program would violate the Establishment Clause, and the court believed upholding the Establishment Clause was a "paramount" interest that trumped free exercise concerns. As support for the paramount nature of the Establishment Clause, the court offered only the fact that the clause "is the first of the several constitutional do's and don'ts contained in the Bill of Rights," and historical writings showing that church-state separation was important to certain founders.

In determining that inclusion of religious schools would violate the Establishment Clause, the federal appellate court focused on the directness of payments to schools, leaving open the possibility that the court might rule differently on a program under which schools received state money only indirectly, whatever that might mean. The court also indicated that the constitutional barrier to funding of religious institutions is greater in the case of elementary and secondary schools than it is in the case of institutions providing services for adults. Thus, although children's educational needs might well be more important than are the interests of adults furthered by state support for other private institutions, the law, as the court of appeals understood it, makes it more difficult, and perhaps impossible, for the state to promote children's educational needs if their parents happen to have placed them in religious schools. Presumably, then, if the state of Maine had *chosen* to include religious schools in the program, because it thought this the only way to protect the educational interests of certain children (i.e., those whose parents would choose religious schools no matter what), this court would have struck down that aspect of the program.

An additional reason why the court of appeals rejected the parents' religious freedom claims was that it construed the parents' rights as entitling them only to the formal opportunity to choose a religious school, and not also to state financial support for such a choice. The Free Exercise Clause provides negative rights against government interference, not positive rights to government assistance, said the court. It is entirely appropriate and fair, then, for parents to bear the costs of their choice. The court gave no consideration to the fact that the children might also bear costs resulting from the parents' choices—namely, the cost of receiving an inferior education because their schools lack adequate resources, or the cost of lost family resources.

The court dispensed with the parents' due process and free speech claims on similar grounds. The parents argued that excluding religious schools prevented them "from using their tuition allotments to expose their children to the educational message which best reflects their morals and values" and "denies parents the right to communicate and instruct their children in the areas of religion, morals and ethics." Given the obvious fact that parents can instruct their children in their morals and values during the 85 percent of children's waking hours spent outside of school, the parents were really claiming an entitlement to instruct their children in their religious beliefs during every waking hour of the children's lives, and to do so with state financial support. The court, rather than challenge the basic premise that parents are entitled to such complete dominion over their children's minds, a premise that is hardly established as a matter of constitutional law, rejected these claims on the basis of the same negative versus positive rights dichotomy underlying its rejection of the free exercise claim. Parents are entitled to do whatever they want with their children's minds; they are simply not entitled to state financial assistance in doing so.

Finally, the court of appeals rejected a claim based on the parents' right to equal protection. The parents argued that they were "being discriminated against on the basis of religion, religious beliefs, speech content, and association." There is no indication in the case that any children had made choices on the basis of religious belief. The issue was whether the state was being fair to parents, not whether it was being fair to any children. The court resolved the issue by again relying on the strictures of the Establishment Clause, which the court treated as an absolute trump over individual rights to equal treatment. Presumably, then, the court would also have rejected an equal protection claim on behalf of the children whose parents placed them in religious schools.

In state court, parents' rights were again the only rights asserted. The Maine Supreme Court, in *Bagley v. Raymond School Department*,[13] reached the same conclusion the federal courts reached, analyzing the parents' claims in more or less the same ways the federal court of appeals did. There are a few distinct and interesting aspects of the state court's opinion, however. First, in the state court litigation, there was some debate over the factual issue of the parents' motivation for choosing to send their children to a Catholic school. The court's analysis made clear that, all else being equal, parents' claims for constitutional protection of their choice of a school for their children are stronger when their choice is motivated by religious belief than it is when they are primarily or solely seeking to secure the best available education for their children. Parents have greater protection under the Free Exercise Clause than they do under the Due Process Clause, and to state a free exercise claim, parents must show that their choice is " 'one of deep religious conviction.' " The court suggested that some of the parents who sued might not have had even a prima facie claim to protection, precisely because they were motivated solely or primarily by a desire to secure the best education for their children. "All of the parents candidly admit," the court stated, "that they are seeking to obtain the best education for their children." Apparently, then, the parents would have been in better stead if they had chosen a school in utter disregard for their children's interests! In the judiciary's adult-centered constitutional universe, parents' religious interests are simply more important than children's developmental interests, even in the context of state support for child-rearing institutions. In fact, the children's interests are irrelevant.

Second, the Maine Supreme Court devoted more attention to the parents' equal protection claim than did the federal courts. Like the federal courts, the state court held that Establishment Clause strictures trump any equal protection rights: "If the exclusion of religious schools . . . is required in order to comply with the Establishment Clause, the State will have presented a compelling justification for the disparate treatment of religious schools, and the parents' Equal Protection claim will fail." In addition, the state court suggested that the parents were simply confused about the nature of the constitutional right at issue. The parents claimed that they were discriminated against on the basis of their religion, but the court saw discrimination only against the school. These parents were free to participate in the voucher program by choosing an eligible school, and it was only the religious school they did choose that was barred altogether from participation. Thus, the parents' "harm" was occasioned not by any discrimination against them but rather by their own choice to forgo the benefit proffered to all parents.

Finally, in its Establishment Clause analysis, the state court stipulated, without evidence, that including religious schools in the program would further children's educational interests. The court then asserted that "the education of the State's children is of such paramount importance that it provides a valid secular reason for state expenditures," and that "[i]ndeed, there are few other governmental pursuits that involve such important public policy considerations." Yet the court went on to find such inclusion impermissible, solely because in furthering that purpose the state would also be "advancing religion." This was so in part simply because the state would be doing *a lot* to help children in religious schools—that is, because the aid was so substantial. In contrast, programs of aid that the United States Supreme Court had previously upheld provided only "specific limited services." It was also in part, though, because the state's payments to schools were "unrestricted"; the program imposed no limitations on how recipient schools used the money. State money could therefore be used to pay for essentially religious activities and instruction. In any event, what is striking is that once the court found that the voucher program crossed a dimly perceived line of permissibility in the United States Supreme Court's tortured Establishment Clause jurisprudence, the vital state interest in furthering the fundamental interests of children disappeared as a consideration. There was no balancing to be done; if the state did choose to include religious schools, it could not successfully defend its decision on the grounds that this was necessary to promote children's welfare. Why that is the case neither this court nor any other has ever explained.

VERMONT   As in Maine, some school districts in low-population areas of Vermont do not maintain public secondary schools, and state statutes require such districts to pay for students to attend a public school in another district or a private school. However, the Vermont program has had a somewhat different history. From 1994 to 1999, school districts in Vermont *were* permitted to pay for tuition at religious schools, following a 1994 ruling of the Vermont Supreme Court, in *Campbell v. Manchester Board of School Directors*,[14] that doing so would *not* violate the Establishment Clause of the federal constitution, at least in certain circumstances. Nevertheless, currently school districts in Vermont may not pay for tuition at religious schools, because the state's supreme court decided in 1999, in *Chittenden Town School District v. Vermont Department of Education*,[15] that doing so violates a provision of the *state* constitution called the "Compelled Support Clause" that more specifically prohibits use of tax dollars to support religious institutions. The 1999 ruling is the final word on vouchers for religious schools in Vermont, absent an amendment to the state constitution, a reversal of position by the Vermont Supreme Court, or a federal court decision invalidating the state constitutional provision.

The 1994 case was brought by one parent, claiming a statutory right to be reimbursed for tuition he paid to an Episcopal high school. The sole issue in the case was whether the school district could defend its refusal of reimbursement on the ground that the Establishment Clause prohibits payment for education at a religious school. The most interesting aspect of the court's analysis is that in holding that the Establishment Clause was not an obstacle to reimbursement, the court emphasized that "tuition reimbursement will involve no greater governmental regulation" of schools benefiting from the program, and that "Vermont has significantly modified its laws with respect to independent schools to avoid excessive entanglement with religion in the regulatory process and protect the free exercise of religion." In other words, the court viewed it as a *good* thing that private schools are not much regulated to begin with and that Vermont required little or nothing of schools by way of academic or other standards as a condition for receiving substantial state funding. And the reasons why it was a good thing had nothing to do with the welfare of children.

After the *Campbell* decision, some school districts changed their policies to provide for reimbursement of tuition paid to religious schools. The litigation resulting in the *Chittenden* decision began when the state commissioner of education terminated state education aid to one of those districts, taking the position that the district's policy, as applied to particular religious schools, violated both the federal Establishment Clause and a state constitutional provision stating that "no person . . . can be compelled to . . . support any place of worship . . . contrary to the dictates of conscience." The school district sued the commissioner and the State Department of Education. Later, two groups intervened. Supporting the school district was a group consisting of parents who sent their children to religious school, but not the children themselves. This group claimed that parents' right to free exercise of religion entitled them to tuition reimbursement and that the fact of parental choice of schools relieved the state of any responsibility for what the state aid supported or promoted. Supporting the state was a group of local residents who objected to use of their tax payments to fund religious schools.

The Vermont Supreme Court stated explicitly at the outset of its decision that it was irrelevant how the program affected the quality of education for children. The case would turn entirely on an interpretation of the Compelled Support Clause in the state constitution and on the First Amendment rights of parents. The court read the Compelled Support Clause to preclude even indirect payment for religious instruction per se, and its holding against the school district turned critically on the fact that the district did nothing to ensure public money was used only for secular education. The court suggested that the outcome might be different if "the amount of the subsidy is so small that it clearly covers only the cost of secular educational expenses," or if the district put in place some kind of "restrictions that prevent the use of public money to fund religious education." Because the court was not ruling that aid may not go to religious schools under any circumstances, it was able to reject the parents' free exercise claim on the grounds that it was not mandating discrimination against religious institutions. The court emphasized that its ruling "requires no one 'to choose between following the precepts of [his or her] religion and forfeiting benefits' that would otherwise be available from the government." One might infer from this assurance that the court would find impermissible any scheme of state financial support for education that did in fact put parents to such a choice—for example, if the state required as a condition for receiving state support that a school promote critical thinking, which some parents might oppose on religious grounds.

WISCONSIN   As noted above, the Milwaukee program was challenged in federal court before it was amended to include religious schools. Unlike any of the suits brought in Vermont or Maine, this federal suit in Wisconsin, *Miller v. Benson*,[16] included children as well as parents among the plaintiffs. The challenge to the program was based on rights to free exercise of religion and equal protection. Although children were named as plaintiffs, the court's analysis of the claimed rights focused entirely on the interests and position of the parents.

The court found that the parents met the threshold requirement of having standing to sue because the program's impact on the parents' "right to direct their children's religious training" constituted a sufficient personal injury. In addition, they stated a prima facie free exercise claim, because "[t]he Constitution protects parents' rights to direct the education of their children, to choose private education over public education, and to choose religious schools over nonreligious schools." The court offered no indication of what the content of the children's rights might have been or what injury they might have suffered from the exclusion of religious schools. Ultimately, the court rejected the challenge to the program, based solely on a conclusion that including religious schools in the program would violate the Establishment Clause. As was true in Vermont and Maine, the court in this case did not balance Establishment Clause concerns against the rights of the individual plaintiffs. Once it found a conflict with the Establishment Clause, that was the end of the matter.

Following legislative amendment of the program to include religious schools, several groups challenged it in state court. The plaintiffs included an organization of parents who had children in, and were committed to, the public school system, an organization of public school teachers, and the NAACP.[17] The defendant was the State Superintendent of Public Instruction. Several groups intervened on the side of the defendant, including individual students and parents who wished to participate in the amended program and who claimed their right to free exercise of religion would be violated if the courts' invalidated the amendment allowing religious school participation.

The plaintiffs in *Jackson v. Benson* argued in part that the voucher program is bad public policy, and the Wisconsin Supreme Court rightly pointed out that it is not the judiciary's role to invalidate programs simply because they are bad policy. The plaintiffs also argued that including religious schools in the program violated state and federal antiestablishment constitutional provisions, as well as certain other state constitutional prohibitions. The Wisconsin Supreme Court rejected all of these constitutional arguments. Accordingly, it had no occasion to address the intervening defendants' free exercise claim. In any event, the court gave no indication that such a claim, or any other on behalf of students or parents, would influence the outcome if it found a conflict between the amended program and antiestablishment norms.

I note here just two interesting aspects of the Wisconsin Supreme Court's Establishment Clause analysis. First, in applying the "secular purpose" prong of the *Lemon* test, the court did not say that the purpose of the program was to ensure children a better secular education. Rather, the court stated that "[t]he purpose of the program is to provide low-income parents with an opportunity to have their children educated outside of the embattled Milwaukee Public School system." The focus, then, was on providing something for parents.

Second, in applying the "excessive entanglement" prong of the *Lemon* test, the court emphasized that schools participating in the program are subject only to the same "minimal standards" to which they would otherwise be subject. Under the Establishment Clause analysis, as the courts have framed it, it is a good thing that the state does not closely monitor schools and "does not involve itself in any way with the schools' . . . curriculum, or day-to-day affairs."

OHIO   Litigation surrounding the Cleveland program began in state court, then moved to federal court after the state court found the program did not violate federal or state antiestablishment constitutional provisions. In state court, the plaintiffs were the Ohio Federation of Teachers and individual taxpayers. Intervening in support of the state defendants were an organization of parents and students and an organization of private schools who were registered to participate in the program. At no stage of the state litigation did a court articulate what rights or interests the intervening parties might have had at stake.

In their Establishment Clause analysis, the Ohio state courts, like the Wisconsin state courts, all characterized the purpose of the voucher program as something other than giving children a better education. For the trial court, the purpose of the program was "providing financial assistance to parents who choose to send their children to private schools."[18] For the intermediate appellate court, the purpose was "to provide low income parents with an opportunity to have their children educated outside the embattled Cleveland City School District."[19] The focus in both lower courts was thus on giving something to parents. The Ohio Supreme Court's discussion of the secular purpose requirement did focus on the children, but not explicitly in terms of ensuring them a better education. The court stated: "On its face, the School Voucher Program does nothing more or less than provide scholarships to certain children residing within the Cleveland City School District to enable them to attend an alternative school."[20] Parental choice and movement from one school to another were thus viewed as ends themselves, rather than as means to the end of securing a better secular education for children. The courts' characterization of purpose in this way no doubt mirrored the way the parties to the litigation characterized it. It might well be that the parties and the judges were reluctant to say the program's purpose was to ensure a better secular education for children, because then it might become necessary to investigate whether the program did actually result in children's receiving a better secular education. And it might become necessary to revise or eliminate the program if in reality it merely facilitated choice and movement without making children better off educationally.

The state courts' analysis of the "primary effect" prong of the *Lemon* test also reflected a focus on the interests of adults. The courts placed a great deal of emphasis on the fact that while the program authorized payment for children to transfer to public schools in the suburbs, no suburban school districts had agreed to accept children from the inner city. The import of this fact had solely to do with the effect it had on parental choice and parental control over children's minds. The intermediate appellate court bemoaned the fact that "[a]s a result of the lack of public school participation in the scholarship program, benefits in the program are limited, in large part, to parents who are willing to send their children to sectarian schools." This was unfair to some parents: "[T]he Pilot Program does not make a single type of benefit available to all parents. Rather the Pilot Program facially provides qualitatively and quantitatively different benefits to parents who choose to send their children to private, mostly sectarian, schools [than it provides] to those who send their children to Cleveland City School District schools." This unfairness, in turn, could coerce some parents into making a choice contrary to or in tension with their religious beliefs: "the Pilot Program creates an impermissible incentive for parents to send their children to sectarian schools." For this reason, the intermediate court would have struck down the program as a violation of the Establishment Clause.

The Ohio Supreme Court, in *Simmons-Harris v. Goff*, rejected the conclusion that the program violated the Establishment Clause. The court invalidated the program anyway, but on the basis of a state constitutional provision having to do with legislative procedures rather than antiestablishment concerns. The state legislature was able to reenact the program immediately after the court's decision, in a way that complied with that state constitutional provision. In terms of Establishment Clause analysis, the only thing the Ohio Supreme Court found troubling about the program was a part of the enacting legislation that established priorities for choosing parents who would receive the vouchers. One of the priorities was for parents who belonged to the religious organization that sponsored a participating religious school. This was problematic because it "provides an incentive for parents desperate to get their child out of the Cleveland City School District to 'modify their religious beliefs or practices' in order to enhance their opportunity to receive a School Voucher Program scholarship." The court struck down just that one aspect of the program, which it found could be severed from the rest.

With respect to the "excessive entanglement" prong of the *Lemon* test, the Ohio Supreme Court emphasized, as did courts in other states, that requirements for participation in the voucher program were "not onerous" and not significantly greater than the minimal requirements for simply operating a school within the state. It would be a bad thing, under the court's interpretation of the Establishment Clause, if the state exercised substantial oversight or imposed robust academic standards on any religious schools that it funded. Courts have sometimes recognized the tension this creates between the "secular purpose" and "primary effect" prongs of the *Lemon* test, which arguably require the state to do whatever is necessary to ensure that state money is used to provide a better secular education, and the "excessive entanglement" prong as the courts have usually construed it. The Ohio Supreme Court did not, however.

In federal court, challengers to the reenacted Cleveland program included parents of children enrolled in public schools, public school teachers, two church pastors, and a group called "Citizens Against Vouchers." Intervening on the side of the defendant state officials were two groups of parents who wished to send their children to religious schools and a group of private schools. No children were named as parties.

The federal court litigation in Ohio began dramatically. At the end of August 1999, just before a new school year was to begin, the district court hearing the case issued a preliminary injunction against the program as a whole, pending final resolution of the legal claims. Amidst public outcry and media frenzy, the court two days later scaled back the injunction so that it only prevented new participants from joining the program, while allowing students previously in the program to continue. The United States Supreme Court then agreed to review the preliminary injunction decision on an expedited basis, skipping over the Sixth Circuit Court of Appeals. In November of 1999, the Supreme Court issued a stay of the entire injunction, so that the program could proceed in its entirety while the lower federal courts adjudicated the case. One month later, the district court issued its final decision, holding that the program was unconstitutional because it included religious schools.[21]

In its final ruling, the district court spoke more clearly and strongly than has any other court about the interests protected by the Establishment Clause. Most courts do not even mention what interests taxpayer or citizen groups asserting Establishment Clause claims have. The Ohio federal court noted the historical concern that individuals not be subjected to or forced to support "government inculcation of the theologies and doctrines of a faith to which they did not subscribe." It cited Thomas Jefferson's admonition that " 'to compel a man to furnish contributions of money for the propagation of opinions which he disbelieves, is sinful and tyrannical.' "[22] The court also noted James Madison's fear that the slightest breach of the wall separating church and state would lead to more systemic evils: " 'Who does not see that . . . the same authority which can force a citizen to contribute three pence only of his property for the support of any one establishment, may force him to conform to any other establishment in all cases whatsoever?' "[23]

The district court was not much clearer than the state courts had been in articulating the supposed secular purpose of the voucher program. In its initial preliminary injunction decision, it stated vaguely that the program "was enacted by the Ohio Legislature to address an educational crisis in the public schools in Cleveland in the wake of a U.S. District Court-ordered takeover by the State of the administration of the Cleveland City School District." In its final decision, the court stated that the secular purpose, which the plaintiffs did not contest, was "to provide nonpublic school alternatives to low-income students for acceptable reasons."

However, the district court squarely addressed an argument by the state and its supporters that the primary effect of the program was to provide children with a better secular education. The defendants asserted that the private schools receiving vouchers better educate students than do the public schools, and argued that " 'the mere fact that . . . [the] school also teaches religion to its students cannot mean that the private school now suddenly serves the State's secular goals less well than if it did not add religion to its teaching.' " As explained later in the book, while the proposition that the addition of religious teaching to the curriculum does not necessarily diminish the secular educational value created is true, the premise that all voucher schools provide a superior secular education is false. But the district court did not reject the state's position because it was unsupported by evidence regarding the quality of education voucher students received. The district court rejected the state's position because it deemed the quality of secular education irrelevant. All that mattered was whether the program advanced the religious mission of sectarian schools to any degree: "[E]ven if it could be demonstrated that students participating in the Voucher Program receive a superior education to children in the Cleveland Public Schools, this fact does not obviate this court's duty to further question whether the Program also has the direct and immediate effect of advancing religion."

The court, purporting to follow Supreme Court doctrine, identified a line between aid that has such an effect and aid that does not, and found that the Cleveland program fell into the former category. In part, this was because the tuition grants "are unrestricted and can be used for any purpose a school finds necessary"; "the grants . . . are not restricted to supporting only secular functions of a participating school's educational program." As such, "the Voucher Program results in government-sponsored religious indoctrination," which is impermissible regardless of what secular benefits to children the program might also create. Unfortunately, the court gave no indication of what measures the state might take to ensure that use of the tuition grants was properly restricted.

The voucher program had the effect of advancing religion also because state money went directly to schools rather than only to parents, as would be the case with a tuition reimbursement scheme, where parents pay the tuition themselves and then seek reimbursement in one form or another from a state agency. Many other courts and many commentators have also focused on the degree to which parental choices and actions intervene between state action and the monetary benefit to religious schools. From a child-centered perspective, this focus is faintly ridiculous, and more than faintly perverse. Requiring indirectness furthers Establishment Clause values only to the extent that it diminishes the perceived "symbolic union" of church and state. (In whose eyes? The courts do not say.) Whether the state sends money directly to schools or gives money to parents because they send their child to a particular school, the state is choosing to subsidize education in religious schools. And requiring that the subsidizing take place in the form of tuition reimbursement, tax credits, or tax deductions rather than in direct up-front payments to schools is perverse because it effectively excludes from the benefits of the program the children likely to need those benefits the most—namely, those whose parents are too poor to pay private school tuition up front themselves or whose parents are not sufficiently motivated to go through the procedural steps necessary to recoup up-front outlays. The regressive consequences of the indirectness requirement must be either unnoticed by the courts or implicitly deemed irrelevant, because they are never mentioned.

Finally, the district court emphasized, as had the intermediate state court, the fact that no suburban public schools had agreed to accept voucher students and the fact that the great majority of participating private schools were religious. Because of these facts, "parents and their children do not have a significant choice between parochial and nonparochial schools." Unlike other courts, the district court referred to children choosing schools, and did so numerous times, as if the court believed that children generally decide where they go to school and that coercion of children's choice of schools is problematic. At other times, though, the court used the more common characterization of vouchers as facilitating parental choice, with children as passive objects of the choices. In any event, the court's emphasis on the lack of choice under current circumstances left open the possibility of a different outcome should the circumstances change. The court noted that the state has the power to order suburban public schools to accept inner city children with vouchers. Apparently, though, the political will has never existed to do that, and conservative groups that tout vouchers have not urged the state legislature to do so.

Although the district court was unequivocal in its decision, it elected, with the agreement of the plaintiffs, to stay its injunction against the voucher program pending review of the case by the Sixth Circuit Court of Appeals. A three-judge panel of the court of appeals ruled in December 2000, in *Simmons-Harris v. Zelman*,[24] that the Cleveland program, *as presently constituted*, does violate the Establishment Clause. The appellate court applied Supreme Court Establishment Clause doctrine rather mechanically, and stated explicitly, without explanation or justification, that the aim of avoiding infringements of the Establishment Clause is more important than the acknowledged "need to establish successful schools and academic programs for children." The court of appeals emphasized the same contingent features of the Cleveland program that the district court had emphasized—especially, the limited range of choices for parents, because no public schools and very few nonsectarian private schools participated in the program, and the fact that there were no restrictions on how schools used the voucher money, making it possible for schools to spend the money on religious instruction and materials. The court thus left it open to the state legislature to reenact the program in a way that avoids these problems— for example, by ordering suburban school districts to accept some voucher students, by increasing the amount of vouchers to make the program attractive to more schools, and / or by placing restrictions on how schools use the money they receive from the state. In fact, the court said explicitly that it was putting aside the question of "what might be legally acceptable in a hypothetical school district."

There were a few additional interesting facets of the Sixth Circuit's opinion. The court discussed at some length the mission statements of the participating religious schools. These showed that "most believe in interweaving religious beliefs with secular subjects" and that the schools require that "all learning take place in an atmosphere of religious ideals." The court did not find that such interweaving diminished the quality of secular education. There was apparently no evidence submitted on the issue for or against that conclusion. Rather, the interweaving was relevant only to the question whether the state was in some sense subsidizing religious instruction. The court also noted that the schools require all students to receive religious instruction and to attend religious services, but never indicated how that was relevant to the analysis.

The most interesting part of the opinion, though, was the court's charge that the program was "designed in a manner calculated to attract religious institutions" disproportionately. The program did this by establishing a relatively low amount for the value of the vouchers and prohibiting schools from charging parents using vouchers any tuition over and above the voucher amount. As a result, religious schools, which on average receive much more in private donations—typically through church congregations—than do nonsectarian schools, can better afford to take voucher students. Private schools without such private subsidies would lose more money on voucher students, relative to religious schools with comparable per pupil expenditures, and so have a greater disincentive to register for the program. An additional concern raised by the low tuition cap, which the court did not consider, is that it could also result in a predominance, among the schools available to students leaving public schools, of those that operate on a shoestring budget, which would tend to be the lowest-quality private schools.

A cynic might suppose that the Ohio state legislature, by establishing a low voucher amount and a tuition cap, was in fact trying to steer children to religious schools, or simply trying to solve its educational problems on the cheap. The fact that the state also authorized payment of only $2,250 per pupil to suburban schools that accept children from the inner city supports that supposition. However, the legislature might have established a low value for private school vouchers in an effort to ensure that vouchers would not cover the entire per pupil cost at any religious schools, in order to avoid the charge that it was paying for religious instruction. And the legislature might have prohibited recipient schools from charging tuition higher than the voucher amount in order to ensure that the poorest parents could participate in the program. The legislature was in a Catch-22 situation, both in terms of satisfying Establishment Clause strictures and in terms of appearing to act justly. .

The state requested Supreme Court review of the Sixth Circuit's decision, and as this book goes to press the nation awaits the Court's decision as to whether it will accept this case for review and thus finally resolve the tremendous uncertainty that revolves around the constitutionality of vouchers.

FLORIDA   Litigation in Florida began as soon as the state legislature created the Opportunity Scholarship Program (OSP) in 1999. The plaintiffs in the initial state court action included individual parents, acting in their own behalf and as representatives of their children, the NAACP, a Citizens' Coalition for Public Schools, a statewide parent-teacher association, teachers' organizations and unions, and individuals as taxpayers. They advanced claims under the federal Establishment Clause, under a state religious establishment constitutional provision, and under two state constitutional provisions dealing specifically with education.

The initial court decision concerned only one of the education provisions in the Florida constitution, article 9, section 1, which mandates that the legislature create "a uniform, efficient, safe, secure, and high quality system of free public schools that allows students to obtain a high quality education."[25] This provision, which is similar to constitutional provisions in many other states, also pronounces that it is "a paramount duty of the state to make adequate provision for the education of all children residing within its border." A Florida trial-level court held that the OSP violated this provision because the provision directs that public schools be the exclusive means through which the state fulfills its "paramount duty." In other words, the court made "uniform" the decisive term in the constitutional language, rather than any of the other possibilities. Because it found that the OSP violated article 9, section 1, the court found it unnecessary to address the other bases for challenging the program.

By finding that the state could seek to fulfill its duty to provide good elementary and secondary education only through funding of public schools, the trial court implicitly interpreted the state's duty as one of simply making a high-quality education available for parents to choose if they so desire. Florida, like every other state, confers on parents the power to waive their children's right under state law to state-provided schooling and instead to place their children in any private school, whether the private school provides a good education or not. The "paramount duty" set forth in the state constitution must therefore be seen as one owed to parents rather than children. The state apparently violates no duty by allowing some children not to receive a good education and by failing to do anything, such as subsidizing underfunded private schools, to try to prevent this from happening. Notably, the defendants did not argue that the state was *required* to provide for all children, including those whose parents would under any circumstances send their children to a private school. The defendants argued simply that it was permissible for the state to do so. The defendants might themselves have viewed the state's duty as running to parents, and as therefore *requiring* only that a free and high-quality public school education be available to all parents, and might have disagreed with the court only on the significance of "uniform."

An intermediate Florida court, in *Bush v. Holmes*,[26] reversed the trial court decision, holding that article 9, section 1, was not meant to establish an exclusive means of state support for elementary and secondary education. This court would have struck down the OSP only if article 9, section 1, explicitly prohibited state payment of private school tuition or if the OSP defeated the purpose of the constitutional provision. The court found that the OSP actually *furthered* the provision's purpose, "by raising expectations for and creating competition among schools." The court also suggested that state support of private schools might be limited to situations where such support is necessary to fulfill the state's responsibility to see that a good education is available to all. This might mean that the court would find a more expansive voucher program, one that facilitated transfer of students out of *good* public schools, would defeat the purpose of article 9, section 1. On the other hand, one could plausibly argue that the fact that some parents are legally permitted to and do in fact choose underfunded private schools for their children also creates a necessity for state funding of private schools, and that the OSP could be expanded to include children who were already attending a private school before applying for an opportunity scholarship, without violating article 9, section 1. That would, however, appear to run directly contrary to other provisions in the Florida Constitution, particularly article 1, section 3, which provides that "[n]o revenue of the state or any political subdivision or agency thereof shall ever be taken from the public treasury directly or indirectly in aid of any . . . sectarian institution." This court endorsed a flexible approach to constitutional interpretation, stating that the state constitution's " 'dominant note is the general welfare; it was not intended to bind like a strait-jacket but contemplated experimentation for the common good.' " However, getting around such an explicit prohibition on subsidizing religious institutions would require something more intellectually athletic than a mere exercise of flexibility.

Legal Academic and Public Policy Analysis

The legal scholarship and public policy writing on vouchers is too voluminous to describe fully. There has been enormous interest in the topic for many years. By and large, this literature has taken at face value, and worked within, the analytical framework that the Supreme Court has established in aid-to-school cases and that the lower courts have applied to voucher programs. The arguments typically track those made by lower court judges on either side of the issue.

Most of the legal academic writing comes from constitutional law scholars, and in particular from experts on the religion clauses, rather than from scholars of education law or family law. For that reason, it may be unsurprising that this writing has focused almost exclusively on Supreme Court Establishment Clause doctrine, on the interests of taxpayers, and on the First Amendment rights of parents and religious organizations. It is one more manifestation of the fact that our national constitution was not written with children at all in mind that a legal debate about a fundamental aspect of child rearing should center exclusively on the religious rights of adults. Although the Supreme Court has of late acknowledged that children are persons, the constitutional text itself and the Court's interpretation of the text provide little material for a child-centered constitutional jurisprudence. Nevertheless, it *is* possible to construct constitutional arguments to further the interests and moral rights of children. I offer arguments of that kind in later chapters. Because this is possible, even constitutional scholars can be faulted when they ignore or undervalue children's welfare and claims to justice, and when they fail to point out and protest the courts' adult-centered approach to child-rearing controversies like that over school vouchers.

Most of the public policy writing comes from or is sponsored by national organizations that advocate for a variety of conservative religious or economic causes or for liberal civil rights causes. One does not find much policy writing on vouchers emanating from child welfare organizations. The greatest interest in vouchers has been among perennial defenders of conservative causes. The same groups and individuals that have defended school prayer, parents' demands to withdraw their children from aspects of public school instruction to which the parents object, and the Boy Scouts' discrimination against homosexuals, and that have opposed values clarification and sex education in public schools, have come out in full force to advocate for vouchers.

Proponents of vouchers in the legal academy and in policy circles rest their case on principles of equality and rights of religious exercise—equality among parents, equality between religion and secular society, and the right of parents to choose a comprehensively religious upbringing for their children.[27] The arguments closely resemble the claims made by the plaintiffs in the Vermont,

Maine, and early Wisconsin litigation. All insist that if a state does provide financial assistance to private schools, it must provide assistance evenhandedly to both religious and nonreligious private schools. Otherwise, the state would be discriminating among parents who choose a private school, based on religious motivation, or discriminating against religious organizations. Thus, voucher proponents would oppose a new voucher program for poor children if it allowed participation only by nonsectarian schools, even if this were the only politically feasible step that could be taken to benefit those children at the time. Many voucher supporters go even further, and insist that states *must* go beyond funding only public schools to also provide financial assistance for private, including religious, schools. A no-voucher regime, in their view, discriminates against religiously motivated parents, those whose religious convictions prevent them from sending their children to public school. It also coerces less affluent parents to send their children to a public school that teaches things contrary to the parents' religious beliefs. Thus, even if all public schools were wonderful, these writers would insist that parents are entitled to vouchers, to state financial support for their preference to keep their children out of public schools.

Like the courts, supporters of vouchers manifest little interest in whether voucher programs are established in such a way as to ensure that children who attend a private school using a voucher actually receive a good education. While there is occasionally glancing recognition of the constitutional requirement that a voucher program in fact serve the supposed secular purpose of improving secular education, there is no discussion of what sorts of regulation would be needed to make sure that happens. Most often, voucher supporters treat parental choice as the ultimate end, thus rendering irrelevant what the consequences are for children's education. Vouchers are about parental power, at least for those parents who prefer religious schools. At times, supporters of aid to religious schools appear to assume, without support, either that states already ensure that all private schools are academically sound or that parents would always choose a superior secular education for their children if given the opportunity.[28] The former assumption is, as I have indicated, patently false.

The latter assumption, that parents are intelligent consumers of schools and driven to choose schools with the best secular education, lies at the core of the "vouchers produce competition and competition improves education" argument that defenders of parental freedom of religion have happily borrowed from conservative economists. Yet this assumption is clearly not true in all, or even many, cases. Even if one assumed that parents typically obtain substantial information about available schools before enrolling their child in one of them, which is not the case, and even if one assumed that all parents are capable of judging the respective merits of different schools, which would require overlooking the tragic deprivations so many parents have themselves suffered, one must acknowledge that some parents simply have aims for their children's education that are inconsistent with the state's aims. Many parents who choose a religious school do so primarily to ensure an ideologically orthodox environment for their children, and many are in fundamental disagreement with the basic aims of public education. Indeed, the same people who support vouchers champion the right of parents to make that choice for that reason. Given that many parents do exercise that right, these supporters of vouchers ought to recognize that the "parental choice leads to better education" argument is problematic. If a better education is defined simply as one that parents prefer, then the argument is circular. If a better education is one that the state views as superior, then parental choice clearly leads in many cases to a worse education.

Voucher proponents do occasionally speak of children's rights, but never as conceptually distinct from parents' rights. Children's rights are really parents' rights in disguise. At best, then, they are meaningless. At worst, they are a ploy to distract attention from the ways in which children's interests are ignored. Proponents speak, nonsensically, of children's having a right to choose to leave bad public schools, when the plain fact is that six-year-olds do not make such choices, and when no existing or proposed voucher scheme has ever tied participation to the willingness or request of students themselves to move to another school. Less often, a voucher proponent might speak of a child's right to a good education. But it is difficult to interpret this as anything more than window dressing when the speaker manifests no interest in whether children in religious schools actually receive a better secular education, and when this supposed right of the child is implicitly treated as entirely defeasible by the choice or negligence of the parent. If a parent leaves a child in a bad public school because she lacks the wherewithal or motivation to negotiate the voucher application and private school admission process, or if a parent chooses a religious school that provides little or no secular education because in her religious worldview secular education is of no value or is harmful, that is perfectly acceptable to voucher proponents. The child's right to a good education vanishes when it does not coincide with parents' choices.

On the other side of the voucher debate are, in addition to teachers unions and others who fear adverse effects on public schools, organizations who have been fighting the religious right on a number of issues and who view vouchers as another attempt to put the power of the state in service to the hegemony of conservative Christianity. These organizations have taken a hard line against Bible reading in public schools, against religious displays on public property, and against special exemptions for religious groups and individuals from a variety of regulations and legal prohibitions, and they are reluctant to give an inch to religious conservatives on school reform, even though they recognize that children's basic welfare is on the line.[29]

One concern voucher opponents have is that parents might be coerced into sending their children to religious schools, because states, rather than fixing bad public schools, create programs of support for private education in which nearly all the choices available are sectarian schools. They also speak of children's being indoctrinated, but the real concern is not with the welfare of children; the objection is not that religious instruction is harmful to children or that children will miss out on a good education. They readily concede that parents are entitled—without state subsidy—to choose a religious school for their children, and they manifest no more interest than voucher proponents in whether children in religious schools receive a good education. The real concern is that with vouchers more children might be indoctrinated with conservative religious beliefs than would otherwise be the case. This might change the religious composition of our country, giving the religious right more political power, and few things are more frightening to liberals.

Voucher opponents are also concerned that taxpayers might be forced to subsidize religious institutions. No-aid separationists echo the absolutist Madisonian line, sometimes cited by courts invalidating aid to religious schools, that "the same authority which can force a citizen to contribute three pence only of his property for the support of any one establishment, may force him to conform to any other establishment in all cases whatsoever."[30] *Any* infringement of Establishment Clause values is unacceptable, because once there is the slightest crack in the wall of church-state separation, there will be no stopping a wave of religious tyranny from smashing through.

This Madisonian rhetoric is hyperbolic, and it fails to distinguish the Establishment Clause and the values it protects from other constitutional provisions and the important values they protect. In other areas, courts allow infringements on constitutional rights and principles where the infringement is more or less necessary in order for the state to further important competing interests or values. The Free Speech Clause, for example, is also an essential bulwark against tyranny, yet free speech doctrine allows for a balancing of competing state interests against the values underlying the clause and upholds state action and state programs that restrict speech when such restriction enables the state to further important state aims.

Indeed, in light of the role the Establishment Clause plays in the Bill of Rights, it is quite ironic that it has been elevated to a position of lexical priority over all other constitutional values and all competing aims. The Establishment Clause is a complement to the Free Exercise Clause, with both intended to protect religious freedom. The Free Exercise Clause, as interpreted by the Supreme Court, does this directly, by conferring rights on individuals against state action that threatens their religious liberty in direct ways—for example, laws that proscribe certain religious practices. The Establishment Clause, on the other hand, protects religious liberty indirectly, by prohibiting the state from favoring any particular faith or favoring religion in general. This protects adherents of other faiths or adherents of no faith from incidentally feeling disfavored or disadvantaged, or being presented with incentives to change their beliefs or practices, and thereby feeling more subtle coercion of belief and practice.[31]

The irony is that the Supreme Court has of late interpreted the Free Exercise Clause—the provision that protects individuals from direct and substantial incursions on their religious freedom—in a far from absolutist way. Following the Court's 1990 decision in *Employment Division v. Smith*,[32] facially neutral laws that burden religious practice—for example, a drug law that has the unintended effect of making virtually impossible the religious ceremonies of some group—trigger only rational basis review, the form of judicial review that is most deferential to legislative action. Under rational basis review, a law survives so long as the state can show some connection between the prohibition and a legitimate public purpose—for example, that prohibiting use of a particular drug might reduce the incidence of disorderly behavior or worker absenteeism. Even laws that are not facially neutral, that target particular religious groups—for example, a prohibition of ritual animal sacrifice in a jurisdiction that allows killing of the very same animals for the purpose of consumption—are not automatically invalid. The group discriminated against must show that the law burdens its religious practice to a significant degree, and then the state has an opportunity to show that its discriminatory prohibition is necessary to further a compelling state purpose. This is the "strict scrutiny" test that is also seen in cases of racial discrimination, and while laws rarely survive this rigorous form of judicial review, the possibility does exist that the free exercise values will be sacrificed in order to serve some other important value. If, for example, the particular way a religious group's ceremonial killing of animals takes place presents a serious public health threat, a court might well uphold a law prohibiting the killing of animals in that way.

In contrast, when courts find that a law to any degree infringes the Establishment Clause—a constitutional provision whose connection to individual religious liberty is sufficiently tenuous that courts do not even interpret it as generating individual rights[33]—they invalidate the law automatically, without allowing the state to demonstrate that the law is necessary to further an important state interest. I am suggesting not that the Establishment Clause is an unimportant constitutional provision, but rather that since its connection to individual liberty is more tenuous than is that of the Free Exercise Clause, the Free Speech Clause, the Due Process Clause, and several other constitutional provisions, its strictures should be more lax than those of the other provisions, not more stringent. It is therefore all the more troubling that voucher opponents cite the Establishment Clause as the basis for their opposition, without even considering whether the purported state purpose of helping children in destitute circumstances is more important than their establishment concerns. I develop this point further in later chapters: in Chapter 3, when I discuss the relative importance of human interests at stake in the voucher debate, and in Chapter 5, when I discuss application of Establishment Clause doctrine to vouchers.

Many opponents of vouchers, particularly representatives of teacher unions, rest their case on the supposed adverse effects of voucher programs on public schools. To the extent their concern is with the welfare of the children who would remain in public schools, rather than with the vested interests of school employees and state officials, it is child centered. One wonders, though, why those who claim to be concerned about the fate of children focus exclusively on the children who would be left behind in public schools, rather than considering also the potential gains for those who would transfer to private schools, as well as the potential benefits for children who are already in private schools. Is there a conflict of interests between groups of children? Should there be a weighing and balancing of those competing interests? Such questions go unaddressed. Whenever one group of children is singled out for concern while other groups of children with important interests at stake are ignored, there is cause for suspicion that adult-centered rather than child-centered thinking is at work. In any event, I address this concern about the fate of public schools in Chapter 3.

Finally, there is also reference in the antivoucher literature to the common school ideal of civic education. Some claim that dispersion of more children into private schools captive to particularist ideologies would thwart the aims of civic education. This concern has been the subject of extensive and careful discussion in philosophical circles, and it warrants separate treatment. Chapter 2 is therefore largely devoted to that topic. I note here simply that this concern is about the welfare of society as a whole, rather than about the welfare of individual schoolchildren, and rests on an instrumental view of children's lives—that is, a view that children's education is important insofar as it can be used to further diffuse societal interests.

In sum, both proponents and opponents of vouchers in the legal academy and in public policy circles manifest little interest in the welfare of the individual children whose healthy development is at stake. All treat the conflict as one between groups of adults—parents versus state officials and teachers unions supposedly hell-bent on secularizing children and clinging to power, or the religious right versus the rest of society, including parents who would be coerced by a voucher program to send their children to a religious school. Both sides invoke constitutional provisions to support their cause, provisions courts have interpreted without giving any serious consideration to the place of children in the overall constitutional scheme, or to the impact their rulings will have on children.

Conclusion

The nation holds its breath waiting for the Supreme Court to decide once and for all whether voucher programs that include religious schools are permissible. But will the Court approach the issue in the proper way? Should the normative status of state support for the education of certain children turn solely on antiestablishment concerns? Does the lexical priority given to antiestablishment strictures accurately reflect the relative importance of the various human interests at stake in this matter? Does it make sense to give Establishment Clause plaintiffs the power to thwart measures to advance children's fundamental interests? What rights, if any, do other people have in connection with state funding of private education? If there are any, should they not be balanced against Establishment Clause concerns, and is it not possible that in some contexts antiestablishment values are simply less important than other values? The courts have not answered these questions, and commentators have generally overlooked them as well. Instead there is endless debate about what the Establishment Clause test currently is or should be. I have something to say about that as well, but I will primarily be concerned to address vouchers from a broader perspective that recognizes the full range of human interests, rights, and values at stake in this important societal issue, and that assesses their relative importance in as objective a way as possible.

[2]

Education Reform and
Adult-Centered Political Theory

Debates concerning education reform have also raged in philosophical circles in the past decade. Much of the debate has focused on public school curriculum and on parental objections to specific aspects of curriculum that local political majorities favor. Most recently, though, there has been substantial interest in vouchers for private school attendance. Political theorists have their own, unique take on education reform issues. In their writings, the Establishment Clause and its underlying values have played little role. Philosophers have instead focused more on the abstract problem of preserving liberal democratic institutions while also accounting for and responding to the fact of ideological diversity and the objections of nonliberal cultural groups to the hegemony of those institutions. The conversation political theorists have had about children's education has been dominated by a debate between proponents of "civic education" and defenders of parents' rights and pluralism. In this chapter, I describe this debate and explain why it is misguided.

The Dominant Conversation among Political Theorists

Discussion of education policy by political theorists in recent years has focused largely on the problem of stability, on what a liberal society must command by way of children's education to ensure that succeeding generations support the institutions of a just liberal society. This concern has led some theorists to advocate using public schools to foster civic virtues and to create the right kind of future citizens. Will Kymlicka and Wayne Norman herald "an explosion of interest in the concept of citizenship among political theorists," resulting from increasing concern that commitment to democratic cooperation is evaporating, as evidenced by such things as voter apathy, welfare dependency, and "the failure of environmental policies that rely on voluntary citizen cooperation."[1] These developments

> have made clear that the health and stability of a modern democracy depends, not only on the justice of its "basic structure" but also on the quality and attitudes of its citizens: for example, their sense of identity and how they view potentially competing forms of national, regional, ethnic, or religious identities; their ability to tolerate and work together with others who are different from themselves; their desire to participate in the political process in order to promote the public good and hold political authorities accountable; their willingness to show self-restraint and exercise personal responsibility in their economic demands and in personal choices which affect their health and the environment. Without citizens who possess these qualities, democracies become difficult to govern, even unstable.[2]

For those most concerned about the problem of stability, vouchers are of interest because they draw students out of democratizing "common schools" and into sectarian schools that might not instill civic or democratic virtues and that might insulate their students from persons whose beliefs and identities are significantly different from their own. The principal counterpoise to this concern among political theorists has been a concern for the rights of parents and nonliberal cultural minorities whose adult members wish to pass on their beliefs to their children and thereby preserve their particularist way of life. Eamonn Callan, in a book entitled *Creating Citizens,* captures the essence of this two-sided struggle when he writes:

> If the role of the state in education is to keep faith with its constitutive morality, a path must be found between the horns of a dilemma. The need to perpetuate fidelity to liberal democratic institutions and values from one generation to another suggests that there are some inescapably shared educational aims, even if the pursuit of these conflicts with the convictions of some citizens. Yet if repression is to be avoided, the state must give parents substantial latitude to instill in their children whatever religious faith or conception of the good they espouse. Similarly, the state must permit communities of like-minded citizens to create educational institutions that reflect their distinctive way of life, even if that entails some alienation from the political culture of the larger society.[3]

Thus, the philosophical debate over educational authority has treated children's schooling as an instrument for serving ends of society as a whole and ends of parents and adult members of religious groups. The participants in this debate divide into liberal statists, who give primacy to creating the right kind of future citizens and to empowering citizens to participate in the process of shaping future generations, and those I will call "pluralists," who give primacy to protecting the power of parents and minority cultural communities to create the kind of future persons they want. Theorists on both sides occasionally take note of children's interests as individual persons whose lives are at stake, but only as an afterthought or as a secondary concern. By no means are children's interests and rights driving the theories, nor is any serious consideration given to what children's interests and rights might be. The contest is conceptualized as one between competing groups of adults who want to control children's education to serve their own ends.

The nature of this philosophical debate, and the concern it raises, might be better understood by considering an analogy to decision making about child custody in divorce proceedings. When a divorcing couple has children, state statutes command that judges allocate "legal custody" (that is, authority to make major decisions such as where the child will attend school) as well as physical custody (i.e., time spent in each postdivorce household) on the basis of the best interests of the child. This command is consonant with the view, sometimes expressed by judges in this limited context, that child rearing is first and foremost about the welfare of children, and that children have the most important interests at stake in the custody decision. Nevertheless, in practice judges sometimes fail to maintain a focus on the child's welfare and instead slip into a mode of reasoning that focuses on fairness to the parents or on giving each parent some share of victory—splitting the baby. These judges are acting contrary to the law and to its moral underpinnings. Political theorizing about education has resembled this illicit form of judicial reasoning about legal custody, insofar as it has focused on arbitrating the competing claims of adults rather than on promoting the welfare of children. The question arises, then, whether such a focus is any more appropriate in debating education policy than it is in resolving custody disputes between parents.

The Liberal Statist Position

Amy Gutmann's *Democratic Education* exemplifies the liberal statist view. In that seminal work, Gutmann argues that the liberal state can justifiably demand of all parents that they allow their children to be taught certain virtues, such as mutual respect, necessary to preserve liberal democratic society. Certainly one *could* argue for teaching virtues on the basis of children's welfare. Instilling respect for other persons, for example, promotes children's ability to interact harmoniously and constructively with a wide range of people throughout their lives. Like other liberal statists, however, Gutmann does not approach questions of school curriculum by asking what best serves the interests of children or what children are entitled to as a matter of justice. Rather she asks how children's education can serve the interests of liberal society as a whole and the "right" of adult citizens to participate in "conscious social reproduction."[4]

To be sure, how society as a whole fares is important to the welfare of today's children as well as today's adults, so children presumably benefit in some way from policies that advance the good of society as a whole. The problem is that in the liberal statist approach to education, children's welfare has no special place, is not the focus of moral attention, and is satisfied *only* to the extent that children share with all other citizens in the good of a stable liberal society. Whether promoting particular liberal aims for society as a whole, or promoting liberal aims by particular means, is entirely consistent with children's educational interests, and if not whether those societal aims could be served by some other means, and whether children's interests require more by way of education than liberal societal aims require, are questions left unexamined.

Gutmann explicitly rejects in *Democratic Education* an approach to education policy whereby the state would impose on all schools requirements designed to give each child the best education reasonably possible, so that today's children might have happier, more fulfilling lives.[5] Of course, there are often substantial difficulties in determining what is best in terms of education for children, even from a single perspective, as well as practical difficulties in implementing any education policy that some parents and cultural communities oppose. Gutmann discusses those difficulties, but ultimately they are not why she would not require that all children receive an education comporting with the best current understanding of what is a good education. Rather, she objects that this approach would violate "the right of citizens to deliberate collectively about how to educate future citizens."[6] The overriding point is that adult rights to control the lives of children are not distributed broadly enough; not only adults-as-parents but also adults-as-citizens deserve such rights.

Gutmann's citizen right of participation in social reproduction is not inherently inconsistent with the conclusions a child-centered approach would generate, but it is also not inherently consistent with a child-centered approach. It might be that children's welfare in general is best served by a decision-making process for education policy that relies substantially on democratic deliberation. But Gutmann's project is not one of showing that to be the case, as a child-centered argument for democratic control would strive to do, nor is it necessary to her position that this supposition be true. Her ultimate standard of acceptable decision-making procedures is whether they treat fairly the groups of adults who disagree[7] and whether they gratify the desires of adults both as parents and as citizens to shape the future of our society, to participate in social reproduction.[8] Thus, if any of Gutmann's conclusions in *Democratic Education* are in fact consistent with children's welfare on the whole, it is coincidental rather than compelled by her approach.

In fact, there is reason to believe that the decision-making procedure Gutmann recommends would sometimes generate outcomes contrary to children's welfare, and that Gutmann views that as entirely appropriate. This would appear to be a necessary implication of her position that even if the wisest educational authority knew what is good for children, that authority should not be able to act to secure that good if it conflicts with the interests of adults. In creating education policy, the state must "tak[e] our good, both as parents and as citizens, into account. . . . [W]e shall want some assurance from even the wisest educational authority that our good as parents and as citizens, and not just the good of our children, will be considered in designing the educational system for our society."[9]

More recent work by Gutmann and other liberal statists continues the theme of citizens' rights versus parents' rights, but focuses more on the content of education, rather than just the procedures of decision making.[10] The content they would prescribe for children's education, typically characterized as "civic education," is "an education adequate to exercising their basic rights and responsibilities as free and equal citizens."[11] It would include such things as "skills of literacy, numeracy, and critical thinking, as well as contextual knowledge, understanding, and appreciation of other people's perspectives," in addition to "virtues that . . . include veracity, nonviolence, practical judgment, civic integrity and magnanimity."[12] It would be easy to mistake this prescription as one grounded in the rights of individual children, because those items all sound like things children might benefit from acquiring, but it is not. It is a prescription grounded in the abstract "democratic ideal" of a universal "commitment to treating adults as free and equal beings."[13] In other words, a political theory of democracy dictates that all or nearly all adult citizens must possess certain skills and virtues, including the capacity to deliberate rationally and to respect the equal citizenship of others, in order for our liberal society to persist. Children's education is primarily about fostering those virtues, for that purpose. Whether it is also entirely consistent with children's developmental needs liberal statists do not ask.

What is most troubling about the liberal statist account is what is left out of its prescriptions for education, as a result of its limited focus on diffuse societal aims and on the rights of adult citizens, and as a result of the concessions it makes to parental rights. For example, Gutmann responds to pluralists' arguments for plenary parental rights over children's education by arguing that local majorities should have the *discretion* to mandate certain practices that would be in the interests of children. If local majorities elect not to act to promote children's welfare, then parents' rights control. Thus, for example, whether schools in our still pervasively sexist society affirmatively promote gender equality would be a matter of discretion for local polities, dependent on how adult citizens in any given locale choose to exercise their right of participation in social reproduction.[14] The moral rights universe contains only adult citizen rights and parental rights. There is no consideration of whether girls (and boys) in all schools might possess a right to instruction that promotes gender equality.

Liberal statist views on funding and regulation of private schools likewise reflect a focus on the claims of parents and citizen majorities rather than on doing justice for children. When discussing school vouchers, Gutmann's analysis is couched in terms of subsidizing parental choice: "Democratic education calls for the choice of an effective school for every parent whose child is not now receiving an adequate education in a neighborhood public school."[15] Why, one might wonder, should the transfer of children from bad schools to good schools depend on parental choice? If subsidized transfers to private schools are necessary, why not do it on the basis of random selection among all students, not just those whose parents apply for vouchers, or on the basis of individual educational need or ability to benefit from the transfer?[16] Operating from a child-centered perspective, one would not simply assume that only children whose parents affirmatively seek a better education for them should receive one. Similarly, when discussing children already enrolled in private schools, Gutmann writes that it is not unfair to their parents that the state make them bear the cost of their (the parents') choice.[17] From a child-centered perspective, one would instead ask whether it is fair *to those children*—many of whose schools are resource poor and many of whom miss out on educational experiences outside school because of tuition costs—that they do not share in the benefit of state funding for education.

Finally, when discussing imposition of educational standards on schools, Gutmann implies that only public schools and publicly subsidized private schools should be subject to such standards,[18] as if it is not fair to parents to regulate the schools they choose when the state is not giving them financial support. Do the children attending private schools that are not receiving public subsidies have no claim to state protection of their educational interests? From a child-centered perspective, one might well conclude that the state has an obligation to regulate those schools as well, because that is necessary to protect those children's developmental interests.

In sum, while there is no necessary or inherent conflict between the liberal statist approach and children's welfare, there is also no necessary or inherent identity between the sets of policies the liberal statist approach yields and the well-being of children. There is in theory a single standpoint—that of the state—from which all issues are assessed, and again in theory it is possible that the state could, though focused on serving democratic ideals, reach decisions on all child-rearing matters that are consistent with the welfare of children. The problem is that nothing in the liberal statist approach guarantees that. Liberal statists advance certain aims for education, such as instilling liberal virtues, that might well benefit today's children, as individuals and as members of a society

[53]

that benefits from stable liberal institutions. But they have little to say about children's other, unique interests as developing individuals, which are quite important and which might conflict with particular means of pursuing liberal statist aims.

Further, in addition to identifying particular aims for schooling, "democratic education" specifies, to some degree, decision-making procedures regarding education policy, but there is no reason to think those procedures will always, or even more often than not, produce decisions conducive to children's welfare. It imposes no substantive criteria for majoritarian deliberation about education, and there is certainly reason for concern that local adult majorities will reason on the basis of, and vote so as to promote, interests other than those of children.[19] Finally, liberal statists typically posit as the principal, and sometimes only, constraint on majoritarian decision making the supposed rights of parents and cultural communities—that is, the competing claims of other adults.[20] They frequently make concessions to those adult rights that potentially sacrifice the welfare of children.[21]

The Pluralist Position

The pluralist view is even more troubling from a child welfare perspective, because it *does* entail an inherent conflict between children's welfare as the state—which ultimately must create an education policy—sees it, and adult interests. William Galston is among those who give priority to pluralism and parental and community rights, as against the state's views of what are better and worse forms of education. In reasoning about conflicts over schooling, Galston takes as his point of departure the need "to take deep diversity seriously as an abiding fact of social life."[22] Diversity is not simply to be accepted out of necessity, though; it is to be valued, because it protects personal liberty, the ability of individuals to live their lives by their own lights.[23]

Galston accordingly posits that parents have a right to presumptive authority over their children's education. This right is predicated not on an assumption that it is in children's interest for parents to have that right, but rather on parents' desire to pass on their way of life to their children.[24] This right is limited only by the bedrock needs of the liberal polity—specifically, by society's need for citizens to be self-sufficient rather than social burdens, and in possession of the minimum liberal virtues, consisting of respect for the law, "willingness to coexist peacefully with ways of life very different from one's own," and "the minimal conditions of reasonable public judgment."[25] For the liberal state to require anything for children's education beyond these "functional needs of its sociopolitical institutions" would constitute an unwarranted infringement of the right of parents.[26]

Thus, for pluralists as for the liberal statists, two values really matter in resolving parent-state conflicts over education—stability and diversity, or in other words, social reproduction and individual or community reproduction. Education is not principally, or at all, about promoting the welfare of individual children. Only after general societal aims and the desires of current adults have been balanced is there any consideration of the well-being of today's children, and then only to assert, with little or no analysis, that the conclusions reached are consistent with, or at least not terribly at odds with, children's welfare.[27]

On the topic of school reform and vouchers, pluralists are naturally inclined to emphasize parental choice even more than are the liberal statists. They support school voucher schemes that contain only the barest of regulatory conditions and are particularly reluctant to accept any conditions that would influence the content of instruction. In the pluralist view, such conditions would threaten free exercise rights by coercing religious groups to sacrifice their religious mission to some degree, and would threaten equal protection rights by disadvantaging some religious denominations relative to others in seeking public subsidy.

Why the Conversation Needs to Change

What is wrong with the prevailing philosophical discourse as I have described it? Why should the conversation about children's education be any different? After all, adults do have interests at stake; we want the future of our society and the future of our own offspring to reflect our vision of the good life. Children's education is a particularly propitious means of accomplishing this end. Why not approach education policy with these ends foremost in our minds? Indeed, is that not how common schooling arose in the first place—to serve the public interest, the ends of democratic society, and to create the right kind of future citizens?

The most straightforward response is to point out the obvious fact that among all the interests potentially affected by children's schooling, none are more important than those belonging to the children themselves. In fact, as discussed further in Chapter 3, they are the only persons who have immediately at stake interests that are truly fundamental. Schooling is about shaping minds, fostering skills, providing socializing activities, and generally preparing young people for adult life. The minds that are being shaped belong to the children, not to us adults. The skills reside in them and largely determine their life prospects, not ours. They are the ones being socialized, not us. And they are the ones who will live the adult lives. Ordinarily when we debate policies affecting the fundamental welfare of some group of individuals today, those individuals—*their* rights, *their* interests, *their* claim to justice—are the focus of moral inquiry. The interests of other persons—and typically other persons do have interests at stake as well—are at best of secondary importance, and consideration of them might even be ruled out.

This is especially important when the persons whose fundamental welfare is at stake are nonautonomous. Making decisions about the lives of such persons on the basis of societal aims or the rights of their caretakers is fraught with danger, because of their inability to protect their own interests and because of the historical tendency to undervalue or altogether ignore their interests. Our current practice with respect to nonautonomous adults is scrupulously to guard against this danger; the law mandates that decisions about their lives be based solely on their interests and rights, even though it is often quite difficult to define their interests and rights.[28] Even in regard to adults who have never been autonomous, we believe that ordering their lives so as to further the interests of other people, or to advance general societal aims, would be immoral and incompatible with a proper respect for their personhood. Imagine, for example, someone proposing that all the mentally disabled adults in a town be paraded down Main Street waving flags, for the purpose of shaming nondisabled adults who are insufficiently civic-minded. We would regard such instrumental treatment of persons to serve collective interests as immoral, regardless of whether the disabled adults were harmed in any way. In fact, we would say that it is worse to use incompetent persons than it is to use competent persons to serve collective ends, precisely because the former are more vulnerable and less able to protect themselves from harm.

Admittedly, our heightened sensitivity to instrumental treatment of nonautonomous adults is a relatively recent development; the history of this society's treatment of the mentally disabled is not one of which we can be very proud. But the fact that our practices today are much different suggests that there has been a transformation of our moral attitudes toward nonautonomous persons in recent times, and that we believe our current practices ought to match our current moral principles. We do not look to the original reasons for having institutions for the mentally disabled and insist that the same aims govern their treatment today. To the contrary, we repudiate the original aims and insist on treating these people in a manner consonant with contemporary understandings of our moral obligation to dependent persons.

Why is it, then, that political theorists do not give priority of place to the welfare of children when discussing child rearing? It is not that they deny the personhood of children or explicitly assert that children's welfare does not matter. As with nonautonomous adults, children today have a different moral standing than they did just a half century ago; while many adults do still think of and even treat children as property, the moral beliefs we voice publicly condemn such an attitude. Thus, no political theorist today openly asserts that it is appropriate to treat children's lives instrumentally, as simply means to further collective ends or the ends of particular adults, such as parents. The reason they do not in practice give children the attention and solicitude that the children's interests should command, if children are to be given their due as persons, appears to have much more to do with the history of philosophy itself and the difficulty of breaking old habits. The basic theories political theorists operate from developed historically in contexts involving only competent, self-determining adults and historically have been applied almost exclusively to real world contexts that involved only—or were treated as involving only—such adults (e.g., property rights, distribution of wealth, freedom of speech, punishment of crime). The principal theories in the tradition of political philosophy depend to a substantial degree on the premise that all the individuals about whom the theories must concern themselves are autonomous adult individuals. Thinking about nonautonomous persons is unfamiliar terrain, and most political theorists likely find unattractive the prospect of revamping wholesale their intellectual apparatus, so they do not.

Another, related explanation of the general disregard for children's interests is that many theorists are understandably squeamish about discussing individuals' interests rather than, and independent of, individuals' choices. Theorizing about the "standard" problems of political theory—i.e., conflicts between competent adults or between competent adults and the state—is made easier by taking at face value individuals' expression of their own interests. Liberal theory presumes that in most instances competent persons are the best judge of their own interests. Thinking about less competent or incompetent persons makes this presumption less appropriate or impossible. It becomes necessary either to make a judgment about their interests or to treat their interests as irrelevant. Theorists tend to do the latter in discussing children's lives, without acknowledging that they are doing so and without justifying that choice.

For these reasons, it seems, political theorists ignore or bracket child welfare questions when initially formulating a position on education or other child-rearing issues, preferring instead to conceptualize the issues as involving simply a conflict between adults—parents on the one hand and other adult citizens (represented by the state) on the other. But these explanations do not amount to a justification. It does require a substantial effort to rethink one's basic theoretical approach in order to address properly the lives of nonautonomous persons, but their equal moral standing as persons demands that the effort be undertaken. Reasoning about what is better or worse for persons who cannot determine that for themselves *is* a complicated matter, but that does not mean that legislatures and courts can have no confidence in any judgments they reach. The difficulty hardly justifies abandoning the welfare of dependent persons as the primary aim of decision making about their lives. As noted above, that fact is generally understood with respect to nonautonomous adults. It is equally true of children.

Eamonn Callan directly responds to the position that a child-centered approach is the only proper approach to defining the bounds of state and parental authority over child rearing. He rejects the position for three reasons. All three rest on claims parents might make, but one can easily imagine comparable claims by adult citizen taxpayers, though these would presumably have less force because any individual citizen's interest in how children are educated is presumably less than that of a parent. Callan's first reason for not adopting a child-centered approach to education policy is that child rearing is of tremendous personal importance to most parents, a "cardinal source of self-fulfillment,"[29] so they have interests at stake sufficient to generate rights, including a right to make bad choices for their children. The second reason is that parents expect a reward from their child-rearing labors that includes realization of certain educational ends in the lives of their children. Parents "do not experience the rearing of a child merely as unilateral service on behalf of a separate human life." And the third reason is that, although Callan stops short of saying that children are not in fact separate persons, he finds moral purchase in the supposition that "we are tempted to think of the child's life as a virtual extension of our own." He quotes Robert Nozick for the proposition that one's children " 'form part of one's substance' " and " 'are organs of you.' " Accordingly, he treats child rearing as a component of adults' "personal sovereignty."[30]

These reasons do not do the work Callan assumes they do. The first reason fails in part because it is simply not the case that we are entitled to whatever is of tremendous subjective importance to us. Many things can and do constitute a cardinal source of fulfillment for people—marrying a particular person, controlling the life of one's spouse, pursuing a particular career, securing political office, preventing pregnant women from having abortions, and so on.[31] In none of these other cases does the subjective importance of a preference or aim itself give rise to any entitlement. The first reason also fails because Callan overstates the importance of the parental interests at stake. I suspect few parents would say that their own interests in connection with their children's education are, objectively speaking, more important than their children's interests. It would thus be peculiar for the law to presume that the parents' interests are more important. This becomes clearer when one compares regulation of schools with other contexts where the state limits parental authority. The most common situation is when married parents divorce or when parents were never married, and a court assigns legal custody—the power to make major decisions in a child's life—to just one parent. There is no widespread outrage in reaction to courts' denying noncustodial parents any power whatsoever to control their children's education. If that is not tragic or a grave injustice, how can regulation of schools be tragic or unjust?

In addition, it is deeply problematic to attribute to anyone a right—an *entitlement*—to direct the life of another human being.[32] Of course, with nonautonomous persons, some one or more persons must as a practical matter direct their lives. However, in the case of nonautonomous adults, the caretaker and decision maker is viewed as a fiduciary, effectuating rights of the non-autonomous persons, as construed by the state. This is so even when the caretaker is ideologically opposed to the standards of care or decision making the state imposes, and even when the caretaker has made enormous sacrifices for the nonautonomous adult (indeed, that adult might be the caretaker's offspring).[33] There is no good reason why parents should not also be viewed as fiduciaries rather than as owners holding title to the lives of their children.

The second reason fails in part simply because it is unsupported; Callan cites no evidence as to what parents expect. Personally, I view my parenting as "unilateral service on behalf of a separate human life," rather than as an investment of labor for which I demand a return, and consider myself quite ordinary in viewing the matter that way. Deeming control over a child's life as payback for parenting efforts makes a virtue of self-centeredness. This is not to say that parents must be martyrs and sacrifice all their own, *self*-determining interests for the sake of their children. We parents reasonably expect to reserve a fair portion of our time and family resources for our own projects, and we have a right simply as persons, rather than as parents, not to be harassed by state actors in our daily lives. But control over children's education is not about balancing parents' *self*-determining interests against children's welfare. Nor is it about state officials intruding into the home or seeking to control parent-child interactions. It is about parents' desire to determine how their child's life will go and to have their own views of a child's interests trump the state's views in setting education policy. There is a child-centered case to be made for allowing parents' views to trump in some instances, and in fact Callan offers one,[34] but Callan has not shown that a child-centered approach should not also be used to determine when parents' views should *not* trump.

Callan's third reason for rejecting a child-centered approach fails for similar reasons. Some people might be tempted to view their children as mere extensions of themselves, but many might not, and arguably any such temptation should be resisted rather than protected with a legal right. If Callan can make the case that children actually *are* extensions or organs of their parents, so that control over my children's lives really *is* a matter of my *personal* sovereignty, that would be quite significant. But he has not made that case.

In fact, theorists on both sides of the civic virtue / pluralism debate purport to accept the separate personhood of children. The problem is that they do not fully realize the implications of that moral assumption. In addition to the general lack of attention to children's individual interests described above, this problem is often manifest in writing rendered incoherent by an unacknowledged eliding of the distinction between parent and child. Many theorists, in constructing their core arguments, implicitly and mistakenly treat parent and child as a single entity or as having a complete identity of interests. Legal and policy writing on education reform is also rife with this conceptual confusion. Ignoring the separateness of children allows one to view conflicts over education as involving only two parties—parents and the state—so that questions of children's welfare never come up. The situation can then be analyzed in familiar and simpler ways, as just another type of conflict between (competent adult) individuals and the state.[35] The result, however, is a conceptual muddle. Avoiding such confusion is another reason to abandon adult-centered thinking about education policy.

Sometimes the elision of parent-child separateness is manifest in an ontologizing of families. Theorists will speak of the rights or claims of families, and of families' choosing a form of education,[36] even though it is plainly the case that parents typically do the choosing, with little or no consultation of children, especially when choices turn on basic values or ideology.[37] Speaking of family rights and family decisions allows theorists to ignore the fact that child-rearing policy is a matter of the state's supervising what some private individuals (parents) do to other private individuals (children), and not a matter of the state's restricting the *self*-determining behavior of private individuals.

At other times, the separate personhood of children is masked by simply speaking very abstractly about rights, freedoms, and choices, without identifying any entity as the holder or source of the rights, freedoms, or choices. Callan, for example, argues as follows against the view that children might be owed as a matter of justice an education that maximizes their development of autonomy:

> Acknowledgment of the great variety of lives that people permissibly lead under free institutions is fundamental to our pre-reflective understanding of liberal politics. But we cannot square that acknowledgment with a reading of personal sovereignty that protects only lives that aim to meet the maximal demands of autonomous reflection and choice. I think the point of trying to understand rights in relation to the "adequate" rather than the maximal development of the moral powers is to seek a reasonable threshold that would be responsive to the range of lives that a free people could accept as worthy of political protection.[38]

Once one recognizes that the lives in question when discussing primary and secondary education are lives of persons who are presently children, this passage becomes incomprehensible. A child does not yet have a life that can sensibly be said to aim or not aim at meeting demands respecting autonomy. The question education policy raises is not whether society should protect already formed lives that are relatively nonautonomous, but rather whether society should foster for today's children lives that are relatively more autonomous. Callan in this passage must really have in mind protecting parents, some of whom do not value autonomy. Yet it is not clear how children's education has any bearing on the autonomy of current adults.

Similarly, Galston, in arguing against moral autonomy as an aim of public schooling, asserts that "liberal freedom entails the right to live unexamined as well as examined lives."[39] Galston would likely incur little objection to an assertion that current adults, including parents, who are living unexamined lives have a right to be left alone, to be free of efforts to force them to examine their lives. But that assertion would be irrelevant to a discussion of children's schooling. What Galston needs to assert, if he wants to say something relevant to education policy, is that today's children have a right to live unexamined lives. That would be a very peculiar, and arguably incoherent, assertion. Galston makes his claim about unexamined lives appear coherent and plausible by omitting the subject of his statement, glossing over the fact that it is the lives of today's children, not the lives of today's parents, that are under discussion.

Until political theorists give full effect to the separate personhood of children, return to their basic theories to address questions about child rearing, and reason about child-rearing policy on the basis of sound general principles, their reasoning about parent-state conflicts over education cannot be anything but ad hoc. At its worst, such ad hoc reasoning produces unthinking philosophical treatment of children and children's lives in ways we would clearly deem morally unacceptable for other groups of persons. Galston at one point implicitly treats children's lives as a commodity to be bargained with; he urges that the liberal state allow parents in nonliberal religious groups to put their children in the kind of schools the parents want, because this will give the parents "redress for various types of informal establishment and cultural hegemony."[40] It is as if to say, "We are sorry your conception of the good is disadvantaged in the liberal public square, so we are offering you as compensation the freedom to do whatever you want with your children." If the topic were spousal abuse, and a conflict arose between liberalism and religious beliefs that support physical chastisement of wives, would anyone think about the conflict in the same way? Would Galston recommend exempting men in certain religious communities from domestic violence laws as a way of compensating them for the disfavoring of their beliefs in the political realm? Why is it morally appropriate to bargain away children's lives but not the lives of any other persons?

The tendency unreflectively to treat child rearing in anomalous ways is hardly confined to pluralists. Peter de Marneffe has presented an argument for deciding the content of children's education in such a way as to ensure competing groups of adult citizens an equal opportunity to politick children for their future votes on contested political issues.[41] In deciding whether to allow children access to sexually explicit materials, public officials should, according to de Marneffe, take into account that excluding sexually explicit materials from schools and libraries is unfair to adult citizens who favor sexual freedom and who want to persuade others to think similarly. Those adults have a right to freedom of expression that should give them equal access to children as future voters. It is difficult to imagine anyone's making a comparable argument that, for example, habilitation decisions for mentally disabled adults should be made in such a way as to give other citizens an equal opportunity to influence the disabled adults' voting. Such an instrumental view of the lives of dependent persons is inconsistent with basic moral and legal principles.[42]

In both examples just given, theorists treat children instrumentally, rather than as ends in themselves. That is the basic problem with so much of the writing and rhetoric about education today. Just because it is possible to use children's education to serve collective ends or the ends of individual adults does not mean that it is appropriate to do so. And it certainly does not mean that it is appropriate to make those ends the primary focus of one's theory. Both the liberal statist and the pluralist approaches to children's education are so at odds with our moral intuitions and practices in cases involving other groups of less able persons that their proponents should be expected to offer an extensive justification for approaching child rearing in such an anomalous way. Yet they offer none.

Toward a Child-Centered Approach to Child-Rearing Policy

The remainder of this book applies a child-centered approach to the particular topic of school vouchers. It begins with the basic assumption that any reasoning about who should possess authority over children's lives must recognize and give full effect to the distinct personhood of children. Children must not be subsumed under the identity of parents, and it should not be assumed that children's interests coincide with those of parents. In addition, child-rearing issues should not be treated as tangential to theories of justice. Child-rearing institutions should be treated as part of the basic structure of society whose features are to be mapped out in accordance with basic principles of justice. A child-centered approach would place children alongside adults when asking in the first instance what rights and other goods people should generally receive as a matter of justice.[43] It would arrive at conclusions regarding rights and duties by reasoning from general principles, principles concerning what a proper respect for individuals qua persons entails and concerning proper treatment of nonautonomous persons specifically. In addition, it would focus first in evaluating any child-rearing policy on children's developmental interests and would assign those interests presumptive trumping power over conflicting adult interests, in recognition of the plain fact that children generally have more important interests at stake in connection with their upbringing than do any group of adults, and in fact are the only persons whose affected interests are "fundamental" in the true sense of that word. I offer further support for this presumption in Chapter 3.

This is not to say that the task of deciding what kind of education is most conducive to children's well-being is easy or simple. There are genuine difficulties both in specifying what the aims should be—for example, to maximize happiness, to promote autonomy, to protect identification with family and community of upbringing, and / or something else—and in figuring out the best means of accomplishing the selected aims. But the difficulty of a task does not make it the wrong one, or lessen its importance. Greater attention must simply be paid to it.

Further, that a child-centered approach to education policy will yield policies that are nonneutral relative to the array of conceptions of the good that today's adults hold is irrelevant. Any education policy, no matter how derived, will be nonneutral. Even a policy of empowering parents and schools to do whatever they want is nonneutral; it privileges a particular conception of the place of children in our society, of what children and parents are respectively entitled to, and of what the aims of education are (i.e., to serve the ends of parents). What matters in the context of child-rearing policy is not neutrality but justice. If one particular, necessarily nonneutral education policy appears most conducive to children's welfare, then an impartial balancing of the interests at stake will likely show that the policy is just, regardless of whether it is disturbing to parents or other adults. That some parents will be upset, feel affront, fear for their children's salvation, and / or become dismayed at the prospect of their children's rejecting their beliefs and way of life in and of itself should not be controlling.[44] Children's interests trump. That some religious conservatives object to a liberal education out of fear that it might undermine their efforts to ensure that their children think as they do is, in and of itself, relatively unimportant. It is not their basic welfare that is at stake; it is the children's. What advocates for nonliberal religious groups need to argue is that *the state* should conclude that *the children* are harmed by a liberal education. They have yet to do so.

Outline of a Child-Centered Assessment of School Vouchers

A child-centered approach to state education policy will yield conclusions concerning both curricular issues (the content of a good secular education) and distribution issues (how education benefits are distributed). While the curricular issues are of tremendous importance, the remainder of this book focuses on distribution issues. There is some excellent recent child-centered theorizing about what content the state should require for children's education—in particular, Meira Levinson's *The Demands of Liberal Education*, Harry Brighouse's *School Choice and Social Justice*, and Michael Pritchard's *Reasonable*

Children. I take the core conclusions of these writers about curricular content, which are generally consistent, as starting points for an analysis of distribution questions—that is, questions about which children should receive an education with that content. I will assume that the state endorses the curricular aims for which these writers argue and that promoting those aims is the secular purpose a state would have in acting to support particular schools. The basic distribution question, then, assuming some such conception of what constitutes a "good secular education," is whether and how the state *may, must, or may not* act to ensure that education for some or all children. From a child-centered perspective, this is *the* question raised by school vouchers.

In answering this question, the chapters that follow rest on an additional factual assumption about state involvement in children's education. That assumption is that while regulation is often seen only as a burden rather than as a benefit, it is generally true that regulation is actually a benefit for some, while constituting a burden for others. Restrictions on air pollution, for example, burden factory owners but benefit consumers of the air. Similarly, while school regulation is a burden for school operators, it can be a benefit for children. It follows from this that not just material resources, but also regulation, can be a good whose distribution is a matter of justice. State-imposed requirements for instruction and treatment of students and standards of achievement, as much as state-provided funding, are a benefit to children, insofar as they induce schools to provide a better education. While state education agencies are often criticized for imposing too much regulation and for imposing regulations that do not seem to serve any good purpose, widespread cries for higher standards and greater accountability in public schools make clear that most people recognize that regulation and oversight are necessary to ensure that children receive a good education.

Thus, in the chapters to follow, I assume for the sake of analysis that the state can identify some components of a good secular education and that these are quite substantial. I spell them out more in the next chapter, but will say here that they would include fostering many cognitive skills such as critical and creative thinking, generating understanding of methods of inquiry in a variety of disciplines, and imparting a robust body of knowledge. I further assume that this education would, from the state's perspective (since we are talking about state decision making), be good for all children in our society, including many whose parents would object to it on religious grounds. Given this set of assumptions, how would a child-centered assessment of distributional issues differ from the prevailing adult-centered approaches?

First, a child-centered approach would not presume any set of adult rights or claims for or against vouchers or attendant regulations. In the analysis that follows, I begin at square one, with no preconceptions about who has what sort of claims on the state, and offer an assessment of how the voucher question would be resolved if children's interests were given their due in a moral or legal analysis of vouchers, and if adult interests were weighed objectively. Second, a child-centered approach would determine the content of children's rights relating to state funding and oversight of education without (direct) reference to parental choices, preferences, or beliefs. In recognition of the fact that child and parent are two distinct persons with potentially conflicting interests, a child-centered approach would not simply assume that what is good for a given child is whatever the parent thinks is good for the child or what the parent wants for the child. As with mentally disabled adults, the state would make a determination of children's interests independent of the views of their guardians. This second difference has several important implications.

It means that the state must look out for all children, not just for those whose parents make claims for a better education on their behalf. It means that parental choices cannot simply be assumed to serve as an adequate proxy for children's interests; whether they should be treated as such in particular circumstances requires analysis. In addition, it means that the state must ultimately decide what the interests of children, individually or collectively, are. Many philosophers and legal scholars overlook the fact that what is ultimately at issue in child-rearing policy debates is state decision making. Conservatives, in particular, are likely to claim that their position, favoring greater parental freedom, is an alternative to state involvement in child-rearing issues. But that is false. If the state allocates power over children's lives to parents by passing laws that protect parental freedom and confer decision-making power on parents, it is involving itself in child rearing. It is making a decision about children's lives—a crucial one.

Thus, in arguing for laws that confer plenary parental rights or rights to exercise religion through children, conservatives as much as anyone else are asking the state to endorse certain beliefs about the content and importance of particular human interests—for example, that parents' interests in using their children's lives to practice their religion are more important than the interests of the children, or that parents' views of their children's interests are always superior to the state's, or that children's interests even as the state sees them are in general best served by giving parents complete control over children's lives. One or more of these beliefs might be correct, but that needs to be shown to the satisfaction of the state actors who are being asked to create a particular legal regime. Conservatives must show why *the state* should endorse *their* beliefs about the importance of parental interests or about what is best for children. I do not presume any such set of beliefs to be true, but instead undertake in the remainder of the book to model the state's reasoning about the content and importance of the human interests and rights at stake, from a starting point free of preconceptions.

[3]

A Utilitarian Assessment of Vouchers

Imagine a voucher program that does the following: The state offers to pay, for any student whose family's gross annual income is less than a certain amount, 100 percent of the per pupil cost of an eligible nonsectarian private school, or 80 percent of the per pupil cost of an eligible religious school, in either case up to the amount of per pupil spending in the local public schools. For students from families with higher income, the state will pay gradually lesser percentages as income rises, until the benefit phases out entirely at a level of income where the subsidy would have no appreciable effect on a child's education. Private schools are initially eligible if they presently satisfy, or demonstrate a likelihood of soon satisfying, robust curricular requirements reflecting the state's view of what constitutes a good secular education and a code of student treatment reflecting the state's view of what constitutes proper respect for the personhood of students. The state monitors participating schools in effective ways to ensure ongoing compliance with those requirements and revokes the eligibility of any school that ceases to satisfy them.

The curricular requirements go far beyond basic reading, writing, and math.[1] They include training in critical thinking, in problem solving, and in the methods of inquiry in a variety of disciplines—for example, the hard and social sciences, advanced mathematics, and logic. They require instruction in the core facts, theories, and principles of a variety of subjects and training in synthesis of complex information. They require schools to encourage students to think creatively and to develop their own original ideas about the world. They require in the secondary grades exposure to intellectual debates in a variety of subject areas and exercises in independently critiquing competing views to distinguish good and bad arguments. In addition, they require that schools afford students a substantial measure of physical and intellectual freedom, foster tolerance, demonstrate a commitment to eradicating racism and sexism from their curriculum and other practices, and otherwise protect students' emotional and psychological well-being.

Under a voucher program like this, one might accurately picture any participating religious school by first imagining a nonsectarian private school that aims to provide students with the best possible secular education, and then adding certain religious dimensions. All participating religious schools teach subjects other than religion primarily from a secular perspective and with the same sort of curricular materials one would find in good secular schools. Unlike public and nonsectarian private schools, however, religious schools also offer students religious activities and instruction. The school day might begin with a voluntary worship service, each class might begin with a voluntary prayer, and students, at least in the upper grades, might have the option during one period each day of either taking a course in the tenets of the school's religion or taking some other elective course, such as journalism or typing or car repair.[2] Apart from these religious additions, though, the school remains the same as the paradigm nonsectarian school.[3]

I do not mean to suggest at this point that a voucher program must require all these things, or in other words that a school should be entirely like that just described in order to receive vouchers. I put off until later parts of the book consideration of what sorts of regulations or conditions for participation in a voucher program are essential, which simply desirable from the state's perspective, and how rigidly they should be enforced, as well as the question of whether a school that interweaves religious instruction or discussion into state-mandated courses should be eligible. At this point, my purpose is to posit a kind of voucher program in which all eligible schools, whether religious or nonreligious, strive to advance the educational interests of their students *as the state sees it,* and then to explore the moral and legal implications of such a program. I also do not mean to suggest that what I have described is all that constitutes good schooling. I have intentionally left the regulatory requirements somewhat unspecific and simplified, glossing over questions about what specific content should be taught, what pedagogical methods should be used, what noncurricular requirements would be desirable, and how educational aims would differ from one age group to the next. The point here is simply to posit an approach to vouchers that has sufficient safeguards in place to ensure that recipient religious schools would advance the state's aim of giving children a better secular education. Within the boundaries of those safeguards, schools might in practice have a great deal of freedom in deciding how they go about achieving the educational outcomes required by the state.

If a voucher program contained the requirements outlined above, the enacting state would clearly be correct in believing that the program would improve the secular education children receive. First, the program would facilitate transfer of students from overburdened and underperforming public schools or from lower-quality private schools to better private schools. Second, the program would substantially increase the resources participating schools have for educating students who are already enrolled in them, and would thereby enable the schools to give those students a better secular education.[4] For some schools, let us assume, vouchers would make the difference between success and failure at this goal, because without vouchers the schools are inadequately funded, as many religious schools today are. The increase in a religious school's total resources (state provided and privately raised) might also allow the school to enhance the religious aspects of school life, because less of the privately raised money is needed for secular instruction, but the primary effect of vouchers for a qualifying school would be to enhance the quality of the state-mandated curriculum, because that is what the school necessarily devotes the vast majority of its resources to providing in order to satisfy the requirements for participation.

Thus, the voucher program described would clearly serve a legitimate state purpose—namely, improving the secular education children receive. How should a legislature go about deciding, then, whether it should enact such a program? And how should courts decide whether doing so is constitutionally permissible? Does the fact that the program would help children in and of itself make it morally or constitutionally permissible? Or mandatory? Or do competing considerations outweigh the benefit to children? Remarkably, there has been little serious consideration of such questions. Few participants in the debate recognize the full range of legitimate interests at stake, and few subject their own presuppositions about what the most important considerations are to critical scrutiny.

I do not believe these questions can be adequately answered without taking a very broad perspective, examining them from several directions, and attempting to take into account the full range of human interests and moral and legal considerations at stake. This chapter and the three following it undertake such an approach. They pursue several different modes of analysis of the same questions about the same sort of voucher program, and in each case attempt to keep the moral compass wide to give all persons their due, to give all interests and rights their appropriate weight.

First, in this chapter and the next, I take a moral theoretical approach, assessing the permissibility of such a voucher program based on considerations of justice rather than on the basis of constitutional provisions or judicial statements of legal rules. In this chapter, I undertake a utilitarian assessment of whether the program would on the whole do more good than harm, taking into account all the human interests at stake. In Chapter 4, I attempt a moral-rights-based determination of whether the state (i.e., members of society collectively) has a moral obligation to any particular group of persons to create or not create such a program.[5] Then, in Chapters 5 and 6, I examine the program through the lens of general constitutional principles—specifically, antiestablishment and equal protection principles.

Both the moral theoretical approaches and the analyses based on constitutional principles have certain weaknesses. The former necessarily rely to a substantial degree upon intuitions; utilitarian analysis of any policy issue inevitably entails a somewhat subjective valuation and balancing of interests, and rights-based theory similarly involves somewhat subjective judgments about whether the prerequisites to possessing a right are satisfied. However, it is possible using either of these moral frameworks to shed new light on the debate by improving our understanding of the interests and rights at stake, in part just through fleshing out in detail what they are, and by exploring the implications of making different assumptions about people's interests and rights.

This exploration should enhance not only policy discussions but also constitutional analysis. It is no secret that people, including judges and legal scholars, are driven to adopt particular views on the constitutionality of vouchers by preconceptions they have about what human interests are at stake and which are most important, and about what particular people are entitled to as a matter of justice, preconceptions they do not articulate or even recognize themselves. It is unlikely many people undertake an entirely detached inquiry into the meaning of the Establishment Clause or of other constitutional provisions before forming an opinion about whether voucher programs ought to be permitted or required. This is especially so because Supreme Court Establishment Clause doctrine is so notoriously incoherent, providing fodder for almost any position one might wish to take, not to mention that all standard methods of constitutional interpretation are indeterminate and that choice from among them is generally driven by a predisposition to favor or disfavor the outcomes one believes they produce rather than by a well-reasoned foundational jurisprudence.

It should be fruitful, therefore, to step back and reexamine beliefs about the interests and moral rights at stake, to try to think objectively about how important each group's interests are and how sound the various claims of moral entitlement are. That is the aim of this chapter and the next. I am not aware of any other work along these lines, and so must write on a clean slate. Most discussion of interests and moral rights in legal and policy writing about children's education is simplistic and un-self-critical. This might be in part because the very enterprise looks inevitably and thoroughly subjective. But we will not know that for sure until we make a serious effort. It might also be in part because it is a somewhat tedious exercise to articulate carefully what each group's interests are and to assess in a reasoned way which are weightier than others. It is much easier to focus only on the interests of one group and to advocate for that group. But if justice, rather than advocacy, is the aim, we must take off the moral blinders, roll up our sleeves, and spend some time thinking through each group's position.

[69]

The argument from constitutional principles, on the other hand, while it draws on more concrete raw material, makes the analysis turn to some extent on contingent historical facts about the law—namely, what principles or rules have previously been recognized and assigned a given importance—and these facts may not track what is rational, reasonable, or fair. In Chapters 5 and 6, I try to achieve a balance between, on the one hand, taking as given widely accepted understandings of certain constitutional rules and principles, and, on the other hand, substituting what I believe to be a more sensible and fair understanding of constitutional rules and principles, and leave it to the reader to judge whether the balance is an appropriate one.

We are assuming, then, that all religious schools that could receive vouchers are ones that strive to provide the best possible secular education and would use state financial assistance to do this better. They all share the same goals for education that state education officials have adopted for public schools. In the absence of state financial support, many religious schools are much less successful at pursuing these ends than they would like to be, and perhaps struggling to provide even a minimally adequate secular education, solely because of a lack of resources.[6] What can we say about the justice of providing or failing to provide vouchers for use at those religious schools?

Utilitarianism has been characterized as "the most influential—and still most widely accepted—way of attempting to resolve moral conflicts that arise in the making of public policy."[7] The basic idea is to consider the consequences of a policy for the welfare of individual citizens and to choose those policies that maximize the overall net gain in human welfare. Welfare can be defined in terms of interests, satisfaction of preferences or desires, happiness, pleasure and the absence of pain, or some combination of these. A utilitarian approach to vouchers thus takes a broad view of a policy's effects on our society, considers all groups of persons whose welfare the voucher program described above might affect, and then determines what result an impartial balancing of their interests would yield. A utilitarian analysis of vouchers thus coincides in substantial measure with what we expect our government to do, to the extent that it does anything—that is, to enhance the well-being of members of our society and to make decisions impartially, treating all members of society as equal persons, entitled to equal consideration and respect.[8]

My aim here is not to defend a particular version of utilitarianism or to demonstrate the virtues of such an approach relative to others. The aim is more practical—to suggest new ways of looking at a real world conflict, rather than to decide any foundational philosophical issues. My strategy will be to articulate the human interests at stake in the voucher debate and to suggest what their relative weights are, in the hope that this will at least generate a greater understanding of the full range of potential consequences of a voucher program designed to improve the secular education of all participating children.

It might also yield a tentative conclusion as to whether such a program is on the whole a good thing, based upon a balancing of all interests at stake. If nothing else, the discussion below of who has what sort of interests at stake and how important those interests are might demonstrate the need to refocus the debate and might provide reason to rewrite constitutional law in this area to track the relative importance of the decision for the welfare of different groups of persons.

Basis for Ranking Interests

Before articulating and attempting to assign weights to the interests of different groups, it is useful to have some criteria for ranking, to reduce as much as possible the subjective and impressionistic nature of the enterprise.[9] Fortunately, some leading philosophers of our time have devoted attention to this issue, and they are consistent in the guidance they provide. Their conclusions converge around the idea of distinguishing basic human needs from nonbasic interests—that is, satisfaction of desires for things beyond basic human needs.

For Joel Feinberg, the distinction is between "welfare interests" and "ulterior interests."[10] Welfare interests are those aspects of well-being one must have in order to carry on in life, preconditions for pursuing any higher aims. In Feinberg's terms, they are "the 'basic requisites of a man's well-being,' " "generalized means to a great variety of possible goals and whose joint realization, in the absence of very special circumstances, is necessary for the achievement of more ultimate aims." They are a person's interests "shared by nearly all his fellows, in the necessary means to his more ultimate goals." Feinberg gives as examples physical health, the integrity and normal functioning of one's body, basic intellectual abilities, emotional stability, "the capacity to engage normally in social intercourse," some minimum of financial resources, and "a certain amount of freedom from interference and coercion." Feinberg argues that from an objective perspective these "are the very most important interests a person has," even if most people tend not to think about them much because they are taken for granted. Because of their great importance to an individual's well-being, they "cry out for protection, for without their fulfillment, a person is lost." Invasion of a welfare interest is the most serious kind of harm a person can sustain.

Ulterior interests, in contrast, are connected with the higher aims that people form for their lives, "a person's more ultimate goals and aspirations." Even though these aims have great subjective importance for people, and may be what people spend most of their time thinking about, frustration of these aims does not undermine a person's well-being in the same way or to the same extent as does harm to welfare interests, and frustration of one aim may be compensated for by fulfillment of another. Feinberg gives as examples of these interests "such aims as producing good novels or works of art, solving a crucial scientific problem, achieving high political office, successfully raising a family, achieving leisure for handicraft or sport, building a dream house, advancing a social cause, ameliorating human suffering, achieving spiritual grace."[11] For the most part, our laws reflect the belief that these interests do not deserve the kind of protection we give to welfare interests; the law protects the basic freedoms and capacities necessary to pursue such higher aims, but does not treat frustration of those aims as a legal wrong. For example, the law protects the freedom (for most adults) to run for political office, but does not seek to ensure that individuals who have the aim of holding political office succeed, regardless of how strongly they want to achieve that end—that is, even if it is subjectively the most important thing in life to them.

John Rawls draws a similar distinction among interests with his concept of "primary goods."[12] Primary goods are aspects of well-being "which it is supposed a rational man wants whatever else he wants," and that "have a use whatever a person's rational plan of life." "With more of these goods," Rawls writes, people "can generally be assured of greater success in carrying out their intentions and in advancing their ends, whatever these ends may be." Rawls thus concludes, along with Feinberg, that our most important interests, the interests that present the strongest claim to legal protection, are those the satisfaction of which is for every person prerequisite to pursuing his or her individualized, self-defined goals in life. Rawls contends that gauging welfare by reference to these basic goods "seems the most feasible way to establish a publicly recognized objective measure, that is, a common measure that reasonable persons can accept." In contrast, "there cannot be a similar agreement on how to estimate happiness as defined, say, by men's success in executing their [individualized long-term plans of life], much less on the intrinsic value of these plans."[13]

Rawls's list of primary goods resembles Feinberg's list of welfare interests. It comprises basic self-determining liberties—including some measure of religious and moral freedom, freedom of thought and expression, and physical freedom, and also education, opportunities for careers, powers to influence political decision making and to invoke mechanisms for enforcement of one's legal rights, income and wealth, self-respect, and "health and vigor, intelligence and imagination." Rawls particularly emphasizes the importance for each individual of having the preconditions for developing for himself a rational plan of life that "call[s] upon his natural capacities in an interesting fashion." This is necessary to "a person's sense of his own value." Life activities that do not fully realize one's abilities "are likely to seem dull and flat, and to give us no feeling of competence or a sense that they are worth doing."[14]

Thus, philosophical accounts of the priority of interests converge on the notion that persons' basic, universal needs (welfare interests or primary goods) are inherently more important, and warrant greater protection, than persons' higher aims in life (ulterior interests or nonprimary goods). This distinction is also captured in the more familiar terminology "fundamental interests" and "nonfundamental interests," when those terms are properly used. In evaluating below the importance of the interests various groups have in connection with vouchers, I rely in several places on this distinction. I assume that fundamental interests are of a greater magnitude and have a greater claim to protection by the state.

Beyond this division of interests into fundamental and nonfundamental ones, we might identify some criteria for assigning relative weights within those categories. Because fundamental interests are "generalized means to a great variety of possible goals," we might distinguish among them based on how general they are, or in other words how many possible goals they are prerequisite to. With respect to nonfundamental interests, I note that many of the interests impacted by a voucher program are interests simply in being satisfied with an external state of affairs, rather than in receiving some concrete good or opportunity. For example, one of the interests taxpayers that challenge voucher programs have is in being satisfied that tax money is being used properly. One of the interests parents have is in being satisfied that their children are getting what the parents believe to be a good education. Such interests in being satisfied with the way the world operates or with the way others' lives are going would seem to be of the ulterior, nonprimary sort. That satisfaction is not a basic prerequisite to pursuing other aims in life or a generalized means to a variety of ends. The fact that such preferences are so changeable supports this conclusion; it would be odd to say one has a fundamental interest in the world's conforming to one's beliefs, or in another person's life going as one prefers, when the next day one might change one's beliefs or preferences. In contrast, a person's interests in receiving adequate nutrition and a good education are fixed, not susceptible to being extinguished by a moment's reflection.

The relative weight of such interests in satisfaction with external states of affairs would appear to depend on two things—first, the degree to which actual states of affairs approximate one's preferences, and second, the depth of one's concern about the states of affairs. Thus, a given policy issue might have greater implications for one group of persons than for another, even though the interest of both is simply in being satisfied with external states of affairs. This could be so either because the alternatives being considered threaten a greater departure from the states of affairs preferred by one group than from those preferred by the other, or because one group of persons feels more strongly about the outcome.

A final point before proceeding: No doubt there will be many reasons to criticize my articulation of people's interests and to disagree with or be skeptical about my conclusions regarding relative weight. But not all possible bases for criticism are legitimate ones. In particular, objections based on a conflict between my conclusions and certain religious beliefs will not be persuasive. Any argument for the existence or weight of a particular interest must be one that the state could accept, and in our system of government the state does not pass judgment on religious truth and so cannot accept conclusions that rest on theological premises. Specifically, the Establishment Clause, and the ideal of the secular state underlying it,[15] preclude consideration by the state of anyone's supposed spiritual interests. The state may not assume, for example, that it is inherently in any child's interest to receive religious training, or that parents have a particular interest because of divine commands. To do so the state would have to assume the truth of particular religious beliefs, which it may not do.[16]

I would also caution against the mistake of assuming that prior pronouncements of courts about people's interests are true or even plausible, and of concluding from the fact that the courts have said certain interests are fundamental that they are in fact so. The Supreme Court, in particular, has manifested great confusion, across a broad range of contexts, about what makes an interest fundamental. This is nowhere more evident than in its decisions regarding children's education, which it has incomprehensibly deemed a matter of fundamental interest for parents but not for children. I suspect few parents would, on reflection, agree with this ranking of interests by the Court.

Clarifying the Interests at Stake

At least ten groups of people potentially have significant interests at stake in the decision whether to institute the voucher program I have described: (1) the children who would use the vouchers; (2) the children who would remain in public schools after the voucher program is in place; (3) the children who would attend nonqualifying private schools; (4) parents of the children who would use the vouchers; (5) parents of the children who would remain in public schools; (6) parents of children in, and operators of, nonqualifying private schools; (7) public school teachers and administrators; (8) operators, teachers, and administrators of qualifying schools; (9) taxpayers / citizens who oppose government support for religious schools; and (10) taxpayers / citizens who favor government support for religious schools. There is some overlap in membership between groups, but it is useful to describe the interests of individuals qua members of each. I consider each group below, beginning with those who object to vouchers or whose interests might be thought contrary to a voucher program of this type.

Taxpayers Who Oppose Government Support for Religious Schools

Taxpayer groups have brought legal challenges to voucher programs that include religious schools because they do not want their tax dollars used to subsidize religious institutions and do not want their government supporting religious institutions. They believe our government ought to operate in a certain way—namely, based on the principle of church-state separation, as they understand it. Some (though certainly not all) feel antipathy toward religion or toward particular religious groups and resent being forced to support in any way a phenomenon they regard as harmful to society and perhaps hostile to them personally. Some might feel that government support for religious institutions makes them outsiders or second-class citizens or exerts a subtle pressure on them to adopt a religious faith.

If one were to judge from the courts' legal analysis of state aid to religious schools, one would think that the interests of this group were the most important of all, easily trumping the interests of children, parents, and teachers. It is difficult to see, though, how that could be the case. Absent appreciable coercion of their beliefs regarding religion, the interest secularist taxpayers have at stake in the voucher debate is largely an interest in being satisfied with external states of affairs, and the states of affairs are ones that would appear not to affect immediately or profoundly anyone's life. Government violation of constitutional restrictions on spending can really irk us, even make us incensed, but we carry on with our lives nonetheless. It is worth noting again here that the Supreme Court treats such an interest in most contexts as too insubstantial even to give rise to standing to challenge the allegedly improper state action, let alone to an individual right that would warrant personal redress. Unsurprisingly, there are no reports that taxpayers in any of the states where voucher programs exist have been traumatized and debilitated. In addition, the voucher program under discussion here would not represent a substantial departure from the state of affairs the strict separationist desires. Although state money would flow to religious institutions, it would do so only to support their secular functions, and the program is designed—by limiting voucher amounts for religious schools to 80 percent of per pupil operating costs—so that the state aid covers no more than the secular component of a school's budget.

Moreover, it is inconceivable that the voucher program described at the outset of this chapter would work a perceptible coercion of any adult bystander's religious beliefs. What is at issue is whether the state will take one particular action that some secularists might construe as an implicit endorsement of religion, even though the action is taken only after assurance that it will advance an important secular purpose, and that in turn might have some slight effect on their sense of freedom in religious belief. It is not a matter of the state's ordering anyone to adhere to some religion or explicitly endorsing religion or conditioning

[75]

an important state-conferred benefit on espousal of some religious belief. The taxpayer's situation is a far cry from that of a child in a public school classroom where prayer is mandatory and peers ridicule anyone who does not join in. A claim of religious coercion would simply have no credibility.

Taxpayers might also object that misuse of state funds wastes their tax money and that the voucher program therefore harms them financially. That objection would not be plausible under the factual circumstances assumed here, because the tax money is producing secular good—improved education for children—and most likely a secular good that is much greater than the money spent, if the two things can be compared. Spending on children's education happens to generate a great return for the rest of society, in enhanced productivity and lessened pathology. In any event, even if a voucher program did waste tax dollars, the loss to any given individual taxpayer would be highly speculative and minuscule.

Public School Teachers and Administrators

To listen to voucher proponents, one would think public school teachers and administrators are monsters who want to hold children captive to their selfish desire to retain their jobs without having to do any work. Many will rankle at the thought that these individuals have any legitimate interests at stake. Rather than speculate about the "real" motivation for teacher groups' (I will refer just to teachers below) objections to vouchers, I will take at face value the concerns they express.

The concerns public school teachers voice do include selfish ones. A voucher program might cause a significant number of children to exit the public schools, and if a lot of students leave, school districts might decide to employ fewer teachers or to cut costs in other ways. Teachers fear that they will lose their jobs or experience a cut in salary or classroom resources.[17] Losing one's job can certainly be traumatic, psychologically and financially, though it is not always so. It can substantially disrupt one's life, even if one is able to find work elsewhere. A person who is laid off might have to relocate or embark on a new career path and is likely to suffer a financial setback, even if only temporarily. The harms associated with losing one's job typically extend throughout one's family, perhaps forcing other family members to change jobs or schools and to make many other sacrifices.

This harm some public school teachers might suffer as a result of vouchers seems a more severe harm than simply having one's desires thwarted as to how the government should operate or as to how other people's lives (even one's children's) should go. As a parent, I might be quite upset if I were unable to secure for my children what I think is the optimal educational setting for them, but it would be worse for me and my family if I lost my job and could not easily find another in the same locale. There are several reasons, though, to believe the interests of public school teachers would not be much affected by a voucher program.

First, vouchers themselves would probably not cause a significant reduction in the rolls of public school teachers. They would cause students to leave, but the state could well respond to this by proportionately reducing class sizes, so that the same number of teachers would teach a smaller number of students. This would certainly be warranted in overcrowded inner city schools. If the state chose not to do this, but instead chose to cut costs by firing teachers, *that* decision would be the cause of teachers' losing their jobs, not the decision to provide vouchers. The same might be said of any salary decreases or loss of classroom resources; the fault would lie not with vouchers but with a conceptually (though not necessarily politically) independent decision by state officials as to how much money they would appropriate for public schools.

Second, teachers are protected by tenure and by unions, so any reduction of teaching staff in public schools is likely to occur through attrition rather than dismissal. Of course, this would adversely affect potential new entrants to the teaching profession, but failing to secure a particular job in the first instance is generally less traumatic than losing a job one already has. Third, the movement of children to private schools presumably increases the need for teachers in that sector. Some teachers now in public school, and some potential new teachers, might actually prefer to teach in a private school. They might, as a result of vouchers, be hired by a religious school, as religious schools grow in number and size. Moreover, vouchers might enable many private schools for the first time to pay teachers a competitive salary. A sufficient number of teachers might be voluntarily drawn from the public schools that no teacher in the public schools would be forced to leave.[18]

In sum, then, the concern about lost jobs seems overblown, and in any event any adverse consequences for some public school teachers would be the result of state officials' independent decision as to funding of public schools, not the result of the voucher program itself. In fact, public school teachers might actually end up much better off, if states enacted voucher programs with new money while holding funding of public schools at least at existing levels and reducing class sizes. They would then have the same resources and fewer students. Thus, public school teachers may actually have no self-interest at stake in connection with the decision to create a voucher program. Their real concern lies with the state's separate decisions about what to do for the students and teachers who remain in public schools.

Public school teachers also express concern for the welfare of children left behind in public schools, and there is good reason to assume this concern is genuine. Teachers are, after all, people who have chosen a career of educating children—not the sort of thing one would be tempted to do if one did not care about children's well-being. I consider below how vouchers would actually affect those children. The teachers' concern represents an interest in an external state of affairs—that is, how certain other people fare in life. This is inherently a nonfundamental interest, as is true of taxpayer concerns about how government operates. It seems weightier than that interest of taxpayers, but not as weighty as the interest parents have in how their children's lives go. Teachers' concern is for people with whom they have personal and often very affectionate relationships, and so is likely more deeply felt than a concern about how the government spends tax dollars. But the relationships are generally not as close as those parents have with their children.

Children Who Remain in Public Schools

Children have a fundamental interest in receiving a good education. That is incontrovertible. One's own elementary and secondary education is the foundation upon which most life opportunities are built; the early education one receives determines one's life prospects to a great degree. A bad education, while not insurmountable in some sense, is a tremendous handicap. A good education, as that concept is understood by state education officials and by leading educational theorists, creates an "open future," the possibility of living a self-determined and fulfilling life, reaching one's full potential.[19] A bad education cuts off innumerable opportunities, undermines basic self-respect, and consigns persons to lives in which they may never realize their full abilities or exercise their natural capacities in satisfying ways. A good education is also necessary for a person to be able to participate effectively in public life, to protect her interests and the interests of her family and community in the political arena.

It is not enough, though, to say that all children have a fundamental interest in receiving a good education. We need to determine precisely how a particular education reform proposal would affect that interest for particular groups of children. Different groups might be affected very differently, some positively and some negatively, some greatly and some hardly at all. Many opponents of vouchers predict dire consequences for public schools as a result of vouchers. If this were true, then vouchers would conflict with the fundamental interests of a very large group of children, and that might well be sufficient in itself to doom vouchers from a utilitarian perspective. Vouchers would be very bad policy regardless of any benefits they might provide for the children who would be in private schools after the program was in place. In addition, a state would then have difficulty arguing that vouchers serve a legitimate secular purpose.

But, of course, it is not that simple. There are several problems with the doomsday arguments, some of which are recognized and some not. Opponents of vouchers base their predictions on the expectation that vouchers would cause many parents to transfer their children from public schools to private schools. A large-scale transfer, it is assumed, would have three principal effects. First, it would cause state funding for public schools to decline, leaving public schools even worse off financially than they are now. Second, it would mean that the most involved and resourceful parents would no longer have a stake in the public schools, because they are the parents most likely to transfer their children to private school. Third, it would result in "skimming" off the top public school students, an exodus of the best students from public schools to private schools, because the better-performing students are generally those with the most concerned parents, who in turn would be the most likely to seek out a better school for their children.

Voucher supporters, on the other hand, contend that public schools would actually *improve* as a result of vouchers, because vouchers would create stronger competition for public schools and thereby motivate public school teachers and administrators to work harder. Critics of vouchers note, however, that competition has done nothing for the poor in other areas of life, such as medical care. I would add that the competition-based argument rests critically on a doubtful empirical assumption. The assumption is that parents in the relevant market are generally able and motivated to acquire and evaluate all the information necessary to make intelligent educational choices for their children, and then to take the steps needed to move them to the best available schools. This assumption is weakest in the very places where the worst public schools exist—namely, poor urban and rural areas, where parents are themselves poorly educated and likely to be struggling just to survive.

Voucher supporter Joseph Viteritti himself notes the great disparity in the ability of parents to make intelligent choices about their children's education, which is based largely on parents' own level of educational attainment.[20] A reporter who investigated one of the two failing public schools in Florida from which voucher students exited observed that "[t]he reality is that parents in the impoverished neighborhood . . . probably won't do their part. . . . Parents are intimidated by the school, too busy working or simply don't care. . . . Principal David Cunningham said the school has tried and failed to increase parental involvement for years. . . . [P]oor families typically are less involved in their children's education."[21] The competition-based arguments also implicitly assume that public schools are bad because teachers and school administrators are incompetent and lazy. There is undoubtedly some truth to that, though it is worth asking why these schools end up with the least competent and least motivated teachers. But what voucher supporters typically neglect to mention are the many serious problems that children and parents in poor urban areas have that create enormous obstacles for the teachers and administrators in the public schools.

Without presuming to settle that debate, I will assume for the sake of argument that opponents of vouchers are right about the fate of public schools in a voucher environment.[22] This raises the question: Are they identifying a necessary consequence of vouchers, or rather just a likely consequence given certain assumptions about contingent political realities? It seems clearly to be the latter. As noted above in connection with the interests of public school teachers, vouchers themselves could not cause the adverse effects on public school financing that opponents of vouchers predict. By appropriating money that can be used at private schools, the state does not *by that act* reduce spending on public schools, any more than it does by appropriating money for road construction or programs for the elderly. How much the state spends on public schools after a voucher program is in place is a separate matter. In fact, vouchers themselves have an immediate salutary effect on public schools and on the children left in them, insofar as they relieve overcrowding.

Admittedly, the two matters are linked in the minds of many legislators—that is, some legislators believe that the state should not increase total state spending on education and therefore should reduce the public school budget by the amount channeled to private schools. This is clear from the fact that existing programs do precisely that. But spending on vouchers does not logically entail this judgment about total expenditures. The proper target of complaint for those concerned about the education of children who would remain in public schools, therefore, is not vouchers but rather the state's failure to appropriate sufficient money for public schools. Vouchers or not, the state has a moral obligation to adequately fund public schools, for the sake of the children in those schools. State officials should be called to account if they fail to fulfill that obligation, and they cannot justifiably or coherently assert as a defense or excuse that they wanted to subsidize private schools.

Overlooking this fact that vouchers and public school funding are not conceptually linked has impoverished the debate about society's broader commitment to children's healthy development. It has prevented exploration of moral and pragmatic arguments for greater aggregate state spending on education. Legislators might be moved to increase total spending for children by being instructed that doing so would largely eliminate political opposition to the programs. It is worth noting in this context that in recent years many states ordered by their courts to equalize state funding among public schools have responded by increasing aggregate spending.[23] In those cases, the threat of reduced spending lay in the direction of public schools in wealthy districts rather than public schools in poor districts, so the political dynamic was very different. But this does suggest that there are no insuperable obstacles to increasing total state spending on education. Groups that tout vouchers as the salvation of poor children should have the question directly put to them whether they would support voucher legislation that increased total state spending on education.

The parental noninvolvement concern runs into a similar problem. People who predict a loss of committed parents typically do not explain what this loss would mean exactly for the public schools, but it could mean either *(a)* that public school teachers and administrators would do a poorer job, because no one would be pushing them to do a good job, or *(b)* that there would be inadequate per pupil state spending on public schools because no one would be pushing government officials to spend more.[24] The complaint is therefore really that the parents of children who would remain in public schools post-voucher are not sufficiently involved, not sufficiently committed and active to keep teachers, administrators, and government officials on their toes. Vouchers can hardly be blamed for that. All parents have a moral obligation to be involved in their children's education and to act as advocates for their children. If some are not doing this even though they are capable (some are not, of course, because of deficiencies in their own education and preparation for adulthood, or for other reasons), then *they* are to blame, and not a state decision to give financial support to the educational choices of other parents. Vouchers certainly would not cause any parents of public school children to *become* uninvolved. If anything, departure of the most active parents might prod previously uninvolved parents to become involved, because in the past they might have been free-riding on the monitoring and advocacy efforts of other parents.

Moreover, the concern with parental involvement appears to be derivative. Voucher opponents value parental involvement not for its own sake, at least not primarily, but rather because of the positive effects it can have on the public school system, principally through monitoring and lobbying to ensure public school employees and government officials do their jobs properly. And if the ultimate concern is that public school employees and government officials will not do their jobs, then again the cause of the problem is other than vouchers. It is the school employees' and government officials' dereliction of duty, and that is the proper target of condemnation, not vouchers.

The "skimming" concern cannot be as easily dismissed as conceptually unrelated to vouchers. Vouchers do inherently cause an exodus of students from public schools, and the way existing programs are structured, the better-performing students are more likely to be among those exiting, since performance correlates positively with parental concern and relative means. However, the supposed effects of this skimming are unclear and generally unarticulated. It is not clear how students remaining in the public schools suffer from a decline in the average abilities of students in the schools. It might actually be the case that poorer students do better when instruction can be geared more to their particular ability level rather than aimed at a wide range of ability levels.[25] One possible indirect consequence might be that the children left behind would have worse teachers, because the transformation of public schools into ghettos for the neediest children could demoralize teachers. But that is very speculative.

And in any event, skimming is not a necessary consequence of voucher programs. A fairer program would select children for transfer randomly or based on need or ability to benefit, rather than on the basis of parental choice, and either approach should eliminate the skimming problem.

In sum, a voucher plan would not itself adversely affect the interests of children in public schools. If public schools are bad, or even worse, after a voucher program is put in place, the cause should be attributed to the failure of the state to allocate sufficient money to public schools, or the failure of teachers and administrators to do a good job, not to the state's directing aid to private schools. In fact, for public school teachers and for children in public schools, the best state of affairs would be a voucher program that chooses children fairly and that holds stable or increases spending on public schools. Existing programs do not do that and can be rightly criticized for that reason.

Parents of Children Who Remain in Public Schools

The interests of parents of children left behind in public schools piggyback on the children's interests. These parents desire that their children's fundamental interest in receiving a good education be fulfilled. We can assume that for most this is a strong desire. Satisfaction of that desire is, in and of itself, a nonfundamental interest, though one likely to be more important than the similar interest of public school teachers, because of the stronger concern people typically have for their own offspring. In addition, as with the children, what really impacts this interest of parents is not vouchers per se but the conceptually independent state decision not to adequately fund and staff the public schools, or the lack of engagement among other parents, or indeed for many parents their own failure to apply for a voucher (though some might apply but be denied). Thus, the interests of this group are significant but not fundamental and not clearly affected by vouchers per se.

Children Who Would Attend Nonqualifying Private Schools

Under the voucher program under consideration here, some private schools would fail to qualify for vouchers, not because of their religious affiliation or orientation per se, but because they do not satisfy the academic standards established as a condition for participation. Some schools might endorse the state's aims but be so mismanaged that they show insufficient promise of satisfying the requirements even with vouchers. Others might object to one or a few of the requirements on principle—for example, they might embrace the aim of providing a good secular education but reject the principle of gender equality, or they might be willing to teach secular content but refuse to encourage critical and independent thinking. Still others might be altogether opposed to secular education, except perhaps for teaching just reading, writing, and basic math; otherwise all content is made to conform to religious precepts. In any of these cases, the children will lose out on the benefit of state funding for their education, through no fault of their own.

I consider in the later chapters of the book the status of schools that only partially comply—one of the many complexities of designing an actual voucher program that is both fair and consistent with the aim of using state money only to advance secular education. Here we ask how the voucher program I described affects children in any of these nonqualifying schools. The program would not appear to have *any* adverse effect. The program would not make them any worse off than they were before it was in place. If they have a complaint regarding the quality of their education, it is with the current state of affairs, in which their schools are neither regulated nor subsidized by the state, and in which their parents choose to place them in schools that do not provide a very good secular education or any secular education at all. The voucher program only improves education for some private school students; it does not make education worse for any.

In fact, the program might, from the state's perspective, make even students in nonqualifying schools better off educationally. It creates a large incentive for the operators of those schools and for the students' parents to *strive* to comply with robust secular academic standards. It also sends a message to parents and school operators who currently reject secular educational aims that they are doing something wrong, that the rest of society believes they are depriving their children of the kind of education to which the children are entitled—an education that will give them a wide range of opportunities in life, that exposes them to a world other than that of their parents and of their parents' religious community. Sending this message might move the parents and school operators to rethink their approach to child rearing, which would from the state's perspective be a good thing for the children. To see this, one must accept that the children are persons distinct from their parents, with lives they have a fundamental interest in eventually ordering according to self-chosen ends.

Still, there is a kind of discriminating that is going on, and the bases for discriminating are things over which the children presumably have no control. Older students might perceive this discrimination and feel unfairly treated. Even students unaware of the discrimination might be said to be harmed by it in some way; analogously, if the state provided vouchers only for white children, we might say nonwhite children are harmed by the discrimination, by being "stigmatized," even if they are unaware of it and even though they would not be made worse off materially than they were before. With the voucher program under discussion here, though, the persons stigmatized are not the children but the parents and school operators. Any harm relative to the status quo ante, therefore, would have to lie in *feeling* unfairly treated.

[83]

I suggest below that perceptions of unfairness ought not to be taken into account in an analysis of whether something is in fact fair, and that persons should be expected to conform their beliefs to the reality of whether something *is* fair independently of their perceptions. With children, that might be asking too much. Even if we factor in these children's feelings, though, we would have to ask how substantial they are and whether on the whole they are good or bad. It seems unlikely that many would be sufficiently aware of the state of affairs or that those who are aware would be deeply affected by it. Schoolchildren are generally oblivious to their school's relationship with the state and are generally focused on more personal aspects of their lives. In addition, any who are aware of the issue might learn a great deal from trying to understand why the state discriminates in the way it does, so the overall effect might in fact be salutary. And some might regard it as a good thing that the state is trying to induce their schools to change; some students in an illiberal religious school, for example, might wish that something be done to liberalize their schools, to give them greater intellectual and personal freedom, and to prepare them better for life in mainstream society.[26]

Parents of Children in, and Operators of, Nonqualifying Private Schools

The parents of children in, and the operators of, nonqualifying schools will, of course, be acutely aware of the discrimination. Some might understand and accept it. Others might feel very strongly that their exclusion is unfair. They might also feel coerced, not in the same way regulation independent of funding would coerce them, but rather the more subtle coercion of being given an incentive to act differently.

As just suggested, an interest in feeling that one is being treated fairly in government decision making arguably should not even factor into an analysis of whether the program is in fact fair. If a policy decided upon without considering perceptions of fairness reflects a proper balancing of interests (i.e., *is* fair), then a mistaken perception some persons have that this policy is unfair to them should perhaps be disregarded. These persons should be expected to conform their beliefs to reality rather than vice versa. On the other hand, taking into account feelings based on an accurate perception of unfairness would be superfluous; the fact that state action would be unfair independently of anyone's perception of its being so would be enough to rule it out in a fairness assessment. I will therefore put aside this consideration, while acknowledging that many parents feel acutely that it is wrong for the state to take tax money from them to use at schools to which they do not send their children, while refusing them any share of state support at the schools they choose.

What might make the voucher program I have described truly unfair to these adults, independently of their feelings of unfairness, in a utilitarian assessment, is if it would harm them without providing benefits to others that outweigh that harm. As with the children in nonqualifying schools, the schools' operators and parents are not financially harmed by the program. They are not made any worse off than they were before in that respect. The only harm might come from the subtle coercion the program effects, the inducement to change their practices. Those who value a good secular education but simply have not gotten their act together would experience pressure not to change their beliefs but rather just to do better, and we typically do not regard incentives to improve one's performance as a harm. They would feel a great sense of accomplishment if they did do better what they were already striving to do, so the financial incentive might even be seen as a benefit even if they do not yet get the payoff.

The strongest case for harm in this group is therefore the indirect coercion some will feel to change their beliefs or to act contrary to their beliefs. Those who do not value, and perhaps explicitly reject, the state's aims might complain that they are effectively penalized for their beliefs. In addition to the financial penalty, or denial of financial benefit, there is also the implicit condemnation of their practices. That penalty and condemnation might be justifiable when all is said and done, but the question here is simply whether they are harmful because of their coercive effect.

One could argue that adults who take an illiberal approach to raising children would actually be better off, from a secular perspective, if moved to reconsider their illiberal ways. There are psychological rewards that come from recognizing and respecting the distinct personhood of one's children and quite often gains in the quality of one's long-term relationship with one's children when they appreciate as adults that one tried, in raising them, to respect them as distinct persons with an interest in determining their own aims in life. But such armchair psychologizing is unlikely to persuade anyone and sounds terribly paternalistic. So I will accept that these parents and school operators experience some harmful coercion of belief.

Importantly, though, the coercion goes not to their governance of their own lives but to their governance of the lives of others—their children's lives. As noted above, persons generally have a lesser interest, objectively speaking, in freedom to direct other people's lives than in freedom to direct their own, even though they might subjectively attribute great importance to the latter. In addition, the coercion here is indirect and implicit. The state would not be ordering them to change their practices, and it would not be explicitly condemning their practices. It would be saying, "This is what we value from our necessarily secular perspective, and we cannot consistently say we value this and fund its opposite." In sum, then, there is harm, but it is not substantial.

To summarize the interests aligned against vouchers: Taxpayers, public school teachers, and parents of children who would remain in public schools have nonfundamental interests in satisfaction of their desires concerning external states of affairs—how the government operates and how children left behind fare. The taxpayer interest in how the government operates is quite weak, and the interest of teachers and parents in how children in public schools fare is not clearly affected at all by vouchers. Teachers also have an interest in preserving their jobs and in not suffering a loss of income or worsening of working conditions, but it is not clear that this interest is adversely affected even under programs that do entail a reduction of public school funding, and a voucher program that did not entail a reduction of public school funding would actually make teachers better off.

The children who would remain in public schools have the most important interests in connection with the fate of public schools, but it is not clear that vouchers in and of themselves would have any effect on those interests. Attention should be directed to whether states use new money to pay for vouchers or instead take money out of the public school budget, and voucher proponents who claim to be concerned about the welfare of children should be called upon to support increased total spending on education and a parallel effort to reform the public schools once vouchers relieve overcrowding. Children who would be left behind in nonqualifying private schools would not be harmed by the voucher program itself, and might actually benefit from it if it induces their parents and schools' operators to try harder to provide a good secular education or to rethink their illiberal approach to education. The parents and school operators, on the other hand, can claim to be harmed modestly by the indirect and implicit coercion of belief and practice that their exclusion from the program would create.

Parents of Children Who Would Use the Vouchers

The only group of voucher supporters that consistently appears as a party in litigation over vouchers is that containing parents who already do or who want to send their children to a religious school. They claim an entitlement to do so, under the Free Exercise Clause and / or the Equal Protection Clause. I consider whether these parents do in fact have moral or legal rights at stake in later chapters. Here I focus on precisely what their interests are.

More often than it is expressed in terms of children's welfare, the voucher cause is said to be about parental choice. Parental power is the ultimate value. In other schooling contexts as well, it is commonplace for judges, political officeholders, political and legal commentators, religious leaders, and everyday folks to assert that parents have fundamental interests in making choices regarding their children's education. Few, however, have any idea what they mean by a fundamental interest; they do not, and most likely could not, articulate criteria they would use consistently to distinguish fundamental and nonfundamental interests. The criteria set out at the beginning of this chapter suggest that this rhetoric about parents' interests is nonsense.

It is true that many parents have strong *desires* regarding the nature of their children's upbringing. This is likely to be particularly true for those parents who sacrifice a great deal financially to send their children to a private school. For some, the desire to have their children attend a school where instruction is consistent with the parents' religious beliefs is quite intense. For most, I assume, the desire that their children simply receive a good education is very strong. However, a strong desire is not a fundamental interest; the fact that people often strongly desire things that are not in their interest at all should make that plain. People do have an interest in satisfaction of their desires per se—that is, an interest in experiencing the satisfaction of knowing that they have secured a certain outcome in the world, that the world is in harmony with their preferences. But achievement of such preference satisfaction or choice effectiveness in every instance is not fundamental to well-being (though a complete denial of such satisfaction in a person's life might fatally undermine his or her basic well-being). This is particularly true when the preferences or choices have to do not with one's own life but with the life of another person, even if that other person is one's offspring. Satisfaction of such desires is clearly an ulterior interest or nonprimary good.

Bear in mind that we are not considering parents' interest in simply being parents—that is, their interest in their children's not being taken away from them. Nor are we considering whether parents will have *any* discretion in child rearing. In fact, as a *formal* matter, even the particular parental freedom to choose what school a child attends is unaffected by the voucher decision; the legal right to choose a private school remains intact either way. And for parents who can afford a religious school without vouchers, that aspect of freedom is unaffected as a substantive matter as well. Nor is parents' interest in teaching their religious beliefs to their children at stake. Even in the absence of vouchers, parents have been and will continue to be free to teach whatever they want during the 85 percent of children's waking hours spent outside of school, and to have a religious school teach their beliefs if they can afford it. Moreover, under the assumption that any religious school that would be eligible for vouchers must provide a secular curriculum that closely resembles that offered in good nonsectarian schools, parents do not have a great deal at stake ideologically in the issue of whether they will be able to send their children to a religious school. In other words, in terms of just their preferences regarding the ideological nature of their children's school, their desired external state of affairs is not so far from the existing state of affairs in a no-voucher environment.

In addition, we are certainly not talking about the sorts of basic liberties—physical freedom, freedom to think and speak freely—that all people must have in substantial measure as a prerequisite to pursuing any life plan. Rather, we are simply considering whether certain parents will receive state financial support for one particular child-rearing preference they have. No parent has a fundamental interest, or even a particularly important interest, objectively speaking, in seeing that happen. Confusion abounds on this issue because people fail to distinguish *parents'* interests in connection with children's upbringing and *children's* interests in connection with their upbringing. Only the latter are fundamental.

Parents who send their children to religious schools do have a financial interest in the outcome of the voucher conflict as well, however, and for many it is a substantial one. They might be sacrificing a great deal to afford the tuition of a religious school. Vouchers might save them thousands of dollars each year. This financial interest is certainly significant. Assuming these parents have sufficient other resources to meet their basic needs, however, it too is not a fundamental interest, and it is not an interest courts have ever treated as fundamental. These parents have a greater financial interest than taxpayers concerned about waste of their tax dollars, but probably a lesser financial interest than public school teachers have in connection with their jobs. Unlike the taxpayer and teacher financial interests, though, this financial interest of parents is directly affected by vouchers.

Parents in this group also have an interest in feeling that they are being treated fairly by their government. This interest finds expression in the equal protection claims some parents of parochial school students have advanced against past voucher programs that excluded religious schools. Parents might believe it unfair for them to pay taxes to support public schools when their children attend a religious school. Some also assert that exclusion of religious schools from public funding for education reflects governmental hostility to religion and that this offends them.

In some circumstances, this kind of interest, or one akin to it—namely, an interest in avoiding stigmatization—can be quite significant.[27] Chapter 6 analyzes the equal treatment argument in some depth, and the present utilitarian analysis is itself aimed at determining whether it is fairer in a certain sense to enact or not enact the kind of voucher program I have described. As discussed above, an analysis of whether the program is in fact fair arguably should exclude from consideration persons' interests in feeling that they are being treated fairly. I therefore put aside this consideration, while again recognizing that many parents now feel acutely that it is unfair for the state not to subsidize the schools they choose.

In sum, then, the interests parents in this group have at stake in educational debates are not, as is generally supposed, fundamental interests. They are certainly less important than are the interests of children in receiving a good education. These parents want their children's interests to be fulfilled, but that does not make those fundamental interests theirs. Satisfaction of that parental desire for their children's welfare is significant, though, as is the financial interest these parents have, which is directly affected by the outcome of the voucher debate. These two interests might give these parents themselves a weightier position than that of any of the groups whose interests are thought to cut against vouchers. This is not to say that their interest in their children's lives counts for more than that of the similar interests of other parents, or is weightier than the interest of teachers in maintaining their livelihood. The relative ranking rests instead largely on conclusions that vouchers themselves do not necessarily have any negative effects on public schools or nonqualifying private schools, and that even if one includes the independent decision about public school funding and staffing in the overall reform issue, the negative effects of a decision to reduce public school funding by the amount devoted to vouchers are speculative and likely modest.

Children Who Would Use the Vouchers

The children who would actually benefit from vouchers are rarely named as parties in litigation, and when they are courts pay little attention to what distinct claims they might have or what interests they have at stake. As noted above, education is a fundamental interest of children. If a voucher program were designed so that only schools that strove to provide the best possible secular education could participate, then presumably all or at least most children who received vouchers would experience a significant increase in educational quality as a result. This improvement might occur because vouchers enabled their parents to transfer them from a public school to a better-performing religious school and / or because the recipient religious schools were able to provide a better education than they did without vouchers. Given the terrible condition of many inner city public schools and the financial difficulties many religious schools now struggle with, the improvement could be quite dramatic for many. Vouchers would thus directly advance a fundamental interest of this group of persons.

Studies of actual voucher programs have not demonstrated a significant improvement for children who transfer from public schools.[28] Opponents of vouchers seize upon this fact, and argue that it shows that the problem lies entirely in the social environment the children live in and the disadvantages they bring with them to school, not in the public schools themselves. However, the actual programs do nothing to ensure that participating private schools are even trying to provide a good education, let alone that they succeed to any particular degree. The better conclusion at this point might be that some children are simply moving from bad public schools to bad or barely adequate private schools. Moreover, at this point the existing programs are not large enough or structured to appreciably affect the total resources of private schools. In addition, the studies do not look at effects on families, for whom tuition savings might create opportunities for new learning experiences for children outside of school. Moreover, the studies tell us nothing about the potential for vouchers to do good in other geographic areas—for example, working class neighborhoods in smaller cities or poor rural areas.

It remains entirely possible that nothing can significantly improve the life prospects of children in the poorest urban areas, short of transforming their socioeconomic circumstances, and that any education reform in those places is futile. It remains true that it is unjust for children to have to grow up in circumstances like those in East Cleveland, and that anyone involved in the voucher debate who genuinely cares about children ought to be committed to eradicating that injustice. It would be premature, however, to conclude that vouchers cannot make a difference, based simply on early studies of the flawed programs now in place. In the absence of political will to overhaul public education in poor areas, our moral obligation to these children requires that we explore promising alternative strategies, and the idea of using state aid to create better educational opportunities in private institutions still holds promise.

Operators, Teachers, and Administrators in Qualifying Schools

The remaining two groups—persons connected with the operation of qualifying private schools and citizen / taxpayer supporters of vouchers—have not played a prominent role in voucher controversies. Groups of religious schools have appeared as parties in one or two court battles. The courts in those cases did not identify what institutional interest the schools asserted, but presumably it was a financial interest or an interest in equal treatment, or both. These interests would ultimately be those of members of the sponsoring religious organization. They naturally would like more money for their projects, and a large-scale voucher program might free up quite a bit of privately raised money now devoted to the organization's schools. In our scheme of government, however, the state simply cannot adopt as an aim increasing the coffers of religious organizations per se. Religious groups' interest simply in having more money, then, should not factor into the analysis. The interest in fair treatment might be more significant, but it raises the same problem raised by the parental interest in fairness discussed above—we ought to determine whether a particular state of affairs is fair independently of whether it is perceived as fair, at least in the first instance.

Adult members of religious organizations that operate schools also have interests in the welfare of children and in the long-term vitality of their organizations. To the extent their schools thrive, these interests are advanced. These interests are akin to those of parents discussed above, simply weaker because the relationship the adults have, qua members of a religious organization, with children is not as intimate. And for both parents and members of sponsoring religious organizations, the ideological stakes are not that great in a regime where schools that would receive vouchers would have to provide a secular education substantially like that in nonreligious schools.

Teachers and administrators in private schools that might receive vouchers are never heard from in the voucher debate, but they have interests at stake as well, and no doubt many of these persons are quite hopeful that vouchers will come. They might benefit from vouchers to the extent the vouchers increase their school's resources and ensure the schools' long-term survival—a real concern for many religious schools today. They might receive a substantial increase in salary, other personal benefits, and classroom resources as a result of vouchers. These benefits connect with other interests teachers have—for example, quality of life, living in a certain geographical area, and sense of personal fulfillment. Their interests are thus quite similar to those public school teachers have at stake, and appear more clearly or directly affected by vouchers than are those of public schools teachers. The interests of this group are not fundamental in the sense discussed above; better compensation and classroom resources will not significantly affect their life prospects, and holding one particular job (as opposed to simply holding *some* job) is an ulterior aim rather than a prerequisite to pursuit of many other aims. But their interests are significant, especially the interest in not losing their jobs as a result of their school's having to close for lack of resources.

Citizens / Taxpayers Who Support Vouchers

The final discrete group of persons with interests at stake contains persons who as citizen or taxpayer *endorse* government financial support for private schools because they think it would be better for society and they expect their government to do what is best for society. They might believe that children who attend religious schools receive better training in morality and good citizenship or receive a better secular education and that this benefits everyone. Or they might believe that vouchers would produce greater competition among schools and that this competition will lead to a general improvement in education. They have an interest, then, in satisfaction of these desires / preferences regarding external states of affairs.

Surprisingly, this interest might be in certain respects just as great as, *or even greater than,* that of the citizens and taxpayers who object to vouchers and whose claims courts have given such great weight. In an environment where the state ensures that all schools that would receive vouchers strive to provide a good secular education, members of this group might well be incensed that the government does not take sufficient advantage of the availability of those schools to relieve overcrowding in public schools and get as many children as possible into better schools. They might see government insistence on funding only public schools as very bad policy, and the discussion so far suggests that they would have better support for their views than taxpayer objectors to vouchers would. And they might be just as convinced that a no-aid policy is inconsistent with the Constitution and a proper understanding of church-state relations as taxpayers on the other side are convinced that an evenhanded aid policy is inconsistent with antiestablishment principles.

On the other hand, avoiding offense or a feeling of exclusion is less of an issue for this group. Failure of the state to subsidize any private education cannot reasonably be seen as a slight toward religious groups. Subsidizing only nonreligious private schools has greater potential for giving offense, but the justification state officials give for this discrimination—concerns about violating the Establishment Clause—is plausible under current Supreme Court jurisprudence, sufficiently so for courts in Maine and Vermont to endorse it. Taking offense would therefore require imputing hidden and sinister motives, and I suspect most supporters of religious schools are not so uncharitable. It would also require overlooking the considerable political muscle religious groups wield today.[29]

In any event, the interests this group has at stake are, like those of citizens / taspayers on the opposite side of the coin, nonfundamental and not particularly substantial in comparison with, for example, interests of parents who would use vouchers. Satisfaction of their desires regarding external states of affairs is not necessary to their basic well-being or a particularly important higher-order component of well-being.

Impacts on Society as a Whole?

I did not include in the list of groups above society generally, or in other words persons simply as members of society. Yet voucher programs might have consequences for society as a whole, and not just for discrete groups of individuals who take a personal interest. The kind of program I described at the beginning of the chapter would improve the quality of education for children who attend private schools. All members of society (except perhaps those near the end of life) have an interest in children's receiving a good education, because this tends to enhance the productivity and lower the rate of crime and other pathologies among the next generation of adults. However, how much of a benefit better education for today's children creates for other members of society is quite speculative, and it would be quite difficult to rank the diffuse interest individual members of society have in greater productivity and lower pathology.

On the other side, some would argue that state support for religious schools creates a danger of civil unrest, because it might create the appearance of state support for religion, or for particular religions, and thereby rile certain con-stituencies.[30] The program I have described, however, minimizes such reac-tion by making the perception on which it relies unreasonable. In any event, what public reaction would be in the long term to any given program is ex-tremely speculative, and it would be difficult to rank the diffuse interest in being spared from an intensification of the culture wars (which might actually lead to some form of denouement).

Others warn that state support for private schools will exacerbate white flight from public schools, thereby making schooling in this country more racially segregated and worsening race relations in our society.[31] Voucher supporters respond that many private schools, particularly inner city parochial schools, are more integrated than the public schools.[32] The evidence does not appear to support the claim that parochial schools are racially integrated,[33] but it is true that inner city public schools are already well segregated; there are not many whites left to flee. In any event, as with the concern about intensifying the cul-ture wars, it is entirely speculative how people would react to increased racial division and difficult to rank a diffuse interest in avoiding racial tension.

A related concern, discussed in Chapter 2, is that of liberal political theorists who worry about the consequences for civic education if students exit the com-mon schools, because many private schools do not teach civic and democratic virtues. The program I have described, however, would, for child-centered rea-sons, qualify only schools that reflect certain core liberal values and civic virtues and thereby prepare students for full participation in democratic society.

Another concern is that the kind of state-church interaction that voucher programs would entail compromises the independence of religious institutions, a concern that would be heightened if vouchers were in fact conditioned on compliance with substantial regulations. Carl Esbeck identifies as a potential harm of state aid to religious institutions an "undermining of religious volun-tarism and the weakening of church autonomy."[34] I assume the danger Esbeck refers to is, at least in part, that if the government decides to promote a cer-tain secular good by providing financial assistance to all organizations, religious or otherwise, that provide that good, then religious organizations whose beliefs are in conflict with that secular good—that is, who do not think it is a "good"—might feel pressured to change their beliefs and come around to supporting that secular good so that they can receive the financial assistance. William Galston goes so far as to raise the specter of totalitarianism; for the liberal state to go beyond a civic minimum in imposing requirements on schools would be to impose on everyone "a single debatable conception of how human beings should lead their lives."[35]

Esbeck's concern about the independence of religious institutions, however, is one the state might have no good reason to share in this context. It is difficult to discern how it could be bad for our society that more religious organizations act to promote agreed-upon secular goods. Arguably the state should not care if religious groups modify their practices or beliefs to conform to secular standards for children's education. In fact, it would appear self-contradictory of state officials to say that X is good for children and Y is bad, and at the same time that it is bad that some groups may have to do X and stop doing Y. Perhaps it would not be if the state could identify some harm to society simply in groups' conforming to secular standards and could reasonably conclude that that harm is weightier than the educational deprivation of children. There might be some loss to society if conclusions that state officials come to about what is good for society are not subject to challenge; it is important for us all that there be dissenting voices on value judgments, so that we and our leaders are forced to reason and deliberate about public policies. But there is sufficiently robust disagreement on nearly every policy issue in this society among just nonreligious perspectives that this danger seems illusory. Moreover, it would be ironic if the law treated conformity to secular child-rearing standards as too threatening to social welfare to be permitted when it does not treat conformity to secular standards for adult conduct that does not affect other people as so threatening.[36]

In addition, it is not clear how religious groups are harmed by changing their beliefs in reaction to external circumstances. Religious groups are now and always have been impacted by a host of external influences and pressures, and the history of religions is replete with instances of adaptation to social and legal environment. It would be difficult to demonstrate that religion is any the worse for it. Nor is it clear that the state should care as a general matter about the extinction of particular religious beliefs. On the other side of the issue, one could plausibly contend that religion benefits from the challenge to its beliefs that the conflict between financial interest and principle creates. This conflict might trigger reexamination of beliefs and then either a relinquishing of beliefs that now appear inadequately supported or a reaffirmation of beliefs that give meaning to the members of the religious group and their practices. In fact, one might think it insulting to religious adherents to say that they need to be protected from financial temptations to abandon their beliefs.

With respect to Galston's concern about totalitarianism, the notion that teaching children to think for themselves has the effect of creating a more ideologically homogeneous population is ludicrous. In fact, it might well increase diversity overall—some ways of life might die out, but many others might come into being. Liberal education does not rule out any conceptions of the good. At most, it makes it less likely that anyone will adhere to any conception of the good unreflectively. I say "less likely," rather than "impossible," because compulsory schooling occupies only about 15 percent of children's waking hours from birth to age eighteen, so regardless of what kind of schooling children receive parents will retain complete control over the vast majority of children's waking hours and so will have a much greater influence. Fostering the expansion of liberal education simply gives more children some chance of having a real choice among ways of life and conceptions of the good as they mature.

One final societal interest that might be relevant is the effect on total government spending. How vouchers would affect this interest, though, is entirely dependent on how a program is designed. Some predict lower spending, because the amount of vouchers is generally less than public schools' per pupil operating costs. However, a voucher plan that included students who were already enrolled in private schools before vouchers came along, or that included students who were entering school for the first time and whose parents would have sent them to private schools even in the absence of vouchers, would to that extent increase educational costs for the state. The state would then be taking on much of the cost for private education that would have been borne entirely by parents in the absence of vouchers. In addition, the assumption of lower state education spending as a result of vouchers presupposes that states will or should reduce spending on public schools as some students exit, but that is hardly a necessary concomitant of vouchers, as explained above. Finally, the entire discussion of state spending must operate against background assumptions about what is the most efficient allocation of the costs of education. If vouchers are used to leverage greater investment of family resources in schooling (i.e., by using payment of only a portion of private school tuition to induce some parents to transfer their children from public to private schools and take on some portion of the cost of their children's education), to that extent they save the state money, but this effective shift in financial burden is not necessarily economically efficient or utility maximizing.

In sum, possible societal effects are extremely speculative, often illusory, and in any event so diffuse as to make it impossible to determine how they should factor into the balancing of interests. Some can be dealt with in designing the programs and therefore do not pose a problem for vouchers per se. Thus, in the absence of any rational basis for concluding whether potential widespread societal effects would in fact occur, and if so to what degree, the state arguably should exclude them from consideration and focus on the more concrete interests of smaller groups and individuals and the more predictable consequences of vouchers. Should broader societal effects become more predictable and quantifiable, the state might then factor them into the equation.

Balancing Interests

Spelling out in any detail the interests at stake in the voucher debate might appear a tedious exercise. The hope is that such an exercise can broaden everyone's perspective and sort out some good and bad policy arguments. While the analysis above was undeniably less than fully comprehensive, and to some degree subjective and impressionistic, it did yield conclusions about the relative importance of interests at stake that are at least plausible. Those who disagree should attempt to develop a more plausible account.

The most important conclusion is that children are the only persons with fundamental interests at stake, and ipso facto they are the persons who have the most important interests at stake. This supports the child-centered position that policy debates about vouchers should be primarily focused on children. That conclusion might seem unremarkable. However, there is widespread misunderstanding about the relationship between vouchers and the welfare of children. Most significantly, it is not clear that vouchers per se can have any negative effect on the children who would remain in public schools. In fact, vouchers would seem to create an immediate improvement in their situation, by alleviating overcrowding. Much will depend for them on the state's independent decision about funding and reform of public schools themselves.

In addition, the voucher plan I have outlined also would not appear to have a negative effect on children in nonqualifying private schools, and might actually make them better off, by creating an inducement for their schools to strive to provide a good secular education. Finally, for the children who would receive vouchers, it seems likely that there would be a substantial effect, and a beneficial one, if the state ensured that the participating private schools strove to provide the best possible secular education. Thus, the most important interests at stake—those of children—count in favor of the voucher plan outlined at the beginning of the chapter.

Another conclusion is that teachers' interests surprisingly appear to be the next most important interests. Their livelihood might be on the line. However, as with children who would remain in public schools, public school teachers might actually not be much affected by vouchers per se. The greater threat lurks in the state's independent decision about what to do with public schools after a significant number of students exit. In light of the heightened public interest the voucher controversy has created regarding public schools, and in light of the job protections teachers have, there might be little cause for concern that that independent decision would result in significant loss of teacher jobs. On the other side of the coin, what generally goes unrecognized is that teachers who work for, or want to work for, private schools that would qualify for the voucher program might have as great an interest at stake, and their interest is directly affected, and positively so, by vouchers.

A third conclusion is that while parents do have significant interests at stake, these have been overvalued. They are certainly not fundamental interests, and saying that they are only distracts attention from the children who should be the primary focus. As between parents whose children would stay in public schools and those whose children would attend private schools with vouchers, the interests of the latter group should have more effect on a utilitarian assessment of vouchers for the same reason their children's interests affect the assessment more than those of children left behind. Vouchers per se would not have any clear effect on the interests of parents whose children would remain in public school, but would clearly and directly affect the interests of parents who would use them. A third group of parents, those of children in nonqualifying schools, could incur some harm, from being stigmatized for their choice of school and from feeling coerced to change their beliefs and choices, but any such harm would be more than offset by the benefit to their children from the parents and schools being encouraged to provide what the state regards as a better education.

Finally, taxpayer interests are the most overblown of all interests in the controversy. They are weaker than the interests of all the individuals immediately involved—that is, children, parents, and teachers. Moreover, there are taxpayers on both sides of the issue. The only thing that might give taxpayer opponents of vouchers a greater stake than taxpayer supporters of vouchers is that they have an important interest in not feeling like ideological outsiders in our society. But for clear-thinking persons, that interest would hardly be affected by a state decision to support high-quality secular education in religious and other private schools. Such a decision could not reasonably be viewed as an endorsement of religion; reasonable and thoughtful people should instead view it as fulfillment of a moral obligation to children.

Prioritizing of interests is not itself sufficient to complete a utilitarian analysis. Ideally, when analyzing the effects of a program on different groups of people with defined interests, one also considers how many people belong to each group and how they align. Determining the number of people belonging to some of the groups discussed above would be quite difficult, requiring a great deal of speculation about people's existing preferences and beliefs and about how vouchers would influence choices and attitudes. For example, we know roughly how many children are already in religious schools nationwide (4.2 million),[37] but we do not know how many are in schools that would qualify for vouchers, or how many parents who currently enroll their children in public schools would choose to transfer them to qualifying private schools under the program described. We know how many public school teachers there are now nationwide (2.5 million),[38] but can only guess at how many, if any, would lose their jobs as a result of the program. We know some secularist bystanders feel strongly enough about vouchers to initiate litigation, but it is unclear how one would even go about determining how many of them, and how many other people, would experience some offense or threat to their sense of belonging or intellectual freedom as the result of the voucher program under consideration here, especially since that program is far different from existing programs.

One might conclude from this great uncertainty about the membership of the various groups I have ranked that a utilitarian approach to the voucher issue is not particularly useful; when it comes to application, this approach may not be able to yield results in which we can have much confidence. For several reasons, though, a utilitarian evaluation of this voucher program is not futile. First, even if it is too difficult to do a balancing of interests, simply ranking them can help advance the debate about vouchers. Public debate and legal analysis appear generally to presuppose a different ranking of interests than I arrived at above, so if my account of the relative importance of interests is a plausible one, it may suggest a need for participants in the debate either to demonstrate the superiority of a different ranking or to reassess their positions in light of the ranking I give. If the analysis above accomplishes nothing more than to demonstrate that the children who would attend private schools using vouchers should be the primary focus of moral concern, and that the interests of other groups should receive less attention and solicitude than they currently do, it will have been worthwhile.

Second, the problem of determining how many people have what sort of interests is certainly not confined to the voucher issue; it infects most policy deliberations. Yet we expect our legislators to undertake this kind of analysis every day, to assess the likely consequences of a proposed state program for different groups of people. Crude estimates are tolerable simply because there is often no good alternative. Finally, even if we cannot estimate numbers of people with anything approaching precision, it may nevertheless be possible to demonstrate that there are more people with stronger interests on one side of the issue than on the other, if the alignment of interests suggests a very lopsided result rather than a close call. And for the program I have described, the alignment of interests does appear to produce a lopsided result, one clearly in favor of vouchers. As between groups of children, teachers, and parents—the groups with the greatest interest—the interests of the group in favor of vouchers are more clearly and substantially advanced by vouchers than the interests of the group on the other side are set back. Only as between taxpayers for and against vouchers does the group opposing vouchers appear to have weightier interests. But the proposed program hardly affects those interests. By no stretch of the imagination could the interests of taxpayer opponents of vouchers be said to be decisive in this analysis.

Thus, a voucher program that would aid only schools that strive to provide the best possible secular education, succeed in doing so to a substantial degree, and do not engage in practices harmful to children would, from a utilitarian perspective, be a very good thing. Moreover, if the state is obligated and not merely permitted to increase aggregate utility whenever it reasonably can, then such a program would actually be morally mandatory. This should at least give pause to anyone who believes that existing Establishment Clause doctrine would rule out any voucher program whatsoever. There are clear historical examples—*Brown v. Board of Education* being a particularly relevant one—of the Supreme Court's departing from prior doctrine when it came to realize that prior doctrine, however sound as a matter of textual analysis or original intent, was directly contrary to what was good and right.

[4]

A Moral Rights–Based Assessment

A rights-based analysis simplifies somewhat by narrowing the relevant considerations to only the claims people can make to protection of interests or wants that have sufficient moral force to "trump" utilitarian calculations or majoritarian decision making.[1] Rights-based theories begin by asking who has what sort of rights in connection with a particular decision or conflict, and then typically treat the rights identified as having lexical priority over interests of individuals or of society generally that are not sufficiently important to be protected by rights.[2]

Many people find a rights-based approach more attractive than an approach that looks to aggregate welfare, at least in the context of child rearing, because they believe that matters of such great significance for particular individuals are at stake that it should not be possible for diffuse societal interests to determine the outcome. They might also believe that, in any area of policy making, as between two sets of interests that have equal weight, it is possible for one set to have greater moral purchase than the other—for example, satisfaction of a desire to receive some good, such as a home in a safe neighborhood, for myself should perhaps count for more than satisfaction of an equally strong and independent desire, grounded in antipathy or envy, that some other person not receive the same good. In fact, one might argue that an interest of the latter sort should not count at all.

This chapter undertakes a rights-based analysis that is independent of existing legal doctrine. It focuses on potential claims to moral rights, rather than on rights already recognized in the law. Courts and legislatures often reason to decisions about legal rights by appeal to beliefs about moral rights. They generally do not reason with much care, though, in child-rearing contexts. In contrast to analysis of issues such as abortion and affirmative action, for example,

TOURO COLLEGE LIBRARY [99]

judicial and legislative deliberations about child-rearing issues tend to be terribly simplistic as well as adult-centric. A carefully reasoned analysis independent of what those government actors have done is therefore necessary in order to arrive at sound moral conclusions and to establish a principled vantage point from which to critique what they have done.

Basis for Assigning Rights

We generally assign rights to individuals, in our moral and legal culture, based on their interests.[3] Interests may be defined in a variety of ways: fulfillment of needs, satisfaction of desires, effectuation of choices, basic welfare, human flourishing, or several other possibilities. One very difficult task in legal decision making and political theorizing is picking out which human interests warrant the protection of rights. Unfortunately, legislators and judges typically carry out this task in an ad hoc rather than principled way. Legislators often confer statutory rights simply in response to political pressure. Judges, when not clearly constrained by statutory or constitutional language, often confer common law or constitutional rights in order to reach outcomes consistent with their particular worldviews.[4]

Those who think about rights in a more disciplined and principled way typically determine which interests warrant the protection of rights by assessing the *objective* importance of interests—that is, not what persons are interested in subjectively, but rather what is in their interest. The determination cannot be based on the importance individuals subjectively assign to their own interests, because then every person would be a law unto herself or everyone would have a right to everything he strongly desires. The courts hearing legal challenges to vote-counting procedures in Florida in the 2000 presidential election recognized this when they said that neither of the leading candidates had rights at stake; only the rights of voters were in issue.

The determination of who has moral rights also cannot be made by simplistic assertions about "natural rights" or "human rights," since such assertions simply beg questions of neutral criteria and justification.[5] Relatedly, an additional restriction on the identification of rights in connection with state decision making derives from the fact that the ultimate aim is to determine what the state should conclude about moral rights, or in other words what the state should conclude about which persons are morally entitled to what legal rights. This is the same restriction identified in the previous chapter with respect to identification of interests. It requires that the assessment of the importance of interests that is a necessary predicate to assigning rights be based upon a set of beliefs that it is proper for the state to endorse. We have a secular state that does not decide religious questions, so the assessment must be based on secular beliefs about this world, and not religious beliefs about people's spiritual interests or afterlife. Put simply, for the state to assign legal rights to individuals, *it* has to have a good reason for doing so, and no one can expect the state to have as a reason for any action the dictates of some religious faith. Thus, "God has conferred this right" and "this right is essential to salvation" are not positions one can expect the state to adopt.

Singling out particular interests for the protection of rights thus involves identifying those interests that, from the state's perspective, are so important to individual well-being that they ought to trump subordinate or nonfundamental interests. That is, the interests must be so compelling that they justify requiring the state to satisfy them before it can consider other interests in its policy making, regardless of how many people share those other interests. The importance of interests is generally taken to be a matter of their weight and type. Some interests make up a larger component of individual well-being. And some interests are of a kind that commands greater respect.

With respect to the weight of interests, the fundamental versus nonfundamental distinction advanced in Chapter 3 typically does some work in discussion of rights. One might say that only fundamental interests command the protection of moral rights, or at least that rights protecting fundamental interests trump rights protecting nonfundamental interests. The first task will therefore be to separate out those interests identified in Chapter 3 as fundamental.

With respect to morally superior kinds of interests, a distinction between self-determining interests and other-determining interests noted earlier in passing is particularly relevant in the context of child rearing. In general, people have no entitlement to satisfaction of their desires as to how other people's lives should go. Such desires, some of which could for some people be just as intense as desires regarding aspects of their own lives, simply do not command the same moral consideration. My preferences as to what my pregnant neighbor does with her body do not have the same standing as my preferences regarding what happens with my own body. This is not because it is blameworthy to care intensely about another person's life. Indeed, when the caring is benevolent, rather than malevolent or indifferent to the other person's welfare, it is praiseworthy. Rather, other-determining interests have less moral purchase because of our historical understanding of the purpose of rights—namely, to protect self-determination and personal integrity, of the separateness of persons, and of what it means to respect persons—in particular, that we should not make any person the object of another's rights. This criterion of importance is likely to be consistent with, and to inform application of, the fundamental / nonfundamental criterion, because it seems intuitively correct that an other-determining interest can never be a fundamental interest.

Rights in Connection with Vouchers

In the context of school vouchers, there is likely to be universal agreement that certain of the interests discussed in the Chapter 3 are *not* sufficiently strong or important to be deemed a matter of right—that is, they are not interests in things to which people are entitled regardless of whether their receiving it is consonant with the overall welfare of society. For example, I suspect no one would contend that teachers in religious schools have a moral right to higher salaries, that persons who want to teach in religious schools but have been unable have a moral right to do so, or that citizen supporters of religious schools have a moral right to satisfaction of their desire that religious schools receive state support. I therefore focus below on the groups whose claims to rights in the voucher context have at least superficial plausibility—children, public school teachers, parents, and secularist bystanders.

Children

If the ranking of interests arrived at in Chapter 3 is more or less accurate, then the interests with the strongest claim to the protection of a moral right in the education context are the interests of schoolchildren. Children in public and private schools have a fundamental interest in receiving a good liberal, secular education. Such an education is a prerequisite to enjoying a broad range of career and lifestyle possibilities as an adult, for realizing one's human potential. In addition to constituting preparation for adult life, a good education enhances children's well-being as children, affording them the pleasure of intellectual stimulation and developing their abilities to comprehend and negotiate the world around them. Many states recognize the moral right of children to receive a good education in their own constitutions.[6] One also finds in the work of moral and political philosophers who address education issues numerous articulations of the conviction that children possess this moral right. And one would be hard-pressed to find anyone who denies it. The Supreme Court's reluctance to say that children have a fundamental right to a particular quality of education *as a matter of federal constitutional law* does not undermine this conclusion, because that reluctance stems largely from federalism concerns, not from doubts about the importance of children's interests in connection with education.

I therefore assume that children in general have a moral right as against the rest of society (as represented by the state) to receive a good education. There might be several ways of satisfying that right for any particular group of children. The question vouchers raise is whether they constitute an appropriate or necessary means of doing so for some children.

For purposes of a moral rights–based analysis, it is useful to divide school-children as a whole into four categories, rather than the three used in Chapter 3, by further dividing the children who would receive vouchers into those already in religious schools and those who would transfer from public schools to religious schools with vouchers. I consider first, though, the children who would remain in public schools even if vouchers were available. As explained in Chapter 3, these children do not have a stake in vouchers at all as a theoretical matter, because there is no necessary connection between religious schools' receiving state support and the quality of education children receive in public schools. Stated in rights terms, the moral right of these children to a good secular education is not a factor in the determination of whether vouchers are permissible, because vouchers per se cannot infringe that right.[7] These children possess a moral right to adequate state support for their education, but no right that other children not receive state support for their education. At most, vouchers could affect their welfare by creating a "skimming" problem, if vouchers were awarded on the basis of parental choice rather than randomly or on the basis of need. Even if an interest in avoiding skimming could properly be taken into account in a utilitarian balancing, it could not plausibly be said to generate a right; a right to hold the better students hostage in this way to one's own educational needs would be a perverse sort of right.

Children in nonqualifying schools also have no rights affected by vouchers per se. Like all other children, they have a moral right to a good education, and that right now goes unfulfilled, but the voucher program I described in Chapter 3 would not worsen their educational plight and so would not constitute an additional violation of their right. If anything, the program would induce their parents and teachers to try to do more of what the state thinks they should do. I consider at greater length in Chapter 6 whether any groups of children have an equal protection right to a share of state funding for education. At this point, I will just note that if any children have an equal protection right in connection with school financing, it is not a right that money be spent on their schools per se, but rather a right to equal state support for their secular education. If the school they attend would not use state money to provide them a good secular education, then giving the school money would not fulfill any rights the children have.

The next category of children comprises those now in public schools whose parents would transfer them to a good private school if they had vouchers. For those children, vouchers constitute *one means* of satisfying their moral right to a good secular education. The state can fulfill its duty to these children *either* by ensuring that the public schools provide a good education *or* by enabling their parents to transfer them to a different and better school. Thus, these children have a right not to vouchers per se, but rather to *some* action by the state to ensure them a good education. A properly designed voucher program would be one means of effectuating that right, but not a necessary means.

The last category of children contains those enrolled in religious schools before vouchers become available or newly entering students whose parents would enroll them in religious schools regardless of whether vouchers are available. These are the only children who have a moral right to vouchers per se. For some of these children the reason is in part that vouchers would make the difference between their receiving and not receiving a good secular education, because without the vouchers their schools lack resources sufficient to provide them a good education. Vouchers are the only feasible means the state has for ensuring these children the quality education to which they are entitled, given that compelling attendance at a public school is not politically or constitutionally feasible (or desirable), and closing down educationally inadequate religious schools is not politically feasible. In addition, as discussed further in Chapter 6, most children in this category would have an equal protection kind of right to vouchers. Because the state funds the education of some children (i.e., those in public schools), if it does not fund the education of others (i.e., those in private schools that would use the money to enhance the secular education they provide), it is discriminating against these children in conferring an important benefit. Any children harmed as a result of this discrimination (i.e., those whose parents are not so wealthy as to make the benefit inconsequential) have a right to equal treatment that the state is violating in the absence of vouchers. That harm could include not just attending a school with inadequate resources, but also missing out on important nonschool learning experiences that parents cannot afford because they sacrifice so much financially for tuition.

Thus, remarkably, the case is strongest for attributing rights in connection with vouchers to children who are already in religious schools or who would be so regardless of vouchers; they are the only persons who have a right to vouchers per se. This conclusion seems paradoxical because political debates about using vouchers to benefit children typically focus on children in public schools who might be able to transfer to religious schools as a result. Indeed some existing and proposed voucher plans have contained provisions restricting eligibility for vouchers to only those children who previously attended public school. My point is not that those students deserve less moral attention than they have received, or that children already in private schools are suffering more now than are children in the worst public schools. My intention here is principally to elevate the standing of children in religious and other private schools in our moral deliberations. It is also to make the point that the provoucher position would rest on more solid theoretical grounds if it invoked the rights of this group. At present, voucher proponents' best argument is that vouchers are *one possible way* of fulfilling the moral right of children in bad public schools to receive a better education, which makes them vulnerable to the reasonable response that there are other ways of fulfilling that right that ought to be attempted first.

Teachers

After children in the ranking of interests in Chapter 3 were teachers, including those in public schools who might lose their jobs as a result of a voucher program. I concluded in Chapter 3 that it is unlikely vouchers would actually have this effect, even taking into account the conceptually independent but politically related decision of how much to spend on public schools after vouchers are in place. If vouchers would have that effect, though, teachers who have invested their careers in the public schools might feel that vouchers violate a right they have. Retaining one's job is certainly an important interest. It creates stability and security in one's life, allowing one to carry on one's home life and social life as before. Losing a job can be very traumatic for oneself and one's family.

Nevertheless, our society generally does not attribute to individuals a moral right to retain a particular job or salary or work environment. There are exceptions at the margins: individuals may have morally supported legal rights against arbitrary or discriminatory firing, or rights to notice of planned termination well in advance of being laid off, and minimum wage laws entitle employees in most workplaces to at least a low base wage. These exceptions protect against exceptionally exploitative or unfair labor practices. Individuals are not, however, deemed to have a right to retain a job when an employer can no longer afford to employ them and when the employer gives ample prior notice of termination.[8]

Part of the reason we do not attribute such rights to individuals is that we assume alternatives are available to workers and that people can seek work elsewhere if laid off or if unhappy with their compensation or working conditions. We do attribute certain rights to individuals in relation to their pursuit of jobs or occupations—in particular, rights against interference with their basic freedom to seek work (as opposed to rights to affirmative assistance, although arguably some assistance has become a matter of entitlement). That basic freedom is in the clearest sense a prerequisite to pursuing a variety of aims in life. But as long as people retain that basic freedom, their interest in occupying a *particular* position is not so important as to warrant the protection of a right, a trump over societal welfare.

Thus, persons now teaching in public schools do not have a moral right to retain their jobs. They have a right to *pursue* teaching jobs and to attempt to bargain for greater compensation and classroom resources, but voucher programs would in no way infringe upon that right. Teachers laid off from a public school as a consequence of the transfer of large numbers of students with vouchers to private schools would be free to seek work elsewhere, including private schools that participate in the voucher program. The conclusion that public school teachers do not have any rights that would be implicated by a voucher plan is consistent with popular sentiment. Indeed, even teachers associations opposed to vouchers typically speak in terms of protecting the public school system and the children who will be left in it post-vouchers, rather than in terms of teachers' rights.

Parents

Next in the ranking arrived at in Chapter 3 were three groups of parents—those who already, or in a voucher regime would, send their children to religious schools, those who do and would send their children to public schools, and those who send their children to private schools that would not qualify for the voucher program. Again, it might seem ironic that parents are closer to the bottom of the rankings than the top, since they are the people traditionally regarded as *the* right holders in connection with children's education, and since litigation of voucher programs has typically involved claims of parental entitlement. I explained in Chapter 3, however, why parents' interests—interests in having their children receive a quality upbringing, having their schooling choices be effective, and not feeling coerced into changing their religious beliefs or religiously motivated practices—are actually not as important objectively as they are generally treated, and in fact are less important objectively than are teachers' interests in not losing their jobs. Here I explain why they are insufficient to generate rights. I have written at length elsewhere about why the widespread notion of parental rights is simply illegitimate, unsupported by our general understanding of what rights are for and of why we attribute rights to people, as well as inconsistent with more general legal and moral principles.[9] Here I can only make a few brief points relating specifically to education.

Parents' interest in the quality of their children's education is one instance of an interest all people have in seeing that the lives of other people about whom they care go well. Other instances of this kind of interest are an individual's concern for the well-being of a sibling, parent, spouse, or friend. The interest is in having a certain psychological satisfaction or comfort. Most parents care very deeply about their children's receiving the right kind of preparation for the kind of life the parents regard as good and would be upset by the belief that their children were not receiving that kind of life preparation. However, one could experience the same feelings in the case of one's sibling, parent, spouse, or friend, and with respect to none of these cases do we generally regard the interest as one sufficiently important to give rise to a right. I might be extremely upset about a sibling's being denied her life's ambition, or about a sibling's not remaining within the religious community of our upbringing, but that concern does not mean that I myself have an important interest at stake. For most people who are parents, their concern for their children's welfare is probably more profound than their concern for anyone else's welfare, perhaps even a spouse's. But it is neither conceptually nor empirically impossible that some people could care just as profoundly about someone who is not their offspring, and if this were shown to be the case, we still would not say that those people have any right in regard to how that person's life goes.

In fact, I do not think this is the interest of parents that most people would point to as the basis for their having moral rights in connection with their children's education. Everyone understands, I think, that no one has a *right* to satisfaction of their desires as to how another person fares in life, not even parents. We do have the sense that *someone* must have rights in connection with children's lives. What most people fail to realize is that it makes much more sense, conceptually and morally, to say that it is *the children themselves,* rather than their parents, who have moral rights in connection with how their own lives go. Analogously, we say that incompetent adults are the right holders in connection with their own care and treatment, not their caretakers.[10] Parents can express their profound concern through acting as agents for their children, as advocates for their children's rights, and through carrying out other parental responsibilities.

The second component of parental interests identified above is an interest in the effectiveness of child-rearing choices. This is an interest that many participants in the voucher debate believe does generate rights. We hear constantly about "a parent's right to choose." This interest is one instance of a kind of interest that might be characterized as an interest in *determining* (rather than just feeling good about) how the life of another person will go. It is an interest in having power of a certain sort. We parents all expect and desire some measure of authority over our children's lives, and some people believe parents have a moral right to that.

I do not. I believe that I ought to have some authority over my children's lives, but because that is best for my children, not because I am entitled to it. In other words, I believe the state owes a duty to my children to confer on me some authority over their lives, because the state has good reason to presume that that will produce good outcomes for them. I do not believe the state owes me any duty in this regard. I should not be the object of moral obligation and attention; my children should be. Why is that? It should be readily apparent that the interest individuals have in gratification of their desire to determine how another person's life will go is relatively unimportant, objectively speaking. The interest I have in making life choices *for myself,* in engaging in *self*-determination, is certainly very important and a matter of my rights. Rights of *self*-determination are necessary to human fulfillment and basic well-being. But parenting is not self-determination. My child is not my self. She is her own self.

[107]

My parenting is therefore a kind of "other-determining" conduct. And that kind of conduct should never be deemed a matter of anyone's rights.

An analogy should make this clear. Directing the life of an incompetent adult is, like directing the life of a child, other-determining rather than self-determining conduct. Our current moral and legal practices treat such conduct as a matter of privilege rather than right. No matter how strongly one might desire to have decision-making power in connection with an incompetent adult's life, that desire does not mean that one has an important interest one-self in having that power, an interest that generates an entitlement. Instead we allocate decision-making authority over incompetent adults' lives in the way we think will be best for them, because that is what *they* are entitled to. In fact, we generally regard the very idea of any person's having a *right* to decide how another person's life will go as anathema in our legal and moral culture, as morally repugnant.[11] Claims to such a right in contexts other than child rearing have been resoundingly rejected, not simply because there is no good reason in favor of recognizing them, but also because they conflict with a proper respect for the personhood of those whose lives are at issue, who are typically incompetent adults.[12] The existence of such a right as a matter of judicial doctrine in the child-rearing context is simply the product of a history of disregard for the personhood of children.[13]

My point is not that other-determining conduct is bad; in the lives of non-autonomous persons, it is essential that some one or more persons engage in such conduct. My point is that we generally do not deem such conduct a matter of entitlement in thinking about the lives of nonautonomous persons, and if we are to be consistent in our moral beliefs we should not deem it so in the parent-child context. We should instead regard parenting as a privilege with important attendant responsibilities. Those who would insist that parents have moral rights in connection with their children's education should carry a heavy burden of demonstrating why parents should have a kind of right that we do not attribute to caretakers for nonautonomous adults. This does not mean that parents' views or preferences are morally irrelevant, but rather that parents do not have a moral right to effectuation of their choices. If their preferences control, it must be because their children's rights so require, or because no other person's rights conflict with what parents want and the state chooses to effectuate parents' views for non-rights-based reasons (e.g., to maximize welfare once all rights have been effectuated, and within the constraints of any rights).

In sum, then, an interest in having one's choices about one's child's education be effective is not sufficiently important objectively to generate a right, no matter how important it might be subjectively (for religious or other reasons) to some individuals. An additional reason for rejecting this second aspect of parental interests as a basis for a right is that state financial support for religious schools, or the lack thereof, does not even affect parental decision-making authority in a manner or to a degree that implicates what the legal system and the public generally regard as a parent's right. In the absence of vouchers, all parents still have the authority—the formal statutory and constitutional right—to decide that their children will attend a private school. What is at issue in relation to vouchers is whether the state will remove a financial disincentive or barrier to choosing a private school. Parents' interest in not being financially constrained in making choices about their children's lives is not so important an interest, in and of itself, as to generate an entitlement.

A comparison with the interests of teachers seems to confirm this conclusion. I suspect most supporters of religious schools would acknowledge that teachers who wish to teach in religious schools have no right to a salary equal to that received by public school teachers, or to state support sufficient to make it financially feasible for them to teach in a religious school at lower pay than they could get in a public school. Yet teachers arguably have a stronger interest in not incurring a cost for their choice than do parents, since the teachers' choice is a self-determining one, rather than a choice about someone else's life. While there may be a good case to be made that persons who have no means of basic subsistence have a positive right to monetary or in-kind assistance from the state, a claim by parents that the state must give them thousands of dollars a year that they do not need for basic subsistence—insofar as it is a claim distinct from one about equal treatment, or about not being penalized for making certain choices—finds little support in widely shared moral principles.

Related to parents' interest in directing their children's lives is their interest in religious freedom. This includes an interest in fulfilling what they perceive to be religious obligations regarding the raising of their children and an interest in not having their beliefs about religion coerced. The first component—an interest in fulfilling a religious obligation—cannot be viewed as *inherently* more important, from the state's secular perspective, than is an interest in acting on other kinds of motivation. Religious obligations may be felt weakly or strongly, just as are nonreligious ethical obligations, self-protective desires, love for one's children, and so on. I doubt any parent's sense of religious obligation regarding the rearing of his or her children is felt more strongly than is my love for my children. And as discussed above, *my* interest in my children's leading a good life, as an outgrowth of my love for them, is not sufficiently important objectively to generate an entitlement on my part. *They* are the ones with fundamental interests at stake in their upbringing, not me. They are the ones who have moral rights.

An interest in not being coerced presents a stronger case. In the absence of any voucher program, or with a voucher program limited to nonsectarian schools, all parents who for religious reasons do or would like to send their children to a religious school could contend that the funding scheme exerts pressure on them to act contrary to their religious principles. If a voucher program of the kind I described in Chapter 3 were instituted, parents in nonqualifying religious schools could claim the same thing. Unquestionably, an interest in not having one's beliefs about religion coerced can be sufficiently important—as a subset of one's more general interest in not having one's beliefs about values, life's meaning, and the origins of humanity coerced—to give rise to a right. However, there must be a sufficiently great threat to the underlying interest to say that a policy or legal outcome would infringe one's right; one does not have a right that the state not act in any way that might make it more attractive for one to modify one's beliefs. And it does not appear that any decision about vouchers one way or another would create a significant threat to any parent's freedom of belief.

The threat to parents' interest in freedom of religious belief that funding only public schools, or funding only public and nonreligious private schools, creates does not come close to meeting this threshold. The failure to fund religious schools simply makes it more expensive to act on one particular religious belief—a belief that it is better for one's child to attend a school with a religious dimension. It does not prohibit acting on that belief, and it does not reflect hostility in the minds of state actors toward that belief. I am not aware that any parents have ever actually complained that they felt pressured to change their religious beliefs by the state's not funding religious schools. Any effect on their beliefs must be slight.

Parents who send their children to religious schools that would be excluded from the voucher program I have proposed, because the schools' religious mission is incompatible with the state's educational aims, would in one sense have a stronger position. That program would embody a judgment about certain of their religious beliefs—not a theological judgment, but a judgment that effectuating the beliefs is harmful to children. The education that the parents, because of their religious outlook, believe to be good for their children, the state does not. The state clearly says so by refusing to subsidize schools run on the basis of their beliefs. These parents might feel the sting of condemnation, as well as the pressure of financial incentives to change their beliefs and practices.

Still, though, the state would not, by means of the voucher program, be prohibiting any parents from believing anything or even prohibiting them from acting on their beliefs. It would simply be refusing to encourage and support their choices and practices. The state does this all the time with nearly all its funding programs, at the federal and state level. These programs come with strings attached, and there are probably a great number of programs for which there are people who would like to participate but cannot because they have a religious or other ethical objection to conforming their conduct to what the state requires. Neither the law nor public morality deems such programs a violation of any person's right to freedom of conscience.[14] This is especially clear when the state has strong reasons for imposing conditions, as in the case of school funding. Indeed, under current Free Exercise Clause doctrine, a person's right to religious freedom does not even include a right against outright prohibition of his or her self-determining religiously motivated practices, so long as the prohibition is part of a generally applicable law aimed at serving legitimate public purposes.[15] The appropriateness of that rule is clear when what is proscribed is conduct the state deems harmful to other persons; no one is entitled to a religious exemption from spousal abuse laws, for example. To object to the indirect coercion of parental choices created by excluding from state funding schools whose mission the state views as antithetical to the children's developmental interests would therefore require assuming that children are not other persons relative to their parents.

Finally, people who do believe parents are entitled to vouchers may express the entitlement in terms of fairness. They believe not that parents are entitled in the abstract to money from the state or that having to pay a cost for choices one makes is always wrong, but rather that this particular cost is unfair. This suggests that people view an interest in fairness per se as a sufficient basis for a right, and not that they view an interest in receiving the money as itself a sufficient basis for a right. So if there is a parental interest at stake that might give rise to a right, it is not an interest in choice effectiveness or in receiving money; it is an interest in being treated fairly. In other words, parents who send their children to religious schools do not have a "basic" right to state funding, but rather might have an equal treatment right. I consider in Chapter 6 whether an equal protection claim to vouchers on behalf of parents is in fact colorable, and confine the discussion here to basic rights. The discussion above yields the conclusion that none of the parental interests that the voucher program I have outlined might implicate is sufficiently important, or is sufficiently affected by state funding or the lack thereof, to say that parents have a basic right at stake. Many parents may strongly desire that the state subsidize religious schools, but none incur a significant threat to their own well-being if the state declines to do so.

Secularist Bystanders

Citizen opponents of vouchers express a number of concerns. Some of their concerns are of the same sort that supporters of vouchers have; they want a better society and may also see at stake the perpetuation of a particular worldview (e.g., liberalism or secularism). Such concerns are no more sufficient to generate a right for citizen opponents of vouchers than they are to generate a right for citizen supporters of vouchers.

Opponents of vouchers also have an interest in the government's conforming to a principle of strict separation that they believe is embedded in the Constitution. Of course, if they are wrong in their interpretation of the

Constitution (if it is possible to say that anyone's interpretation is wrong), then their interest in government conformity to the Constitution does not entail an interest in government conformity to a principle of strict separation (as they understand that principle). In fact, it would entail an interest in government *non*conformity with that principle.

Even if their interpretation of the Constitution were correct in some determinative sense, though, an interest in government conformity to general operational principles such as church-state separation or separation of powers or federalism (in contrast to conformity with provisions regarding the government's treatment of an individual) is typically not regarded as sufficient to generate an individual right. The Supreme Court has held in most contexts that such an interest is not even sufficient to confer standing on individuals to challenge government action, and having standing does not put one in as strong a position as having a right. For example, in the analogous case of *Allen v. Wright*,[16] the Court held that African American parents of public school children did not have standing to challenge the IRS's conferral of tax exempt status on racially exclusionary schools, based in part on a conclusion that the plaintiffs' alleged injury from the federal government's "nonobservance of the Constitution" (specifically, of the Equal Protection Clause) was "abstract" and insubstantial. The one area in which the Court has treated such an interest as sufficient to confer standing is the Establishment Clause, but not because the Court perceives opponents of state aid to religious organizations as having a right at stake. The Court has judged that in this area more than others private individuals are in a good position to police the government, to act as "private attorneys general."[17]

However, some opponents of vouchers have a more personal interest, and this interest has competed with parental interests for the center of judicial and public attention. This is an interest relating to one's sense of membership in one's local community and in American society and relating to one's religious freedom. A general interest in belongingness and in perceiving oneself as a full member of community and society, and an interest in basic freedom of belief on matters of ultimate value or importance, are fundamental in the sense that I have assumed. Without a sense of belonging to human society, it would be difficult to pursue any personal life ambitions, because one's sense of self-worth and of one's capabilities would be undermined. Without a substantial measure of intellectual freedom, one cannot even formulate personal aims. It therefore seems correct to say that individuals have a right against state action that substantially threatens their sense of belonging in the community or their intellectual freedom.

However, a well-designed voucher program would not infringe this right of secularist opponents of vouchers. One's rights are not infringed by every action that has some effect on the interests underlying the rights; the effect must exceed some threshold in order to infringe one's rights. For example, I might feel some subtle pressure toward becoming an Episcopalian because the mayor of my town is an Episcopalian and because I think (wrongly, let us assume) that her co-religionists have an advantage in developing a good working relationship with her. That does not make the mayor's religious affiliation an infringement of my right to freedom of religion, because the effect is too slight. People do not have a prima facie right against any and all effects on their psychological well-being or intellectual freedom. In our jurisprudence of constitutional rights, this view of rights is sometimes manifest in a requirement that plaintiffs demonstrate a substantial burden on their freedom before courts will review the constitutionality of a law.[18]

In some contexts, the effect of state action on individuals' interest in a sense of belonging and in intellectual freedom *is* sufficiently large to implicate their rights. For example, a child being raised in the Jewish faith who attends a public school in which Christian teachers and administrators flagrantly and routinely violate the Establishment Clause prohibition on prayer and religious indoctrination might be greatly affected by this. The effect might rise to the point where his sense of membership in the school community and in American society, and his freedom to believe the tenets of the Jewish faith, are substantially undermined.

The effect of a voucher program on the secularist citizens and taxpayers who challenge such programs is likely to be much closer to the first example than to the second. At least where vouchers are solely advancing the secular education of children in private schools, the effect on any clear-thinking secularist's sense of belonging and intellectual freedom cannot be substantial. In those circumstances, no one could reasonably view vouchers as government endorsement of religion or as an inducement to parents to send their children to a school because it is religious. Vouchers would simply remove a financial disincentive to choosing a private school that provides a high-quality secular education, making parental choice between a public school and a private school financially a matter of indifference (more or less). Parents' values and perceptions of relative educational quality, rather than where the state directs its financial support, would drive parents' choice of schools. Vouchers in this context would therefore communicate nothing to agnostics or atheists, or to members of religious groups that do not operate schools, about their standing in the community, nor would vouchers exert any pressure on those people to adopt a religious faith. There being no significant effect on opponents of vouchers, no rights they possess would be implicated.

Conclusion

A well-designed voucher program, one that ensures that all participating private schools provide a good secular education and treat students with proper respect, would impact moral rights only of children attending private schools that would qualify for the program. Claims of parents' right to choose or of taxpayers' right not to have their money go to religious institutions are, as a moral matter, unsupportable. Even the claim that children in failing public schools have a right to vouchers is not quite right. Their rights could, if the political will existed, be fulfilled by other means, such as a complete overhaul of the public schools or a robust public choice program.

In contrast, for children attending private schools that strive to provide a good education but are not succeeding, or not succeeding much, because they lack adequate resources, vouchers appear to be the only feasible way the state can fulfill its moral obligation to ensure those children a good secular education. I have also suggested that these children may have an equal protection right that requires the government to support their education as much as it supports the education of other children (assuming that the support makes a difference in terms of educational quality), and I discuss that possibility further in Chapter 6.

There being no competing rights, the conclusion is straightforward. A well-designed voucher program is a moral entitlement of children who are in private schools that strive to provide a good secular education. Such a program would therefore be not merely permissible, but actually mandatory. This result is consistent with that reached by means of a utilitarian analysis. Thus, the two approaches to a moral assessment of a well-designed voucher program point in the same direction, in favor of the program. A state could therefore assert in defense of such a voucher program, against legal or political challenges, that even if the program infringes to some extent antiestablishment strictures, the program is necessary to further children's fundamental interests and to respect children's moral rights. The next chapter considers whether a well-designed voucher program would in fact infringe antiestablishment strictures.

[5]

Making Sense of Antiestablishment Principles

The two areas of federal constitutional law that vouchers most clearly implicate are religious establishment and equal protection. Free exercise of religion claims have also appeared in a few court cases regarding vouchers; parents claim that funding only public schools or providing vouchers to nonsectarian private schools but not religious schools violates their rights under the Free Exercise Clause. As noted in Chapter 1, courts in Maine and Vermont dismissed such claims summarily, concluding that denial of funding for a freely chosen alternative school does not burden the exercise of religion. They drew support from the Supreme Court's statement that " 'the Free Exercise Clause is written in terms of what the government cannot do to the individual, not in terms of what the individual can exact from the government.' "[1] In any case, the currently prevailing interpretation of the Free Exercise Clause treats it as an equal protection mandate, simply highlighting the protection owed religious minorities when legislation discriminates against them on the basis of their religion.[2] Therefore, I focus in this and the next chapter on the constitutional principles of nonestablishment and equal protection. I do, though, consider free exercise principles in the course of discussing these two areas.

Why address the Establishment Clause at all, given the conclusions of Chapters 3 and 4 that the interests connected to the antiestablishment rule that are relevant to an analysis of vouchers are rather low on the list of importance, and insufficient to generate rights? One obvious reason is that the courts will continue to apply the Establishment Clause to programs of state aid to religious schools, and will continue to treat it as a trump over all other considerations regardless of how senseless that is, unless and until the Supreme Court decides this should no longer be done, and there is little reason to believe the Court will do that anytime soon. Another reason is that a clearer understanding of Establishment Clause principles and how they should apply to state support for the education of children in religious schools might make clearer why the interests of secularist objectors to such aid should carry little weight. Finally, there is confusion on both sides of the voucher issue about certain Establishment Clause principles, and about the particular factors courts have assumed to be relevant to the voucher issue, and some of that confusion stems from a lack of understanding about the reality of children's lives and children's education. A more child-centered look at Establishment Clause doctrine might therefore shed some new light.

Lower court decisions on vouchers have manifested little consistency in applying the Establishment Clause. Decisions on the permissibility of vouchers go both ways, and even among those going the same way there is little consistency in the factors they emphasize or in their treatment of Supreme Court precedent. Courts concluding that vouchers violate the Establishment Clause have most often emphasized the size of the assistance involved, the absence of assurance that aid is used only for secular purposes, and / or the fact that vouchers are used predominantly at religious schools. Courts concluding that vouchers do not violate the Establishment Clause have most often emphasized the indirect nature of the assistance to religious institutions, the neutrality of the program as between public and private and between sectarian and nonsectarian schools, and / or the absence of burdensome regulation. All purport to be interpreting and applying Supreme Court precedent, which in itself suggests Supreme Court doctrine in this area is hopelessly unclear. We can, however, identify some of the more salient and consistent concerns and operating principles that the Court or individual members of it have expressed.

How the Supreme Court Has Framed the Legal Analysis

The relevant Supreme Court precedents are too numerous to describe here. Four decisions relating to religious elementary and secondary schools are of particular relevance: two older cases involving monetary aid, *Committee for Public Education v. Nyquist*[3] and *Mueller v. Allen*,[4] and two recent cases involving "in-kind" aid, *Agostini v. Felton*[5] and *Mitchell v. Helms*.[6] These cases signal both changes in the Court over the past thirty years and the characteristics that have distinguished permissible and impermissible forms of aid in the cases most closely analogous to vouchers.

Nyquist—1973

In *Nyquist*, the Court held unconstitutional three forms of aid that New York State provided for religious schools: (1) direct monetary grants for maintenance and repair of buildings, (2) tuition reimbursements for poor parents who enrolled their children in religious schools, and (3) tax benefits for middle-income parents who enrolled their children in religious schools. Applying the *Lemon* test, the Court first found that there was a secular purpose for all three forms of aid. The building grants promoted the health and safety of students, and the two forms of financial assistance to parents promoted pluralism and protected the public schools from the influx of students that would occur if parochial schools could not survive financially. However, the Court also found that all three forms of aid had the primary effect of aiding religion. The building grants aided religion because they went directly to religious schools and *could be* used to pay for "the salaries of employees who maintain the school chapel, or the cost of renovating classrooms in which religion is taught, or the cost of heating and lighting those same facilities." The financial benefits for parents aided religion for a similar reason; the statutory programs contained no guarantee "that the state aid derived from public funds will be used exclusively for secular, neutral, and nonideological purposes." The Court found in its prior decisions a clear rule that, without such guarantee, "direct aid in whatever form is invalid." The Court then reasoned that the indirect nature of the tuition assistance—that is, the fact that the assistance went to parents in the first instance, rather than directly to the schools—should not be sufficient to save the programs.

One might infer from the Court's emphasis on guaranteeing use only for secular teaching that the Court would approve a program of financial aid that did so. However, the Court also suggested that any program creating "an incentive to parents to send their children to sectarian schools" runs afoul of the Establishment Clause, and appeared to assume that rebating *any* portion of tuition costs would constitute such an incentive. The Court specifically rejected an argument that limiting the amount of tuition assistance to 50 percent of parents' actual payments for tuition at a religious school, which would in turn constitute only 15 percent of educational costs in religious schools, made the aid permissible because it created a "statistical assurance" that the assistance was paying only for secular instruction. As such, *Nyquist* can be read to say that any aid that lowers parents' costs of securing religious schooling for their children is impermissible. Arguably, every form of aid—even bus transportation and secular textbooks—does that, but the Court has approved many nonmonetary forms of aid to religious schools on other occasions, both before and after *Nyquist*.[7] A few lower courts hearing voucher cases have concluded that *Nyquist* is no longer authoritative, because more recent Court decisions appear inconsistent with it.[8] Most, though, have concluded that *Nyquist* is still controlling precedent.[9] It seems fairly clear that the Court would have to overrule *Nyquist* in order to uphold a voucher program.

Mueller—*1983*

Ten years later, in *Mueller,* the Court upheld a Minnesota tax law giving parents a limited tax deduction for expenses incurred in sending their children to public or private school. Allowable expenses included tuition and nonreligious educational materials, supplies, and equipment. The Court found several secular purposes for the deduction: the value of an "educated populace" to the health of the community; the financial relief public schools experience in not having to educate the children who attend private schools; the benefit to public schools from the competition that private schools provide; and the state's " 'legitimate interest in facilitating education of the highest quality for all children within its boundaries.' " The Court noted that the secular purpose requirement is almost always satisfied, because the Court will look for any "plausible secular purpose" that "may be discerned from the face of the statute."

The Court also concluded that the tax deduction passed the "primary effect" prong of the *Lemon* test. It did not have a primary effect of advancing religion, even though it supported attendance at religious schools, because of several characteristics of the deduction. First, it was "only one among many deductions . . . available under the Minnesota tax laws." The Court did not explain the relevance of this fact. Second, it was neutral as between religious and nonreligious persons and schools; it was available to all parents regardless of the school they chose for their children, whether public or private. The Court distinguished *Nyquist* largely on this basis; the tuition grant program in *Nyquist* was not neutral, the Court said, because it was available only for attendance at private schools.[10] The *Mueller* Court did not explain, however, why public / private neutrality rather than religious / nonreligious neutrality is relevant to an Establishment Clause analysis, or why the state's direct payments to public schools would not have created evenhandedness in *Nyquist.* The *Mueller* Court was unmoved by the argument that the vast majority of aid would go to religious schools, which was true because nearly all children in private schools in Minnesota attended religious schools and because parents whose children attended public schools would have little or no educational expenses to deduct. The justices were "loath to adopt a rule grounding the constitutionality of a facially neutral law on annual reports reciting the extent to which various classes of private citizens claimed benefits under the law."

A third characteristic of the tax deduction that allowed it to survive the primary effect test was that it only indirectly aided religious schools, since the direct financial benefit of the tax deduction was to parents rather than to the schools. This meant that "public funds become available only as a result of numerous private choices of individual parents." The Court noted that, with the exception of *Nyquist,* all of the aid programs the Court had invalidated involved "direct transmission of assistance from the State to the schools themselves."

One might read this to mean state aid to religious schools will nearly always satisfy the primary effect requirement if it is indirect. If so, there was a marked increase in the significance the Court attributed to the direct / indirect distinction between *Nyquist* and *Mueller*. The relevance of intervening private choices for the *Mueller* Court was that they obviate any impression of an " 'imprimatur of state approval.' " The Court did not explain, though, how if the state is not approving of recipient schools in any way, improving education could possibly be among the secular purposes for the tax deduction.

The final aspect of the Court's primary effect analysis rested on the empirical proposition, adopted without supporting evidence, that religious schools generate certain benefits for society: (1) competition that drives public schools to improve and (2) a lower tax bill for everyone, insofar as the state's cost of providing public schooling is reduced when more students attend nonpublic schools. The Court failed to acknowledge that because the tax deduction would benefit parents who would send their children to private schools with or without the deduction, it would to that extent increase taxes relative to the situation before the program was implemented.

With respect to entanglement, the *Mueller* Court noted that the only oversight the tax deduction program would entail would be determinations by state officials as to whether particular textbooks qualified for the deduction. The only criterion for qualification was that the textbook be secular rather than religious. This meant state officials had to decide which books were " 'used in the teaching of religious tenets, doctrines or worship, the purpose of which is to inculcate such tenets, doctrines or worship.' " The Court concluded that this single form of oversight did not constitute excessive entanglement of the state in religion, and based this conclusion simply on prior decisions of the Court reaching that conclusion on the same issue.[11] Having survived all three prongs of the *Lemon* test, tax deductions became the first, and to date only, form of state monetary assistance for religious elementary and secondary schooling that the Court has approved. At least one lower court has interpreted *Mueller* as establishing that an educational assistance program that is both neutral and indirect will survive an Establishment Clause challenge, and concluded that a voucher program can satisfy both requirements.[12]

Agostini—*1997*

Fourteen years later a very differently composed Supreme Court endorsed a strong neutrality-toward-religion position on aid to religious schools. *Agostini* addressed the constitutionality of states' sending state-employed teachers into religious schools to provide remedial education to educationally at-risk students, pursuant to a federal aid program known as "Title I." The Court had held in 1985 that doing so violated the Establishment Clause.[13] After that decision, such state-provided remedial teaching for students of religious schools occurred either in a trailer parked at the curb outside the religious school or in a public building, which in both cases was inconvenient and costly. In *Agostini,* the Court, in a 5–4 decision, reversed itself, holding that Title I teachers may now go inside religious schools. In an opinion authored by swing vote Justice O'Connor, the Court explained its reversal by reference to two changes in its factual premises since 1985 and one change in its doctrine, all relating to the "primary effect" prong of the *Lemon* test.

With respect to factual premises, the Court decided, first, that it would no longer assume that state-employed teachers would be inclined to inculcate religious views while teaching simply because they were inside a religious school building. This factual assumption regarding expected teacher behavior was relevant both to whether the aid would advance religion and to entanglement (which the Court subsumed within a broader effects analysis), because an adverse presumption regarding teacher behavior would necessitate a level of state oversight of their teaching that might amount to excessive state entanglement in the operations of religious entities. The Court decided, secondly, that it would no longer presume that the physical presence of state-employed teachers in religious school buildings would create a symbolic union of church and state.

Two aspects of these changes in factual premises are peculiar. First, in neither *Aguilar* nor *Agostini* did the Court have any evidentiary basis for making an assumption one way or the other about teacher behavior or symbolic unions. Nor did the Court claim in *Agostini* that anything in the real world had changed between 1985 and 1997. In both *Aguilar* and *Agostini,* the Court essentially took judicial notice of certain unproven facts about the world, and in *Agostini* simply reversed itself on those points of judicial notice. There seems no explanation for the reversal except that a majority of the current justices are operating on the basis of an assumption that evenhanded aid is permissible, are more charitable in their attitudes toward state-employed teachers, and are less sensitive to symbolic unions. Second, with respect to symbolic unions, the Court gave little indication of whose perceptions were of concern.[14] Is it secularist bystanders? Is it members of religious groups that do not operate their own schools? Is it the children in the religious school? The Court's discussion suggests that symbolic union is an objective characteristic of state activities, requiring no reference to perceiving subjects. But it would be quite surprising if something could have symbolic (and therefore implicit, rather than explicit) meaning independently of any persons' subjective perceptions.

The change in doctrine the Court announced was that it would no longer take the position that "all government aid that directly aids the educational functions of religious schools is invalid." Which sort of direct aid is valid and which is not, and indeed what makes aid direct rather than indirect, the Court did not clearly spell out. But in holding valid remedial teaching by state employees in religious schools, which the Court viewed as direct aid to those schools, the Court emphasized several facts: First, the aid is neutral as to religion, in the sense that it is available to all and only students who satisfy certain nonreligious criteria, without regard to the kind of school they attend. It therefore creates no incentive for parents to choose religious schools rather than nonreligious schools. Second, the aid goes to religious schools only as the result of the independent choices of parents, rather than as the result of a state decision to fund activities in religious schools. Third, no government funds "ever reach the coffers of religious schools." And fourth, the aid cannot "indirectly finance religious education," because it does not "relieve the sectarian schools of costs they otherwise would have borne in educating their students." The third and fourth factors suggested that the Court would view vouchers as impermissible, either because state money would be reaching the coffers of religious schools or because the state would be paying for instruction that religious schools would otherwise have to pay for themselves (i.e., state-mandated subjects) and would thereby, in the Court's view, indirectly subsidize religious instruction. In addition to listing important relevant facts, the Court noted several facts that were *not* "meaningful," including the fact that a large number of religious school students would receive the state-provided services, rather than just one or a few.

The four dissenters in *Agostini,* Justices Souter, Stevens, Ginsburg, and Breyer, made clear that they would find unconstitutional a voucher plan that includes religious schools. In disputing the majority's conclusion that Title I services would not supplant services for which religious schools would have to pay, they stated:

> There is simply no line that can be drawn between the [supplemental] instruction paid for at taxpayers' expense and the [core] instruction in any subject that is not identified as formally religious. While it would be an obvious sham, say, to channel cash to religious schools to be credited only against the expense of "secular" instruction, the line between "supplemental" and general education is likewise impossible to draw.

The dissenters characterized Title I services as "direct state aid to religious institutions on an unparalleled scale," and implied that they would disapprove of substantial subsidizing of instruction that religious schools themselves ordinarily do, even in secular subjects.

Mitchell—2000

Mitchell is significant primarily as further evidence of how the current justices of the Supreme Court are aligned on aid to religious schools. The case involved in-kind aid—educational materials and equipment, including computers—rather than monetary aid. Further, it yielded only a plurality decision; there was not a majority view on what the proper constitutional test should be, but rather just a majority in favor of the outcome upholding the aid program. The case therefore does not establish binding precedent that could control a voucher case.

The plaintiffs in *Mitchell* did not contend that the aid program lacked a secular purpose, so the Court did not decide that issue. The Court needed only to apply the "primary effect" prong of the (modified) *Lemon* test. That prong now turns on three "primary criteria": whether the challenged aid program results in government indoctrination, defines aid recipients by reference to religion, or results in excessive entanglement. There was no claim of entanglement, so the case ultimately turned on just questions of government indoctrination and definition of recipients. And because the program clearly did not limit aid to religious schools, the only real issue was government indoctrination.

The four most conservative justices—Scalia, Rehnquist, Thomas, and Kennedy—joined an opinion favoring upholding the program. They made clear their support for a principle of neutrality, which means for them that aid "is offered to a broad range of groups or persons without regard to their religion." If aid is generally available to "the religious, irreligious, and areligious" alike, "no one would conclude that any indoctrination that any particular recipient conducts has been done at the behest of the government." The fact that aid reaches religious institutions only as the result of private choices strongly supports a conclusion that aid is generally available to all.

The most interesting aspect of this plurality opinion is its implicit references to attendant regulations. Justice Thomas's opinion summarized the rule the justices in the plurality perceived in prior cases as follows:

> *If* the government, seeking *to further some legitimate secular purpose,* offers aid *on the same terms* . . . to all who adequately further that purpose . . . then it is fair to say that any aid going to a religious recipient *only* has the effect of furthering that secular purpose. The government, in crafting such an aid program, has had to conclude that *a given level of aid is necessary* to further that purpose among secular recipients and has provided *no more than that same level* to religious recipients.[15]

This passage suggests, but does not state explicitly, three very important things: (1) the state cannot allow religious entities to participate in programs of aid unless they demonstrably further the secular purpose for which the aid is provided, (2) the aid may not have an incidental effect of furthering religion, and (3) the state must limit the amount of aid to that calculated to be necessary to furthering the secular purpose, and if it does so then the aid does not have an incidental effect of furthering religion. This is essentially the position I defend below.

The other five justices expressed even more strongly that the state must ensure that its aid is used for the secular purpose motivating the program of aid.[16] These other justices principally disagreed with the third proposition implicit in the plurality opinion. They would find aid impermissible if it could be, and in the case of Justices O'Connor and Breyer if aid actually was, "diverted" to religious use. For Justices Souter, Ginsburg, and Stevens, it was enough to strike down the program that the educational materials and equipment could be used for religious purposes. Justices O'Connor and Breyer would require proof of actual diversion, and in this case found only trivial instances of diversion—e.g., local school districts purchasing religious books for religious schools' libraries. In part for that reason, O'Connor and Breyer joined the four in the plurality to uphold the program.

What O'Connor and Breyer now think about monetary aid, which will clearly be determinative in a voucher case, is uncertain. Monetary aid is clearly "divertible," and it is not as apparent as it might be in the case of computers or library books how one would ensure money is not diverted to religious use in practice. At certain points O'Connor and Breyer suggested that diversion of aid to religious use would not matter if the aid was "indirect," in the sense that it reached religious schools as the result of private choices. At other points, however, they emphasized that the statutory program under review contained a prohibition on use of aid for religious worship or instruction, that the aid was supplemental rather than supplanting religious schools' private funding, that no state money ever reached the coffers of religious schools, and that the state retained title to the instructional material and equipment, thus ensuring "that religious schools reap no financial benefit." They also noted that in-kind aid is of less concern than monetary aid, because preventing state financial support for religious activity was "the original object of the Establishment Clause's prohibition." And Justice O'Connor reaffirmed the position she took in *School District of Grand Rapids v. Ball*,[17] finding unconstitutional state payment for religious school teachers to teach secular subjects after regular school hours, on the grounds that "[b]ecause the government financed the entirety of such classes, any religious indoctrination taking place therein would be directly attributable to the government."

Summary

The foregoing Supreme Court precedents hardly send a clear message as to how the Court will treat vouchers. While *Nyquist* invalidated the closest thing to vouchers the Court has ever considered—tuition reimbursements—*Mueller* suggested that programs providing "indirect" monetary assistance to religious schools are permissible if they provide for public school choice as well as private school choice. *Agostini* and *Mitchell* signaled that a principle of neutrality as between religious and nonreligious institutions had come to dominate the thinking of a majority of Supreme Court justices on state aid to private service providers, and also signaled a diminished sensitivity to the potential dangers of state involvement with parochial schooling. However, the *Agostini* decision rested in substantial part on factors that cut against vouchers—principally, whether state money ends up in the coffers of religious institutions and whether state aid spares religious institutions from expenses they would otherwise have to bear. *Mitchell* reaffirmed the basic positions taken in *Agostini,* while perhaps showing Justice O'Connor—the pivotal vote in this area—moving further in the direction of evenhanded aid to all private institutions, and Justice Breyer now joining her. But pinning down O'Connor's position on vouchers from her *Mitchell* concurrence is truly an exercise in reading tea leaves. On the other hand, Justices Ginsburg, Souter, and Stevens are clearly opposed to vouchers.

Some specific aspects of the Court's decisions are noteworthy. First, the secular purposes the Court has recognized for aid to religious schools have included promoting pluralism, sparing public school districts the expense of educating more children, creating an "educated populace" for the health of the community, fostering competition between school sectors, and facilitating education of the highest quality for all children. Second, the most important factors in the primary effect analysis appear to be (1) whether aid can be diverted to religious uses, will free religious schools of educational expenses they would otherwise incur, or will reach the coffers of religious schools; (2) whether the government somehow participates in religious indoctrination; (3) whether aid creates a symbolic union of church and state; and (4) whether aid is indirect and reaches religious schools only as the result of intervening private choices, though the Court has never made clear what makes a payment indirect. Finally, while the Court has consistently manifested a preparedness to strike down programs of aid solely on the grounds that they involved an excessive entanglement with religion, the Court has downplayed this aspect of the *Lemon* test in its most recent decisions, and has appeared increasingly less inclined to find state regulatory oversight of religious institutions constitutionally problematic.

General Principles

Finding little that is consistent or clear in Supreme Court doctrine, legal scholars try to make sense of the Establishment Clause by gleaning bedrock or core principles underlying nonestablishment. Favorite precepts include: no coercion of religious belief, with its subsidiary principles of no government endorsement of religion, minimal government influence on religious belief, and no incentive to believe or not believe; no intermingling of church and state functions; no state-compelled tithing; and no state subsidizing of religion. These various principles, singly or in combination, support a variety of positions on aid to religious schools. The two most popular general positions, which have several variations, are "no-aid" and neutrality.[18] The latter sometimes goes by the name "equal treatment" or "evenhandedness."

The Supreme Court has clearly moved in recent years in the direction of neutrality, as evidenced by *Agostini* and *Mitchell*, although the Court does not appear ever to have taken an absolute no-aid position.[19] The no-aid position emphasizes the threat that state aid for religious institutions constitutes for religious freedom, and so draws on the more general principle of personal liberty said to underlie both religion clauses. The neutrality position emphasizes nondiscrimination and so draws support both from the Free Exercise Clause (since discrimination against religion creates disincentives to belief) and from the Equal Protection Clause and its underlying moral principle of human equality. These two positions are generally assumed to be at odds with each other, but I show below that under certain interpretations of each they can be reconciled.

A Potential Convergence of the No-Aid and Neutrality Positions

On one interpretation of the no-aid position, government simply may not pay for religious practice or instruction per se. First Amendment scholars and Supreme Court justices are united in the belief that the Establishment Clause, at a minimum, dictates this proscription.[20] On this interpretation, the no-aid position is reconcilable with the prevailing interpretation of the neutrality / equality position—namely an interpretation requiring that if the state funds a particular secular activity in the private sector, it may provide funding *for that secular activity* to all organizations that engage in it, regardless of whether the organization is religious or nonreligious. Interpreted thus, both positions permit the state to direct funds to the secular activities of religious entities, and neither permits the state to direct funds to religious activities of religious entities. No-aid adherents might be more sensitive than neutrality proponents to support for organizations that mix secular and religious functions. But both positions can endorse support for all organizations that perform secular functions, or in other words, that promote secular goods favored by the state, provided the support is limited in some sense to those secular functions of any religious organization and therefore solely furthers a public purpose.

Some who incline toward a no-aid position, including the liberal minority of the Supreme Court, believe this last condition limiting support to secular activities means that only certain forms of in-kind aid—namely, things that cannot be used for religious teaching, such as secular textbooks and bus transportation between home and school—are permissible. They argue that monetary aid is impermissible because it could be diverted to religious uses. Some would go further and say that even in-kind aid, or aid targeted for secular expenses, is impermissible because it frees up for religious activities funds the religious entity would have had to use for secular needs.

Richard Posner and Michael McConnell explain why, from an economic standpoint, this stronger no-aid position does not make sense.[21] If it is possible to segregate secular and religious functions of a private entity (this is not always possible, but it sometimes is) and to identify roughly what component of the private entity's budget goes to secular functions and which to religious practice, then monetary support that does not exceed the amount the entity would otherwise devote to secular functions should be viewed as aid solely for the secular functions. For example, if a local government agency supports a homeless shelter run by a religious organization, by reimbursing the shelter for what it spends on meals and bedding, the agency should be seen to be paying only for the secular good that is provided—food and shelter for needy people. The limitation of aid in the voucher program I have outlined to 80 percent of any participating religious school's operating costs, coupled with robust academic requirements that would ensure any participating school was devoting the vast majority of its resources to secular education, is intended to accomplish this purpose of ensuring the aid would support only secular education. If it turned out that a lower (or higher) percentage was a more accurate estimate, then that is what it should be.

Some might object to this economic argument that giving a religious entity money for its secular functions leaves that entity with more privately raised money to spend on religious practices, or in other words frees up private money previously spent on the secular functions so that the money can now be used to increase spending on religion. But this objection is unavailing as a theoretical matter (even if it would persuade some current Supreme Court justices). It is true of all aid to the secular functions of all organizations, religious and nonreligious, and of all aid to individuals for secular purposes, that it frees up privately raised money for other purposes, including religious purposes. For example, if the government pays for my medical care, or reimburses me for money I spent at the doctor's office, I can use more money from other sources to give to my church. Likewise, when the government pays for meals and bedding in the homeless shelter, it allows the shelter to spend more privately raised money on other functions, including religious services. This objection would therefore rule out state aid of all kinds to anyone. Moreover, the government should be indifferent as to whether private money is used for religious or nonreligious purposes. Of course, entities and individuals do not typically maintain separate accounts for secular activities and for religious activities, and it would be silly to require them to do so. The economic argument is a conceptual one, and as a conceptual matter it makes sense to think of state subsidies as going only toward secular activities so long as the amount of the subsidies does not exceed the cost of the activities.

Thus, as a theoretical matter, the fact that state aid substitutes for, and therefore frees up for religious projects, privately raised money should not pose an obstacle to vouchers. One would instead need to argue that it is not possible to identify secular functions as such of religious entities. The voucher program described in Chapter 3, however, would limit participation to schools that clearly and primarily engage in secular education. Nevertheless, the Supreme Court has not embraced this economic view as a body. The three *Mitchell* dissenters clearly reject it. The four justices in the *Mitchell* plurality appear to endorse it. Justice O'Connor has made statements in several of her opinions suggesting that she does not accept it, and Justice Breyer adopted her view in *Mitchell*. Were O'Connor to accept the economic view, that would probably be sufficient for her to uphold a properly designed voucher program. This is therefore a critical issue for the Court. Unfortunately, it is never discussed explicitly in the Court's opinions. As noted in Chapter 1, several lower courts in voucher cases have stressed the lack of regulation that would ensure money could be used only for secular purposes, but they have offered no guidance as to how a state might overcome this problem. With one exception, they have not appeared to accept the economic view any more than has the majority of the Supreme Court.[22]

An Extreme No-Aid Position

On a different interpretation of the no-aid position, no aid of any sort may go to religious entities under any circumstances, even when aid is going to nonreligious private entities performing the same services, because even support for secular activities of religious entities creates an *impression* of state endorsement for religion, or a *symbolic* union of church and state. This extreme version of the no-aid position is not reconcilable with the neutrality / equality position. But it is easy to show that the neutrality / equality position wins in this conflict. First, this extreme no-aid position would base the constitutionality of aid on the irrational perceptions of hypersensitive onlookers, which is not a sound basis for judging the permissibility of state action. If aid to religious entities supports only secular activities—that is, provision of certain secular goods by the religious entities—then it is irrational to regard that aid as support for religion. And it is clear that at least some forms of in-kind aid—state-provided math books, for example—would support only secular functions of a school. It would be irrational to conclude that state provision of math books to religious schools, along with nonreligious private schools and public schools, signals state endorsement of religion. Allowing religious schools to operate without satisfying any standards, as now occurs, might more reasonably be construed as implicit state endorsement of religion. But once the schools are operating, provision of math books should be seen as endorsement only of children's learning math. Once it is shown that such in-kind aid must be permissible, the only obstacle to monetary aid is the divertibility concern, so objection to the proposed voucher program would require rebutting the Posner / McConnell argument against that concern.

Second, this extreme version of the no-aid position puts the state in an impossible religion clause bind. It would have the state exclude only religious organizations from participation in a general program of support for private providers of public goods, and this would create the impression in the minds of other people that the state is hostile to or disfavoring religion per se. The religion clauses also prohibit state hostility to religion. This impression might also be irrational, insofar as it pertains to the *subjective intent* of legislators; in general, legislators at the state and federal level are quite solicitous of religious groups. But insofar as the impression relates to the discriminatory *effect* of the exclusion, it is well-founded.[23] It makes little sense, and certainly cannot be constitutionally required, to create a well-founded impression of discrimination *against* religion in order to avoid an irrational impression of state *endorsement* of religion.

The "No Impact" Position

There is also a more extreme view of the neutrality position, or rather a view that goes under the guise of neutrality but is in fact nonneutral. This position would require the state not only to aid all groups engaging in a certain favored activity, such as schooling, evenhandedly, without regard to religion, but also to exempt religious organizations from any attendant regulations that conflict with their religious beliefs. On this view, then, the voucher program I have outlined is not well designed, because it would make no exception to its participation requirements for schools run by religious groups whose beliefs conflict with those requirements.

Carl Esbeck advocates this position when he asserts that neutrality proscribes "exclusionary criteria requiring . . . charities to engage in self-censorship or otherwise water down their religious identity as a condition for program participation," and that "[f]or faith-based providers to retain their religious character, programs of aid must be written to specially exempt them from regulatory burdens that would frustrate or compromise their religious character."[24] Esbeck claims that this position would not constitute preferential treatment of religion. But that is clearly wrong. If organizations wishing to participate must censor any *nonreligious* beliefs inconsistent with the purpose of the program, or must compromise some aspect of their *nonreligious* identity, while religious organizations need not censor their religious beliefs or compromise their religious identity, then there clearly is favoritism for religion and a coercive effect in favor of religion relative to other motivations, beliefs, and identities.[25] And there is no question that under a neutral program of state support for private providers of social services, the state may and routinely does impose criteria for participation without regard to potential conflicts with nonreligious beliefs or preferences of potential participants. For example, the state might provide money for programs that encourage teens to abstain from sex and that do not teach teens how to use contraceptives, believing (rightly or wrongly) that is the best way to prevent teen pregnancy. In doing so, the state may condition receipt of money on agreement by participating organizations to encourage abstinence and not to teach contraceptive use. The state may do this even though some potential participants might believe that the state is wrong about the effectiveness of that approach or that such an approach is inconsistent with a proper respect for young people.

In addition, under Esbeck's interpretation of neutrality, the state would be required to provide aid to any religious organization that merely *claimed* to be providing the good that the state was seeking to support. It would have to do so even if, from the state's perspective, an organization requesting aid was actually providing something very different from, and perhaps antithetical to, that good, so long as the organization claimed a religious basis for its disagreement about what constitutes that good. That is clearly untenable, and the Supreme Court has unequivocally said so. For example, in *Roemer v. Maryland Public Works Board*, the Court stated that "a secular purpose and a facial neutrality may not be enough, if in fact the State is lending direct support to a religious activity. The State may not, for example, pay for what is actually a religious education, even though it purports to be paying for a secular one, and even though it makes its aid available to secular and religious institutions alike."[26] As noted above, all the current justices of the Supreme Court expressed in *Mitchell* the view that the state must ensure that aid recipients are in fact furthering the secular purpose for which the aid is provided and must restrict aid to the secular functions of religious entities.

An analogy to other activities makes plain why this must be so. If a religious organization claims, for example, to be providing services for crime victims, it should have to provide services that are, from the state's perspective, helpful to victims. Otherwise, the state could not view what it was financially supporting as furthering the secular purpose of the funding program. A religious group might counsel female rape victims that their suffering was caused solely by their failure to follow God's will and to submit to men in all things, and might exhort the victims to accept rape as divinely sanctioned service to men. The group might claim that this was a service to crime victims for which it should receive state aid, and Esbeck's theory would appear to support its claim. But the state cannot regard this as a service to crime victims, because it cannot endorse the religious view motivating the practice and because the likely consequences for the victims and for society generally are ones the state does not value—in fact, the state regards them as harmful. Thus, this religious organization would not be promoting the public good at which the state is aiming, and it should not receive state funding.

The same is true in the schooling context. A religious group might herd its children into a building every day solely for religious indoctrination—or for any other activity (Satan worship, KKK indoctrination, making sneakers for profit, etc.)—and call it a school. Esbeck's interpretation of neutrality would require giving them the same assistance given to parents who send their children to private schools that provide what the state regards as a high-quality secular education. Neutrality cannot plausibly mean this. It cannot mean that the state must give aid to anyone who wants it,[27] or that the state must acquiesce to every private citizen's religiously informed view of what constitutes the desired purpose of the state aid. It means providing the same benefit *for the same secular purpose* to everyone who, in the state's view, serves that secular purpose. A well-designed voucher program would do just that.

The Quid Pro Quo Position

Finally, some supporters of free exercise exemptions and of aid without strings for religious organizations resort to a position that abandons neutrality as between religious and nonreligious organizations in connection with programs of state aid, and instead embraces favoritism for religious groups when it comes to imposing regulations as a condition for receiving aid. These supporters would argue that the state should excuse religious schools from many of the regulations contained in the voucher program I have described, particularly those governing content of instruction and treatment of students.

Many who argue for such favoritism toward religious organizations rest their position on a "quid pro quo" argument that purports to effect an evenhandedness or fairness within religion clause jurisprudence as a whole. On this argument, the state should favor religion in granting exemptions from general regulations, in furtherance of Free Exercise Clause values, because the Establishment Clause disfavors religion.[28] In other words, exemptions are payback for the discrimination against religion that the Establishment Clause supposedly causes. This position is sometimes justified as compelled by the text of the First Amendment, which is said to compensate for special disabilities on religion created by the Establishment Clause with special privileges for religion created by the Free Exercise Clause, even though the words *compensate, special, disabilities,* and *privileges* do not actually appear in the text.

This interpretation of the First Amendment would have very limited plausibility in a no-aid Establishment Clause regime, and has none in a world in which the neutrality principle controls. First, it is peculiar to say that the Establishment Clause, under any of the popular interpretations of that clause, disfavors religion. While the clause does exclude use of religion uniquely for purposes of governing, religion clause scholars are in agreement that the essential purpose of this exclusion is to protect religious liberty.[29] In that sense the Establishment Clause actually *favors* religion relative to other aspects of life. Political beliefs, for example, obviously do not receive the same protection from influence by state action.

Second, speaking in such generality about whether the Establishment Clause favors or disfavors religion is too simplistic to do any work in a moral argument, which is what a quid pro quo argument ultimately is, despite any claims to textual authority. We do not owe moral duties to phenomena, such as religion; we owe moral duties to people. A quid pro quo argument should look to the people affected by judicial or legislative Establishment Clause decisions and ask whether they have been disfavored relative to other persons and whether they deserve some kind of compensation for being disfavored.

In a regime in which religious institutions are permitted to participate equally in programs of government financial support for private entities that provide public goods, the only disparate treatment of people on the basis of religious belief under Establishment Clause rules would arise from the proscription against government speech endorsing religion (including such things as school prayer and religious displays on public property). This exclusion certainly does not disfavor all religious people. Typically, it simply prevents the religious majority in a particular locale from using government power to advance its religious beliefs, and it does so in order to protect religious minorities in that locale. As such, it actually protects many religious people—those in the minority—while having only a trivial effect on the religious majority; no one is harmed in a meaningful sense by not being able to express his religious views through the state. Religious majorities are left free to express their views in myriad other ways, and they typically have ample means of doing so. Moreover, because the Establishment Clause (at least in conjunction with the Free Exercise Clause) prohibits *all* government speech about religious truth, including speech proclaiming the falsity of religious beliefs, it really protects members of *all* religious groups, large and small. All religious and antireligious groups are prevented from using the state to advance their views on religious issues, and so this proscription on religious speech by the state actually does not disfavor *anyone*.

Third, even in an extreme no-aid regime, the quid pro quo argument would unravel once one got beyond the simplistic assumption that the Establishment Clause disfavors religion or disfavors all religious people. It is true that in an extreme no-aid regime, religious entities that provided secular services would be disfavored relative to nonreligious entities that provided the same services and received state financial support. Typically, though, not all religious groups provide a given service, and some, particularly very small groups, may not provide any services of a kind that the state is funding. For example, while there are a couple of thousand religious denominations in this country, only a small percentage of them operate schools. The smaller groups that do not provide the supported service, and that would not do so even if subsidies were available, would not be disfavored by exclusion of religious providers from a general program of aid. In fact, they might actually benefit from such exclusion, if state aid to their religious "competitors" would make it even harder for these smaller groups to attract and retain members.

So even an extreme no-aid rule would not disfavor all religious people; it would typically disfavor larger religious groups relative to nonreligious private providers of services such as schools, while ensuring evenhanded treatment among religious groups. The question would then become whether these larger religious groups deserved some compensation for being disfavored relative to nonreligious private entities. Even if there is a convincing argument to be made for such deservingness, the problem arises that it is typically not the larger religious groups that seek free exercise exemptions, or who are extraordinarily burdened by state-imposed regulations, or whose beliefs are most at odds with mainstream norms. Rather, it is typically religious groups constituting a small fraction of the population in a given area—for example, a Native American tribe, Santerians, Jehovah's Witnesses, or Seventh Day Adventists. These groups, the discussion above suggests, are actually favored by the Establishment Clause, under any of the popular interpretations. Even larger groups such as Fundamentalist Christians are protected by the Establishment Clause, at least where they are in the minority, against imposition of the views of a Catholic or more liberal Protestant majority. It would therefore be difficult to justify a Free Exercise Clause exemption for them as compensation for anything, except perhaps their relative lack of political power (which is not caused by Establishment Clause doctrine). The quid pro quo argument would thus lead to a favoring of religious minorities under both religion clauses, which is not a quid pro quo result at all.

Further, even characterizing the situation as a favoring of religious minorities and a disfavoring of majorities would be too general. It may be that a religious group constitutes a majority in some locale but a minority within a larger political unit. It may be that the religious majority in some state or locality has never attempted or had any desire to co-opt the state to further its religion, and so has never received an adverse court ruling under the Establishment Clause. What would be required, it seems, to make the quid pro quo rationale for free exercise regulatory exemptions the least bit plausible would be to demonstrate in each instance that the particular religious individual or group seeking an exemption from regulation was previously disfavored by the strictures of the

Establishment Clause. To the best of my knowledge, no proponent of the quid pro quo rationale for exemptions has ever undertaken to do this. In addition, the question of proportionality would arise; quid pro quo reasoning generally assumes that the compensation is roughly equal to the loss. If an exemption were a huge benefit for a particular group, and an earlier constraint on conduct by virtue of the Establishment Clause imposed only a slight cost on that group, then the exemption would be unjustifiable. Thus, a defensible quid pro quo approach would likely be unworkable and, even if it were feasible, would rarely support a claim for exemption from regulation.

Finally, returning to the specific context of aid to religious schools in a neutrality regime, the quid pro quo argument would be trying to justify exemptions, sought by certain groups of parents as compensation for a supposed detriment they have incurred in another context, that have the result of creating a detriment for their children (again, from the state's perspective). In other words, the state would be compensating certain parents (it would be implausible to say that their children were being compensated for something) by giving them the power to sacrifice the educational interests of their children. Even if these parents did deserve some compensation from the state for some reason, *this* cannot be an appropriate form of compensation. As persons, children have a right not to be used in this instrumental fashion to pay off moral debts to other persons, regardless of who those other persons are. Those who claim that a voucher program must be free of regulations that conflict with religious belief must overlook the distinct interests and moral standing of children.

Conclusion

One can develop from the best interpretation of the two most popular general positions about state aid to religious entities—the no-aid position and the neutrality position—the following unified position: where the state provides monetary *or* in-kind support to private entities to support their *secular* activities that advance legitimate *state* objectives, the state need not, and may not, discriminate between religious and nonreligious private entities. On the other hand, the state may not financially support religion per se, and when giving support to private organizations, must ensure that they actually engage in the secular activity and advance the public purpose that the state aims to promote, must limit its assistance (in an economic sense) to supporting the secular activity, and must subject religious organizations to the same regulations it imposes on nonreligious organizations.

Applying this position to the voucher program outlined in Chapter 3 yields the following conclusions: Because much of the operation of all participating schools is purely secular, promoting the skills and imparting the knowledge that the state legitimately supports, it is permissible for the state to provide vouchers covering the cost of these secular activities. However, the 80 percent (or some other, more accurate percentage) limit on funding for religious schools is essential. The state may not provide any funding for the religion classes, religious services, prayers, or other essentially religious activities religious schools engage in, and so must calculate roughly what percentage of religious schools' operating costs are devoted to religious activities and must limit the monetary value of the vouchers accordingly. Secularist citizens / taxpayers could have no legitimate objection to a voucher program that does this. Also essential are the academic requirements designed to ensure that the state subsidy is actually being used to provide high-quality secular education. Proponents of religious accommodation could have no legitimate objection to imposing those requirements on all participating schools.

Specific Doctrinal Conundrums

Before moving to equal protection principles, I address a few specific aspects of judicial analysis of aid to religious schools that appear rather muddled. Many people have criticized many aspects of courts' application of the *Lemon* test, yet there are even more criticisms to be made, some of which have particular relevance to the voucher issue and to the adult-centered nature of reasoning about education issues. I group the issues below in terms of their connection with one of the three prongs of the *Lemon* test—secular purpose, primary effect, and entanglement.

Secular Purpose Issues

One perplexing aspect of the courts' Establishment Clause analysis is the slipperiness of the secular purpose requirement. Because the purpose test is ill defined, state officials and judges can fabricate a secular purpose for any state program. One might think the purpose test inconsequential, because most decisions turn on the effect of state aid—the second prong of the *Lemon* test. But the effect analysis is tied conceptually to the purpose analysis; courts typically look to see whether the aid accomplishes the asserted secular purpose. It therefore makes sense to think about what would constitute a legitimate and adequate state purpose for subsidizing religious schools. As shown in Chapter 1 and in the description of Supreme Court precedent above, courts have posited a great variety of secular purposes for aid to religious schools, and little attention is paid to the validity and sufficiency of the supposed secular purposes. It would enhance scholarly and judicial analysis of vouchers to sort out the valid from the invalid, the adequate from the inadequate.

One commonly asserted secular purpose for vouchers is to promote parental choice. Increasing the ability of any group of people to satisfy their preferences can, as a general matter, constitute a secular state aim, because it is likely to be instrumental to the temporal well-being of those people. It may make them happier, make them feel respected, and / or empower them to effectuate their higher-order aims in life. However, one could characterize aid of any kind whatsoever as serving such a purpose, so accepting it as a valid and sufficient state purpose would eviscerate the secular purpose requirement. It would allow a program of state aid to pass the first prong of the *Lemon* test even where the aid is directed to purely religious activities. For example, state payment for construction of churches and for salaries of clergy could be said to promote the choices of people who belong to the congregation receiving the aid. Likewise, a program of funding religious services for children in any church or denomination could be said to have the purpose of promoting parental choice. "Promoting individual choice" or "promoting individual freedom" is clearly too general or abstract to serve as a state purpose. What is required is a purpose to further more concrete and specific secular ends. In other words, the purpose must have to do with the substance of what is to be chosen, rather than choosing itself as a desired end, and the substance of the choices receiving support must be a secular good.[30] We must therefore reject "promoting parental choice" as an adequate purpose for a program of private school funding.

Related to the claim that vouchers promote parental choice is the claim, which has appeared in many proposed voucher bills, that vouchers will increase the level of parents' involvement in their children's education. The claim presupposes that if parents are given more choice in their children's education, it will prod them to become more involved. This too sounds like a good secular purpose, but falls prey to the same criticisms leveled against promoting choice as a purpose. First, this purpose too would justify aid to purely religious activities; state funding for Sunday school and bar mitzvahs might also get parents more involved with their children's lives and learning. Second, just as it is necessary to ask what is being chosen, it is necessary to ask what it is in which parents are getting involved or what effects the involvement will have. Vouchers might have the result of prodding religious parents to become more active in ensuring that their children's schools thwart development of any cognitive skills that might encourage children to question the religious and political beliefs of the parents and restrict their children's knowledge to only the views of the religious denomination. That kind of involvement has no value as far as the state is concerned; in fact, the state must view it as inimical to the children's welfare.

Another purpose occasionally mentioned is promoting pluralism, by fostering growth of schools with a variety of ideological orientations. This purpose, too, is highly problematic. While it sounds benign and secular, what it really means is that the state may promote the inculcation of religious beliefs in children, in order to maintain a variety of religious beliefs in our society. The state plainly may not do that. As with parental choice and parental involvement, if promoting pluralism were an appropriate and adequate state purpose, then any program of aid for any religious activities—building churches, supplying prayer books, paying people to go to church—would have a proper purpose. In addition, the clearly instrumental treatment of children's lives inherent in this purpose is, as explained in Chapter 2, morally objectionable.

A final suspect purpose is that of sparing the public schools from having to educate a group of children. This, too, sounds like a good secular purpose until examined closely. The state certainly has an interest in saving money, but that interest can hardly serve by itself as an adequate purpose for aiding religious schools. There must also be a purpose of enhancing the secular education of students in religious schools. That is, the aid must be designed to encourage parents to transfer their children to schools that are better, not worse, academically. If the aid would not do this, then for some students—those whose parents would transfer them to a worse school—the aid would result in their receiving an inferior secular education, which is, on the whole, harmful to the state (and its treasury) and a derogation of the state's obligation to those students. In the absence of a purpose to improve the secular education of students and assurance that this will in fact occur, a purpose of relieving a burden on the public school system is in effect simply a purpose of abandoning some children. That purpose could be served without funding religious institutions, by simply expelling some children from public schools, and the Establishment Clause would arguably require the state to take that approach to saving money instead of the approach of giving money to religious organizations (the same equal protection problem would arise in either case).

A purpose of enhancing the secular education of children is, then, the only sensible articulation of the secular purpose underlying a voucher program. The state appropriately aims at satisfying the developmental needs of children, as the state sees them. This raises the question, though, whether the state should be able to assert a justifying purpose if it has no reason to believe that an aid program will actually further that purpose, or if it has reason to believe the aid will *not* further that purpose. Suppose a city erected a Christian cross on all its public buildings and claimed that doing so would help improve our nation's relations with China. Should a court accept that asserted secular purpose under the *Lemon* test? If the purpose test is to be at all meaningful, assertion of a purpose must not be disingenuous or fanciful.

Thus, a court should not accept an asserted purpose of enhancing secular education for children—by enabling their parents to choose an academically superior school, by enhancing the secular education religious schools are providing, and / or by generating competition among schools for more empowered parents—if the state has little or no reason to believe that religious schools are academically superior, or that recipient schools would use the vouchers to improve their secular education, or that recipient parents would choose schools on the basis of the quality of the schools' secular education. With a voucher program of the type I have outlined, however, the state *would* have good reason to believe the vouchers would enhance secular education, because it would have regulations in place to ensure that all recipient schools strive to provide a good secular education and use the voucher money for that purpose. Therefore, there *would* be a legitimate and adequate secular purpose for such a program.

Of course, it might be that all the problems, real and potential, with the purpose test are accounted for in the effect analysis. For example, if a proffered secular purpose is just masking promotion of religious indoctrination or would not really be served by an aid program, then courts would likely find that the primary effect is to advance religion. If that is always the case, then the Court might as well do away with the purpose test, as some have urged, since it becomes superfluous. But then courts would just have to ask at the second stage, the "primary effect" prong, the very similar question of what is a proper secular effect. As long as the Supreme Court retains the purpose prong, it ought to make the exercise meaningful by looking at asserted purposes more rigorously. And it should find that promoting the secular education of children is a valid and adequate state purpose, while promoting parental choices, parental involvement, or pluralism is not sufficient. Because the voucher program set out in Chapter 3 does ensure that aid enhances secular education, it satisfies the secular purpose requirement.

Primary Effect Issues

The secular purpose inquiry at least appears to be what its name suggests—a search for a secular purpose for the aid in question. The "primary effect" prong of the *Lemon* test, on the other hand, does not appear to be what its name suggests. In addition, this step of the *Lemon* analysis has spun a complicated web of fuzzy doctrinal strands. Yet this has become the most important component of the courts' analysis, so there is a pressing need to bring some clarity and coherence to it.

IS IT REALLY A *PRIMARY* EFFECT TEST? The Supreme Court has not explained what makes an effect primary, or why a secular effect must be the primary effect of an aid program rather than the only effect or simply a substantial or not insignificant effect. In practice, in cases after *Lemon,* courts have typically not measured the respective degrees of secular and religious effect at all, but rather have found that an aid program fails the primary effect prong if there is *any* effect of advancing religion. Thus, as the courts apply it, the primary effect prong is really more a "solely secular effect" test. In *Nyquist,* for example, the Court concluded simply from the fact that *some* portion of the building grants and financial assistance to parents *might* be used for support of religious activities that the primary effect of those forms of aid was to advance religion,[31] even though in reality the great majority of the aid might be used to support secular activities. In *Mueller,* the four dissenting justices implied that there can be more than one primary effect, and that a primary effect of advancing religion would override a primary effect of promoting a legitimate secular state purpose,[32] which suggests that there is a fair amount of confusion on the Court about the concept of primary effect. In *Aguilar v. Felton,* the Court's entanglement analysis rested on the assumption that the state would be required to monitor religious schools sufficiently to ensure that the Title I instruction had "an exclusively secular effect."[33] And in *Agostini,* the Court, in its effect analysis, did not even use the term "primary effect," but rather characterized the inquiry as "whether the aid has the 'effect' of advancing or inhibiting religion."[34]

Where it is possible cleanly to segregate secular and religious aspects of a religious entity's activities, a "solely secular effect" test makes sense. In that situation, it should be possible for the state to limit its support, in economic terms, to support for the secular aspects (in which case there would be *no* effect of advancing religion). And if the state *can* do this then it *must* do so, because then there is no secular justification for the portion of aid that promotes religion. I consider in Chapter 9 situations where the state cannot segregate these aspects of a religious school's activities.

DIRECT VERSUS INDIRECT AID   An increasingly prominent issue in aid to religious school cases is whether aid is direct or indirect. Laura Underkuffler writes that the theory that intervening private choices between state disbursement of funds and receipt of money by religious institutions eliminates Establishment Clause problems "is now championed by many as the critical theoretical key to properly and easily disposing of what would otherwise be very difficult Establishment Clause challenges to state-aid programs."[35] Although early on, in *Nyquist,* the Supreme Court indicated that this fact was of little consequence, in more recent cases the Supreme Court has placed substantial emphasis on it and lower courts in voucher cases have followed its lead. Some lower courts have viewed the scheme of writing out checks to parents but requiring endorsement over to schools as direct aid to the schools,[36] while others have interpreted it as making the aid indirect,[37] suggesting that there is a fair amount of confusion about what makes aid indirect.

One might think the direct / indirect distinction more relevant to a legislative motive inquiry than to an effect inquiry. The relevance of an intervening private decision is presumably that it obviates concern that the state itself wants to support religious institutions, because in theory all of the private actors could choose to take the aid to nonreligious institutions. The intervening private decisions do not, on the other hand, alter the effect of the aid on religious schools; how money gets to a school's coffers in and of itself is of no consequence to the school's operations. Nevertheless, the courts have used this distinction to decide the effect question, perhaps because the concern is not so much with the effect on school operations as with the perception that aid creates in the minds of members of the public.

The Supreme Court's emphasis on private choices is, for reasons explained below, nonsensical. Even if it did make sense, however, it would not translate well into a direct / indirect distinction, at least as the Court appears to understand that distinction. In light of its past treatment of the issue, the Court would treat as a direct payment state issuance of one large check made out to a school, to cover the per pupil cost of instruction for a large but specific number of students, as would have occurred under some voucher programs proposed in recent years. On the other hand, the Court might treat as indirect state issuance of smaller checks that are made out to individual parents, even if the checks must be restrictively endorsed over to the private schools in order for them to have any value, as is done under existing programs. But in either case state money reaches religious school coffers only as the result of private choices, and the amount of the state payment is based upon the number of private actors (parents) who choose a religious school. And in either case at some point money is transferred directly from the state treasury to religious schools' bank accounts. As noted in Chapter 1, under existing programs, after parents endorse their checks over to the schools, the schools deposit the checks in their own bank accounts. Their banks then submit the checks to the state treasury for payment, and money flows directly from the state treasury to the schools' bank accounts. Thus, to whom the state writes a check is irrelevant to the private choice inquiry, if payments are based on attendance. Far different would be a statutory scheme that gave religious schools a lump sum of money without regard to how many qualifying students they had, but no one has proposed such an approach. Thus, even if private choice were a proper factor, the direct / indirect distinction would not reflect that factor.

Might there be symbolic significance, though, to the distinction between making out checks to schools and making out checks to parents? One might argue that members of the public could perceive issuance of checks to religious schools as reflecting a closer relationship between church and state than does issuance of checks to individual parents. It is unlikely, though, that there would be a substantial difference in their perception, at least if the state made known how it calculated the amount schools received. Moreover, members of the public might actually reach the opposite conclusion—namely, that payment directly to the school raises *less* prospect of state endorsement of religion. They might

[139]

view payment to the school as a contracting out of secular educational functions to a private entity that happens to be religious, and, on the other hand, might view payment to parents as a reward to them for making a religious choice. In either case, any perception of state endorsement of religion would be muted by the fact that payments would also go to nonsectarian private schools or to parents who choose nonsectarian private schools.

The courts have, of course, never looked for or commissioned any studies of citizens' relative perceptions of the two approaches. Instead they have based decisions on the judges' personal hunches about how things would be perceived. Absent real evidence of a substantial difference in perception, the courts should probably place no weight on the method of payment chosen, as long as any method chosen is based on parents' choosing to send their child to a particular school. In any event, it is a simple matter for states to alter the details of the process by which public money gets to private schools, so it is not particularly important what courts decide about whose name should be on the checks.

Having said that private choice is really the relevant concept in the direct / indirect analysis, I will nevertheless argue that emphasizing private choice is itself specious. While parents choose which particular school their child will attend, the state decides which schools parents may choose from among. In other words, the state must decide to which schools it is appropriate for parents to direct state funds; if it does not, then it could not plausibly claim that the aid has a primary effect of improving children's secular education. Under existing voucher plans, states restrict participation to schools that have received some kind of formal state approval (albeit not based on any demonstration of educational quality). But even if there were no such restriction, the state would be implicitly passing judgment on schools simply by allowing state money to flow to them, for an assertedly secular purpose, just as much as if it were sending money to them without regard to how many parents had chosen to enroll their children in them. So the choice is *never* entirely private; some state judgment about the recipient schools is also inherently involved. This would be true of a reimbursement or tax credit or deduction as well; if the state gives parents money based on their proffering proof that they spent some sum for their child to attend a particular school, then the state must have decided that it should subsidize the choice of that school. The state's approval of that school (not necessarily by name, but perhaps simply by category, for example, "all private schools") for inclusion in the range of schools for which reimbursement for expenses could be sought is a but-for cause of the parents', and ultimately the school's, receiving state money.

Moreover, the state knows full well, when it decides that religious schools are to be among the private schools parents may choose, that the vast majority of parents will in fact choose religious schools, because the vast majority of private schools are religious schools and because this has proven to be the case in every program that has included religious schools. The intervening choices therefore do not obviate concerns about the state's intentions. On the other hand, if there is nothing illicit about religious schools' receiving state aid, because the state ensures that any that do provide a good secular education and ensures that the aid supports only their provision of secular instruction, then there should be no concern with the state's intending to aid religious schools. If that is the case, then private choices again become irrelevant.

The Supreme Court should therefore dispense with the direct / indirect distinction and the private choice aspect of its analysis. It should instead focus on the legitimacy of the state's aiding religious schools, in light of what the state knows or does not know about what individual religious schools are doing with respect to instruction and treatment of students.

SYMBOLIC UNION   An additional aspect of the effect test that is perplexing is the importance given to the idea of symbolic union. As noted in Chapter 1, the Supreme Court has usually been very vague about whom symbolic unions affect, which itself suggests this issue is not so critical. In a couple of cases, though, the Court has clearly expressed a concern about the effect of a symbolic union between church and state on the children in religious schools.[38] While not spelled out by the Court, the concern presumably is that schoolchildren will see aid to their school as state endorsement of the school's religious mission, and that the state would thereby influence the children's religious beliefs.

This concern is overstated, if not downright farcical. It is unlikely elementary or secondary school pupils could be much affected by any symbolic union of church and state. In part this is because most would simply be oblivious to any connection between the state and their school; younger children, at least, tend to be entirely immersed in their local surroundings and daily activities. But it is also in part because the effect such a union could have on their minds is minuscule in comparison with the other factors in their lives influencing their beliefs about religion—principally, their parents and their teachers. With respect to children, the symbolic union discussion would benefit from a dose of reality about the minds of children. And if there should be no significant concern about the effect of symbolism on students, then a symbolic union should not defeat an aid program on their account.

The other likely target of concern is the citizen bystander who might perceive state favoritism for a particular religion, or for religion in general, in an aid program. Such persons are typically the plaintiffs in aid to religious schools cases, and some justices of the Supreme Court believe that the principal danger against which the Establishment Clause guards is a message of exclusion or second-class citizenship that outsiders might receive from state aid to religious entities.[39] In accord with the discussion above of the "primary" component of "primary effect," though, it seems that the Court ought to weigh this possible effect along with all others, rather than make it determinative. As discussed in Chapter 3, it seems unlikely that the symbolic union effect would count for much in such a weighing, and it certainly should not outweigh substantial secular educational benefits for children. If state involvement with and support of religious entities were so great, and of sufficiently suspect purpose, as to create an extremely strong symbolic effect, then probably the aid program would fail on other grounds—perhaps because it does not have an adequate secular purpose or because the effect of supporting religious practice clearly outweighs the effect of supporting secular activities. Arguably, then, the symbolic union inquiry, along with the direct / indirect inquiry, should be shunted to the background, if not entirely abandoned.

PERVASIVELY SECTARIAN   Characterization of religious schools as "pervasively sectarian" has played an important, and sometimes decisive, role in litigation over aid to religious schools.[40] Yet the Supreme Court has never rigorously analyzed the concept or applied it with much attention to facts about particular schools.[41] Instead the Supreme Court and lower courts have typically applied a blanket assumption that all religious elementary and secondary schools are pervasively sectarian.[42] The Court appears to mean by this appellation that religious purposes are so infused into everything such schools do that it is not possible to identify any secular activities or goods that the schools provide.[43] In other contexts, such as aid to religious colleges and universities, the Court has been more discriminating, examining the factual record regarding specific activities of individual religious entities to determine whether the activities are essentially secular in nature or are instead suffused with religion.[44] The courts ought to do the same with religious elementary and secondary schools, because the reality is that these schools vary greatly in the nature of their activities and that instruction in some is, even in the absence of regulation, virtually indistinguishable from what takes place in nonreligious schools.[45]

If the "pervasively sectarian" classification is to play an important role in judicial review of aid to religious schools, it ought to track some relevant legal rule or distinction. (Arguably, though, the Court should simply abandon the classification and just examine whether and to what extent aid recipients generate the secular goods the aid is designed to promote.) The analysis above of when aid violates nonestablishment principles suggests a proper way to use this classification. Courts could apply the pervasively sectarian characterization to schools in which essentially religious instruction so predominates, or in which religious beliefs and purposes so infuse and shape instruction in state-mandated subjects, that the state cannot have a legitimate secular purpose in funding that school. A secular purpose could be lacking either because there is so little secular instruction in the school that it is not a good educational choice for children, or because any secular instruction is merely incidental to religious indoctrination. On the other hand, schools in which secular instruction predominates, on the whole and in each of the state-mandated subject areas, would not be pervasively sectarian even if they are run by a religious organization.

Schools eligible for vouchers under the program I have outlined are clearly of the latter sort; religion is supplemental and segregated from the core curriculum. Those schools would therefore not be regarded as pervasively sectarian. This is consistent with a commonsense rendering of the term "pervasive"—if most of what a religious school does is indistinguishable from what a nonsectarian school does, then religion does not pervade the school. Courts should never rule out aid for such schools on the basis of the constitutional proscription of funding religious instruction. Instead, they should permit states to fund the secular portion of the curriculum. In Chapter 9, I consider whether all religious elementary and secondary schools in the real world should be characterized as pervasively sectarian, as courts have uniformly supposed.

To summarize this discussion of the primary effect inquiry, I have suggested that the Supreme Court should do away with, or at least accord less significance to, the direct / indirect distinction and the symbolic union concern, and should be more discriminating in identifying private schools that are pervasively sectarian in the constitutionally relevant sense. What ultimately matters is whether the state is funding secular instruction and only secular instruction. Whose name is on a check and how the public might interpret aid to religious schools are irrelevant to that inquiry. The courts might use the "pervasively sectarian" label to explain why funding of some religious schools is impermissible, but a blanket characterization of all religious schools as pervasively sectarian is unsupportable and should not substitute for an evaluation of when aid would in fact support secular instruction in religious schools.

Entanglement Issues

The Court has generated some confusion about the nature and purpose of the Establishment Clause prohibition by speaking repeatedly in terms of advancing *or inhibiting* religion or religious belief when evaluating aid programs under that clause. This is particularly apparent in the courts' application of the entanglement prong. In *Agostini*, for example, while the Court downgraded the entanglement analysis, it did undertake the analysis, and in reaching its conclusion that there was not excessive entanglement the Court focused primarily on whether having Title I teachers inside religious schools would require burdensome oversight and regulation of religious schools, which would inhibit their operation.[46] The Court had in much earlier cases actually found excessive entanglement to be present where ensuring that aid furthered secular purposes would require

[143]

"comprehensive, discriminating, and continuing state surveillance,"[47] "excessive monitoring,"[48] or "pervasive monitoring."[49] As noted in Chapter 1, several lower courts in voucher cases have emphasized the lack of significant regulation of voucher schools in finding there was not excessive entanglement.[50]

I alluded in Chapter 1 to a paradox this creates, insofar as substantial oversight and regulation may be the only way to ensure that the secular purpose and effect requirements are satisfied. Taking the point further in the present context, if certain regulations are attached to school aid as a means of ensuring that the aid is used for activities that promote students' intellectual growth and autonomy, then treating such regulations as inconsistent with the Establishment Clause would defeat the overriding religion clause aim of protecting religious liberty. Such regulations serve in part to enhance the religious liberty of students.

Justice Rehnquist observed this paradox in a dissenting opinion he wrote in a 1985 case, *Wallace v. Jaffree*.[51] He noted that the *Lemon* Court derived the entanglement prong of its three-part test from a 1970 Supreme Court decision, *Walz v. Tax Commission,* that involved a constitutional challenge to state property tax exemptions in New York for church property used in worship. The *Walz* Court had upheld the tax exemption, after finding that it "did not so entangle New York with the church as to cause an intrusion or interference with religion." Justice Rehnquist observed:

Interferences with religion should arguably be dealt with under the Free Exercise Clause, but the entanglement inquiry in *Walz* was consistent with that case's broad survey of the relationship between state taxation and religious property. We have not always followed *Walz*'s reflective inquiry into entanglement, however. One of the difficulties with the entanglement prong is that, when divorced from the logic of *Walz,* it creates an "insoluble paradox" in school aid cases: we have required aid to parochial schools to be closely watched lest it be put to sectarian use, yet this close supervision itself will create an entanglement. For example, in *Wolman,* the Court in part struck the State's nondiscriminatory provision of buses for parochial school field trips, because the state supervision of sectarian officials in charge of field trips would be too onerous. This type of self-defeating result is certainly not required to ensure that States do not establish religions. The entanglement test as applied in cases like *Wolman* also ignores the myriad state administrative regulations properly placed upon sectarian institutions such as curriculum, attendance, and certification requirements for sectarian schools, or fire and safety regulations for churches. Avoiding entanglement between church and State may be an important consideration in a case like *Walz,* but if the entanglement prong were applied to all state and church relations in the automatic manner in which it has been applied to school aid cases, the State could hardly require anything of church-related institutions as a condition for receipt of financial assistance.[52]

Aside from the internal inconsistency created within the *Lemon* test when courts give the entanglement prong this "advance or inhibit" interpretation, the interpretation also, as Justice Rehnquist suggested at the beginning of the quoted passage, confuses the respective roles of the Establishment Clause and the Free Exercise Clause. The courts' principal concern regarding substantial oversight and regulation has in most cases been that the regulated religious entity will be inhibited in carrying out its religious mission. That is a quintessential free exercise concern, not the kind of concern the Establishment Clause was designed to address.[53] In fact, any religious entity that believes regulations imposed on it—whether or not tied to aid—are excessive and are substantially burdening its religious activities would have a prima facie free exercise claim. The regulations would amount to government action that has a direct and substantial impact on particular persons. Reading a "no substantial burden on religion" requirement into the Establishment Clause test therefore at best creates redundancy. But in fact it is more troublesome, for two reasons.

First, it appears to create an alternative means of challenging regulations, in competition with the Free Exercise Clause, and with different standards of judicial review. Under current free exercise doctrine, following the Court's 1990 decision in *Employment Division v. Smith*,[54] legal restrictions on conduct that are of general applicability and neutral as between religion and nonreligion do not trigger special protection under the Free Exercise Clause. They are therefore subject to judicial review only under a rational basis due process standard, and will be upheld if the state can show merely a rational basis for them; the state need not show a compelling, or even important, interest in imposing the restrictions.

An interpretation of the *Lemon* test that allows courts to strike down laws because the regulations they contain create an excessive entanglement inhibiting religion would supply individuals and organizations with an avenue for bypassing the *Smith* decision when it suited them to do so, because the fact of inhibiting religious practice would be sufficient on its own to defeat a law that imposed regulations. No showing of nonneutrality or the absence of a rational basis would be needed. And this would in theory be true not just of regulations tied to aid but of any regulations; there is nothing inherent in Establishment Clause jurisprudence that requires first showing that a challenged law provides financial aid to private entities. In fact, because each aspect of the *Lemon* test provides an independent basis for invalidating a law, one need not discuss any part of the test other than entanglement, and so might need *only* allege that unwanted regulations create an excessive entanglement inhibiting religion.[55] This might seem far-fetched, and perhaps if the Supreme Court ever addressed an Establishment Clause claim that did not involve any of the usual establishment forms of state action—for example, state aid to religious institutions or use of government property to communicate religious messages—it would establish a rule that any suit brought under the Establishment Clause must challenge those sorts of action. But the Court has never done so.

Second, it is difficult to see what justification there is for striking down aid programs on the basis that attendant regulation burdens the religious organizations receiving the aid when the recipients are not complaining. A religious entity that is adversely affected by regulations tied to aid is able to avoid the regulations by declining the aid. While some might think religious entities are better off if they reject the aid,[56] it is not clear how the ultimate value of liberty is served by paternalistically preventing those entities from accepting the aid and the regulations that come with it if they choose to do so. At the very least, it is paradoxical that regulations imposed universally and involuntarily would survive a free exercise challenge, while the same regulations, when voluntarily accepted and compensated for with state financial assistance, would be invalidated on Establishment Clause grounds, and at the request of persons other than the entities subject to the regulation!

The Court would do well to reassess the respective roles of the Establishment Clause and the Free Exercise Clause and to keep those roles distinct. The two clauses are best seen as working in tandem to protect the same value—religious liberty—but each in its own way, each addressing different ways in which religious liberty might be impaired. The Establishment Clause guards against coercion of religious belief as a result of the government's *favoring* a religion or religion generally. The Free Exercise Clause guards against coercion of religious belief as a result of the government's *disfavoring* religion—that is, by imposing burdens on people because of their religious beliefs that it does not impose on other people. In accordance with this division of responsibilities, regulation that inhibits religious practice should be viewed as a free exercise problem, if it is a problem at all. Establishment Clause entanglement should be interpreted to mean interactions between state officials and a religious organization that *advance* the purposes of the organization or that create a strong impression of state favoritism for the organization's religion in the minds of the public, in addition to state involvement in deciding theological questions. Under that interpretation, courts could not invalidate voucher plans under the Establishment Clause on the grounds that they entail substantial regulation and oversight of religious schools. The entanglement inquiry would be limited to whether interactions between religious entities and state officials might lead to illicit state support for or endorsement of an entity's religious beliefs.

Conclusion

State support for secular education in religious schools is consistent with Establishment Clause principles and with the best interpretations of the no-aid and neutrality positions. Under a well-designed voucher program, all participating religious schools would provide essentially secular instruction in core subjects, so none would be "pervasively sectarian" properly understood. The amount of funding would simply have to be limited to reflect the portion of a religious school's activities that are essentially secular. It should not matter whether aid to such schools arrives in the form of many checks made out to individual parents or one check made out to the school, as long as the amount of money a school receives is based on the number of pupils it serves. States may condition such aid on acceptance of whatever regulation and oversight are necessary to ensure that schools provide a good secular education and do not treat students in harmful ways, and the burden this creates for religious schools should raise no Establishment Clause (or Free Exercise Clause) concerns.

This chapter has demonstrated, therefore, that the voucher program outlined in Chapter 3 would be constitutionally permissible. In the next chapter, I consider whether such a program of vouchers might actually be constitutionally mandatory, as an entitlement of parents who send their children to religious school or of the children attending those schools.

[6]

The Equal Protection Strategy for Compelling Aid to Religious Schools

Were the United States Supreme Court to clear away the Establishment Clause as an obstacle to a well-designed voucher program, the question would arise whether states could be legally compelled to create such a program. In all likelihood, every state in the country would soon find itself in court facing a claim that they *must* provide funding for private schooling. Recognition of that likelihood might itself induce the Supreme Court to hold that vouchers are impermissible, or at least to be very careful, in an opinion holding vouchers permissible, not to provide any fodder for such a rash of suits to compel funding for private schools.

Plaintiffs would have the greatest likelihood of success in seeking to require vouchers with a claim founded upon the Equal Protection Clause of the Fourteenth Amendment of the federal Constitution. As described in Chapter 1, parents in the Maine, Vermont, and early Wisconsin litigation asserted such a right. States defending aid programs of various sorts before the Supreme Court have also advanced an equal protection type argument in defense of their programs.[1] In addition, numerous legal scholars and legislators who support vouchers have asserted that parents who send their children to private schools are entitled as a matter of fairness and equal treatment to a share of state funding for education. They should not be denied this important state-conferred benefit simply because they choose, as is their constitutional right, not to send their children to the state's own schools.

Courts that have considered such claims have summarily rejected them, even in situations where the state was funding nonreligious private schools.[2] In most cases, though, the courts have done so because they assumed that the Establishment Clause trumped the Equal Protection Clause, not because they concluded that equal protection doctrine did not support the claim. Importantly, if the Establishment Clause obstacle were removed, and courts did uphold equal protection claims, this would override any state constitutional provisions prohibiting aid to religious institutions; the federal constitutional right would trump. Thus, if the equal protection claim is viable, every state in this country could find itself faced a few years from now with a court order to create a voucher program.

The fundamental principle underlying the Equal Protection Clause is equal personhood before the state. This means that the state must treat every person's interests as of equal worth.[3] My interest in being free of state-imposed burdens or in receiving state-conferred benefits should count for as much in the state's deliberations as does anyone else's. Another way to state this requirement is to say that the state must be impartial among members of society, not favoring the interests of some over others. In judicial application of the Equal Protection Clause, this principle translates into a requirement that the state strive to treat people equally when they have the same interests at stake. In some contexts, the state must strive harder than in others. Importantly, this requirement clearly applies to both distribution of benefits and imposition of burdens (indeed, it is often difficult to distinguish the two), as is evident from numerous Supreme Court decisions subjecting exclusion of certain groups from public welfare programs to equal protection scrutiny.[4] It would be just as much a violation of the principle of equal personhood for the state to give $1,000 checks to all and only white people as it would be for the state to impose taxes only on nonwhite people. This chapter examines the implications of this equal personhood principle for the fairness claims that are advanced on behalf of parents who send or wish to send their children to a private school. It also considers whether such a claim could be made on behalf of children themselves.

An equal protection claim could arise in three settings: (1) where the state funds only public schools, (2) where the state funds public schools and non-sectarian private schools, but not religious schools, and (3) where the state funds public schools and all private schools that comply with substantial conditions and excludes from funding only private schools that fail to comply with the conditions, as is true of the voucher program I have outlined. I consider each of those settings below.

Equal Treatment of Parents

Michael McConnell articulates forcefully the position that funding only public schools is unfair to parents who, for religious reasons, object to the kind of education and environment public schools provide and elect to enroll their children in religious schools. The argument could easily be extended to cover parents who choose a private school for other reasons. These parents, McConnell points out, "not only must . . . bear the costs of the religious education, but . . . also forfeit *all* public subsidy for education." The failure to fund *secular* education in religious schools, simply because parents have chosen to add a religious component to their children's schooling at their own expense, "extracts a penalty—and a large one—for the exercise of constitutional rights."[5] He compares this to denying all Medicaid benefits to a woman who chooses to have an abortion, in addition to declining to finance the abortion. In both cases, certain individuals themselves pay for a privately provided service they have chosen to purchase (religious instruction and abortion), but then because of their choice are denied their fair share of state money allocated for a different purpose (secular instruction and other medical services). This denial treats those individuals unequally and creates a strong disincentive to exercising their constitutional rights as they wish.

McConnell's factual characterization is accurate. When the state funds only public schools, it is refusing to pay for provision of the same secular good—secular education—by private institutions. As a result, it denies parents who choose for their children to receive that good in a private institution a benefit that it gives to parents who choose for their children to receive the good in a public institution. Parents have a constitutional right to choose a private school for their children, and to choose a private school that adds religious instruction (or yoga, or Chinese-language instruction, or a hockey program) to the school day. Yet when they exercise that right, the result is that they are cut out of a public benefits program, even though the purposes of that program are not inherently incompatible with their purchasing religious instruction or any other supplemental instruction or activity. This clearly creates a disincentive to choosing that one's child receive a secular education in a private setting, in a school that adds the religious or other supplemental component one wants one's children to have. It is not difficult to understand why some parents view this as unfair to them.

Nevertheless, there is little difficulty in demonstrating that funding only public schools does not violate any parent's right to equal treatment. First, it is important to bear in mind that while all members of society have an interest in being treated with equal regard by the state and, in some circumstances, treated the same as other similarly situated persons, this interest is not in all contexts an important interest, or in other words is not substantially affected by all discriminatory treatment. If the stakes are small, because the good that the state is doling out is unimportant and the basis for the unequal treatment is not terribly objectionable, then a slight by the state does not impair one's well-being significantly and arguably does not violate one's rights. For example, no United States president has ever invited me for a private tour of the White House, while many other private citizens have been invited. Other government officials slight me in a similar way on a daily basis. Yet this does not violate any right of mine, because it is not important to my well-being that I receive a private tour of the White House, and because the basis for the slight—my lack of power and wealth—constitutes only a slight attack on my sense of self-worth and standing in society.

On the other hand, where the stakes are high—either because what I am denied is a very important good or because the basis for the state's slight is a substantial attack on my sense of self-worth and standing in society—my interest in equal treatment can properly give rise to a right. For example, if the state guarantees other people a jury trial before they can be sentenced to jail, my interest in also receiving a jury trial before I can be sent to jail is sufficiently weighty to give rise to a right, because my basic liberty is at stake. And a denial of equal treatment to African Americans because of their race constitutes such a threat to their sense of self-worth and standing in society as to give rise to a right. This distinction tracks that which the courts make between denials of equal protection that warrant heightened scrutiny and those that warrant only rational basis review.[6]

As explained in Chapters 3 and 4, a state's failure to fund any private schools does not deny parents who send their children to private school a critical good. Parents retain the formal right to send their children to such a school, and the reality is that it is their children's education that is at issue, not theirs. Nor does the limitation of funding to public schools reflect invidious discrimination. The state's rationale for not funding private schools is perfectly understandable in nondiscriminatory terms. The state is choosing to operate its own program of education, while leaving private organizations free to do the same. As is the case with other government programs, the state elects to fund only its own operations and not parallel institutions in the private sector. It is simply implausible to say that funding only public schools reflects negative attitudes about parents who send their children to private schools; no offense can reasonably be taken.

In addition, the fact that parents' choice to send their children to a private school is a voluntary one, while not as decisive as some courts have assumed it to be, substantially weakens a claim to vouchers based on fairness to parents. Neither the law nor shared moral beliefs support the general proposition that fairness requires that individuals receive state financial support for their voluntary decision to forgo a public service in favor of a private analogue, or to forgo a publicly subsidized private service in favor of a nonsubsidized private service. As a general rule, if people opt out of a state-provided benefit program that is offered to them on the same terms offered to others, they are deemed to be on their own, with no valid claim for state support of their choice. The state treats all persons equally by making the state-provided benefit available to all.

Thus, the state treats all parents equally when it offers them all a free education for their children at a public institution, just as it treats all citizens and visitors equally when it opens the doors of public museums to anyone who wishes to enter. In either case, some persons may not want to accept the benefit offered, for any number of reasons—some religious, some not (e.g., a philosophical objection to the content of what is taught in the public institution, a philosophical objection to the government's teaching anything, a view about the quality of what the government is providing, the inconvenient location of the public facility, etc.). In either case, persons might choose to substitute a private alternative, and they might choose a private alternative that adds some additional dimension—for example, a religious component—to what is otherwise similar to the service provided in the public institution. And in both cases, the government must respect the choices these persons make, but incurs no obligation to subsidize the private alternatives they choose. It leaves them to bear the consequences of their choices, and this is entirely consistent with widely shared moral beliefs about what it means to respect people as moral agents. The state may have an obligation to protect people from adverse consequences of *unchosen* characteristics or circumstances, but as a general rule does not have an obligation to protect people from the adverse consequences of their voluntary choices, or in other words to make their choices costless.[7]

As others have pointed out, the issue comes down to defining baselines. McConnell implicitly assumes that the baseline is equal funding for all schooling choices within the range of parents' constitutional rights. Generalizing this assumption beyond the schooling context makes apparent why it is untenable— it is simply unworkable. The general rule would be that the government must subsidize every private analogue to its own services. Thus, the baseline for funding of protective services would be that the government finances not only a state police force but also all private security services that private citizens, for whatever reason, prefer to use. The baseline for welfare would be that the government finances not only a state welfare office but also the welfare services of any private agency that some poor people prefer to patronize. The baseline for museums would be that the government funds not only a state-operated museum, but also every private museum that, at least in part, serves a secular educational function. Departure from the baseline of equal funding for private and public providers of any service would, on McConnell's view, violate the principle of equal personhood, even though the choice of a private alternative is a voluntary one.

Effectuating this understanding of the baseline, it is easy to see, would spell the end for our government. Indeed, some people might object on religious or other grounds to the government itself, and demand funding for a parallel, private system of governance, or demand the right to pay taxes only to and receive services only from some private organization. This might be entirely consistent with some libertarian fantasy, but it is not the world that any significant number of people want. It is also not a world that is morally superior to the one we have. Under our form of government, the state may undertake programs of its own to generate public goods and to assist individuals, such as children, who are unable to fulfill their own needs. The state may elect to fund only those programs of its own and not private analogues even though some people prefer the private analogues, and in doing so it does not offend the principle of equal personhood, so long as the state program is open to all.[8] The lack of judicial precedent in other contexts on claims of the sort McConnell advances suggests a general recognition that the basic principle upon which it rests does not have even facial plausibility.

In the case of schooling, there are perfectly good reasons for the government to undertake to establish a public program, reasons that even most libertarians would accept. One reason is that in a society where millions of children live in poverty, a great number of children might receive no education in the absence of public schools. Another reason is that common schooling—education in a pluralistic setting, bringing children from diverse family backgrounds together—is of great value to individual children and to our society as a whole, and the state can reasonably assume that it would occur to a much lesser extent in a regime of only private schools.

I noted above that pointing to parents' voluntary choices is not entirely decisive as a response to the equal protection argument against funding only public schools. This is because there must be some limit to what the state can do to make acceptance of benefits from the state unattractive to certain groups. Surely if the state conditioned entrance to the Smithsonian on renunciation of certain religious beliefs, persons strongly opposed to doing so would have a valid objection, under any number of constitutional provisions.[9] And one component of the equal protection argument on behalf of parents is that public schools advance a worldview that some parents do not share. Some parents view the public schools' approach to certain subject areas, such as sex education, as inconsistent with their religious views. Others believe the absence of religious instruction and prayer in public schools implicitly conveys to their children a message that religion is unimportant or mistaken. These parents might contend that it is improper for the state to fund only public schools, because it has made this public benefit too unattractive for them.

There are important distinctions, however, between the Smithsonian example and the reality of public schooling. First, in the former case the government is requiring individuals to express a viewpoint they do not hold. This infringes upon basic personal liberty. In contrast, to send their children to public schools, parents need not express agreement with anything taught in the schools, and no one would attribute to them agreement with anything in particular taught in the schools simply by virtue of their sending their children to the schools. Second, in the Smithsonian example, it is an interest in self-determination that is at stake, while in the case of schooling the interest parents have at stake is, as discussed in Chapters 3 and 4, an interest in *other*-determination—control of someone else's life—and the latter simply has little, if any, claim to protection. Third, in the Smithsonian example, the unattractive feature of the benefit is unrelated to any legitimate state purpose underlying provision of the benefit. In contrast, the aspects of public schooling to which these parents object are ones the state reasonably believes conducive to the underlying and legitimate state objective of providing a good secular education, and in fact are compelled to some degree by constitutional constraints on the state. In short, the hypothetical condition on entrance to the Smithsonian is harmful in ways that public school design is not, and the former lacks the kinds of justification that the latter has.

A final argument parents might make against funding only public schools is that the state is putting its financial muscle behind one ideological view, and disadvantaging the parents' own ideology. If parents cannot afford a religious school, then they must expend effort and family resources to provide religious instruction by some other means, and this makes it more difficult for parents to compete with the state in conveying a worldview to their children. Insofar as this objection is based on fairness to individuals, rather than to worldviews (which do not have rights), it falls prey to the same difficulty that undermines McConnell's equal treatment argument. Requiring the government to fund private analogues to its services whenever someone believes a government service privileges some worldview would be ruinous for our society, and is in any event not compelled by common notions of justice. Additionally, the objection rests on a presumption that different groups of adults are in competition for children's minds (the majority vs. various minorities), which is a morally unacceptable way of viewing child rearing. It treats children instrumentally and so fails to accord them the kind of respect owed to persons. What little merit the objection has lies in a concern about excessive state power, but this is not a fairness rationale and it is not particularly persuasive in this context. Our dual system of public and private schooling has been operating without vouchers for quite a long time, with nearly 90 percent of children attending public schools, and yet there is tremendous ideological diversity in this country and the vast majority of Americans are religious.

A more convincing argument against state funding of only public schools might be made in those areas of the country, particularly poor urban areas, where public schools are not providing an adequate secular education. Parents in those areas have good reason to object to the government's giving the public's money (including their own taxes) only to these schools, rather than to the private schools to which the parents feel compelled, for educational reasons, to send their children.[10] In that situation, the government is taking money from parents and other taxpayers for the purpose of providing some good for their children, but then does not really provide the good.[11] This is not really an argument about equality, however; it is rather a complaint about the government's incompetence and misuse of tax money. An argument that the government should use one's tax dollars instead to subsidize a private school is best seen in this situation as an argument about how the government can better use tax revenues, not an argument that providing only one alternative is per se unfair.

In sum, the principle of equal personhood does not support an objection on behalf of parents to the state's funding only public schools, even in a world where all private schools provided a secular education at least as good as that provided in public schools. What if, as in Vermont and Maine, however, the government funds *nonreligious* private schools as well as public schools and excludes only religious schools from its program of education financing? The state would have decided to go beyond funding its own programs to funding private institutions that provide the same service, to the extent that they provide that service and to the extent that they are chosen by parents. One could also characterize the state as having elected, even though the equal personhood principle did not require it to do so, to provide financial support for parents' choice to opt out of public institutions. The fairness-to-parents argument asserts that once the state takes this step—providing the benefit of a state-supported *private* education, or the benefit of state support for parents' educational choices— it must provide the benefit equally to all who want it, absent an adequate justification for denying it to some. And it asserts that there is no justification for discriminating among parents on the basis of their motivation for opting out or on the basis of their choosing a form of school that adds a religious component to the school day; this would simply be hostility to religion, and it is impermissible for the state to be hostile to religion in general.

However, many of the counterarguments that defeat the fairness objection to funding only public schools also apply to a situation in which a state funds nonsectarian private schools but not religious schools. The state treats all parents equally by offering to all *some* private alternative to public schools. Parents who enroll their children in religious schools are voluntarily forgoing this state-proffered benefit, and the state has no obligation to make that choice costless. Analogously, if the state contracts out some other public service, such as counseling for crime victims, to private providers, it may elect to include only secular providers among the contractors, even thought it could have included religious providers. Users of the service would have no greater complaint than if the state funded only public agencies providing that service.

The state should be required, though, to offer somewhat greater justification for excluding only religious schools from funding for education than it must offer for excluding all private schools. Some might go farther and contend that such a classification on the basis of religion should trigger strict scrutiny in an equal protection analysis. But while there would certainly be a strong case for strict scrutiny if the state facially discriminated among different religious groups (and current free exercise doctrine effectively requires such scrutiny),[12] legislation excluding all religious organizations from a government benefit program would not satisfy the prevailing criteria for applying strict scrutiny.[13] While there is a history in this country of invidious discrimination against certain minority religious groups, there is no history of discrimination against religion in general (in fact, the opposite is true). In addition, religious individuals constitute a supermajority of voters in this country, and so are quite capable of using the political process to correct any legislation deemed to treat religion in general improperly.

Nevertheless, the state ought to have good reasons for excluding only religious providers of a service. But several are available. First, the state might wish to ensure that members of the public can obtain the service without having to get it from a religious institution, just as they can when a public agency provides the service. In other words, the state might aim to secure services as much as possible like those it would provide itself. Second, the state might wish to avoid ideological conflicts with its contractors, which would be likely with some religious groups, particularly if the state conditioned participation on compliance with substantial regulations. Yet the state might also wish not to have to discriminate among religious groups on this basis in awarding contracts. Moreover, on the other side of the coin, the harm from the discrimination is not so pronounced. Contracting only with nonreligious providers would not constitute hostility to religion; the state would presumably also decline to contract with antireligious providers. In funding only nonsectarian private schools, the state would be aiming to subsidize secular education, not secularist education. Thus, even if a state did implement a voucher program but excluded religious schools, this would not be inconsistent with the equal personhood of any parents.

Finally, there is the parental equal protection claim that would be advanced against the voucher program I have outlined. This claim would be advanced on behalf of parents who send their children to private schools, religious and nonreligious, that do not qualify for vouchers because the schools do not satisfy the program's conditions. Let us assume that the reason for a given religious school's failure to qualify is ideological—that is, the conditions for participation conflict with the religious tenets of the school and of parents who patronize it. To some the equal protection claim might seem stronger here than in the case of a program that excludes all religious schools, because here the discrimination is effectively on the basis of religious belief and is likely to exclude adherents of some faiths but not other faiths, with the ultimate results of exerting pressure on parents to compromise their beliefs and of threatening the survival of some faiths.[14]

The claim is actually weaker here, however. First, although the regulatory strings have a disparate impact on different religious groups, this is not sufficient to trigger heightened scrutiny. The voucher program does not on its face single out any particular religious groups for unfavorable treatment. As with any laws that prohibit particular conduct deemed, on a secular basis, harmful to others, or that require particular conduct deemed, on a secular basis, necessary to furtherance of a legitimate state objective, the conditions attached to this voucher program are neutral as to religion and generally applicable. Consistent with the Supreme Court's interpretation of the Free Exercise Clause, then, the conditions should not be subjected to heightened review under that clause or the Equal Protection Clause. As noted above, numerous government subsidy programs attach conditions to participation that some potential recipients object to on religious grounds, but a free exercise or equal protection claim to an exemption from the conditions would fail, so long as the conditions were not designed to disqualify people on the basis of religious belief per se, and so long as the state had a legitimate and rational basis for doing so. And the conditions attached to the voucher program I have outlined clearly have a legitimate and rational basis—namely, to further children's interest in receiving a high-quality secular education. In fact, the courts would say the conditions have a *compelling* basis, insofar as they are necessitated by an application of the Establishment Clause.

In addition, the voucher program I have outlined, when viewed in comparison with the prevailing alternatives, does not give rise to even facially plausible concerns about hostility to religion in general. Relative to the current state of affairs in most jurisdictions—that is, where states fund only public schools—and relative to voucher programs that include only nonreligious schools, the program I have outlined represents a pronounced move toward inclusion of religious service providers and toward recognition of the positive contribution most of them make to the shared public aim of ensuring all children a good secular education. The program I have outlined raises facially plausible concerns about hostility only when compared with programs like those in Milwaukee, Cleveland, and Florida, which give money to virtually all religious takers, without any meaningful conditions attached. But if the program does reflect any hostility, it is not to religion per se, or to any particular religions, but rather to practices, however motivated, that the state deems harmful to children. It imposes the same conditions on all takers, religious and nonreligious, for the compelling purpose of advancing children's developmental interests, and no one can plausibly claim that this violates his rights. Parents who send their children to a nonqualifying religious school have no stronger claim, grounded in fairness, to exemption from the conditions for participation than do parents who send their children to nonqualifying nonsectarian private schools.

[157]

Finally, those who object to regulatory strings might contend that the strings effectively force parents to speak in a manner contrary to specific religious beliefs in order to receive a government benefit, and that the program I have outlined is thus much closer to the Smithsonian example than is a regime of funding only public schools, or even of funding only nonreligious schools. They view religious schooling as parental speech, and the regulations I have outlined would force parents to change the content of their speech.[15] However, this argument has several flaws. First, schooling should not be viewed as adult speech. It is a state-mandated service to children. To view a child as a megaphone for parental expression is morally inappropriate, inconsistent with a proper respect for the personhood of the child. Second, in a concrete sense, parents need not speak at all, and typically do not. It is the teachers in the religious schools whose speech is affected. Teachers clearly have less claim to freedom of speech in communicating with children than do parents. And parents would remain free to say whatever they want to their children. The regulations would simply ensure that children are exposed during school hours to mainstream views in curricular areas and treated as inherently moral equals. Nor would the act of sending one's child to a voucher school amount to expressive conduct, such that others would attribute to parents any particular views of the state that are reflected in the regulations. A person could certainly coherently say: "I choose to send my child to this religious school, even though the state forces its teachers to teach things with which I disagree, because I prefer the school in other respects to the available alternatives, not least of which is its qualification for state funding." Third, teachers and parents are free to go elsewhere; the voucher program I have outlined does not compel universal participation. And finally, the regulations are, in any event, justified by the compelling state interest of furthering the fundamental interests of children and by the aim of avoiding a violation of the Establishment Clause.

Thus, an equal protection claim on behalf of parents in any of the three possible settings—funding only public schools, funding only nonreligious schools, and funding all schools that comply with substantive regulations—must fail. This is true as a theoretical matter, and I would predict that the Supreme Court would reject a parental equal protection claim in the first setting definitely, in the second setting most likely, and in the third setting probably. Dicta in numerous Supreme Court opinions to the effect that states retain the power to regulate all private schools to ensure that they provide a good education give clear indication that the Court would uphold some substantive curricular requirements.[16] How far the Court would allow states to go in conditioning participation in a voucher program is uncertain, but it would almost certainly allow them to go further than if they were imposing regulations involuntarily. If the Court rejects facial challenges to voucher programs, it will inevitably be called upon to decide this question.

In any event, all is not lost for those who believe the state's funding of only public schools, or of only nonsectarian schools, is unfair. The next part of this chapter demonstrates that those who couch a demand for vouchers in fairness terms would have much firmer ground to stand on if they argued that selective funding is unfair *to children* whose parents send them to religious schools, rather than unfair to the parents. This is principally because a child-centered argument is not vulnerable to the response that it is not unfair to make people pay for their choice to opt out of a publicly provided benefit in favor of a private provider.

Equal Treatment of Children

The final question I will address in relation to the idealized voucher program I described in Chapter 3 is whether such a program might be constitutionally mandatory because of the equal protection rights of any children. I concluded in Chapter 4 that a well-designed voucher program is a necessary means of fulfilling the basic moral right of some children in religious schools to a good secular education. Under the constitutions of some states, that might be sufficient basis for a legal claim of entitlement to such a program. However, basic positive rights of that sort are more alien to the federal constitution, as the Supreme Court has interpreted it. There is practical, as well as theoretical, value, then, in considering whether any children have a fairness or equal treatment type of right to such a program. Individuals are often entitled to things as a matter of equality even though they do not have a basic right to those things.[17]

To answer this final question, assume the perspective of a legislator. As a legislator, you look out upon society and the current generation of children, and you determine that children have certain vital developmental interests, including an interest in receiving a good secular education. Because children are unable to secure this or other primary goods for themselves, you and your fellow legislators undertake to guarantee that children receive them. You do that primarily because in our society we believe we have a collective moral obligation to vulnerable, dependent persons generally and to children specifically, to protect their fundamental interests. In fact, it is likely that your state constitution explicitly declares that obligation to children and / or the correlative right of children to a good education. The principle of equal personhood requires that you guarantee this for all children; you may not decide to guarantee it for some and not for others. This conclusion finds expression in the Supreme Court's holding in *Brown v. Board of Education,* and the Court's statement in that decision that "an opportunity [for an education], where the state has undertaken to provide it, is a right which must be made available to all on equal terms."[18] Accordingly, you establish a system of public schools that is available to all children, and you enact compulsory school attendance laws.

Now it also happens that a "fixed point" in the moral and legal culture of your society is that parents are free to enroll their children in a private school instead of a public school. Another contingent characteristic of your society is that some public schools do not provide an adequate education. This leads many parents to want to enroll their children in private schools. However, some cannot afford to do so, and their children suffer educational deprivation as a result. In addition, many private schools that strive to provide a good secular education are failing to do so solely because they lack adequate resources, yet parents send their children to those schools anyway, either because the local public schools are even worse or for religious reasons or both. And for many of the parents who do manage to afford a private school, the tuition places a substantial strain on family resources and forces them to forgo other learning opportunities for their children. Finally, in your society some parents wish, for religious reasons, to send their children to a private school that does not even strive to provide a good secular education, because the parents regard the aims of secular education as antithetical to proper religious development and to compliance with religious commands.

In your society, then, some children are suffering educational deprivation because (1) they are stuck in lousy public schools, (2) their parents choose private schools that strive to provide a good education but the schools lack adequate resources and / or the parents must sacrifice a great deal to afford the private school tuition (I call these "children in type A religious schools" below), or (3) their parents choose religious schools whose aims are contrary to those established by the state ("children in type B religious schools"). For children in the first two situations, vouchers would end the educational deprivation. For some of the children in the third situation, the voucher program I have outlined would induce their schools to change or induce their parents to transfer them to a school that provides a good secular education. For others in the third situation, though, this voucher program would have no positive effect. The question is whether the equal personhood principle creates an obligation on your part, owed to any of these children, to establish the sort of voucher program I have outlined.

At this point, a fact mentioned in the Introduction becomes of critical importance—namely, the fact that children do not themselves choose where they will go to school, and arguably never make an informed and independent choice between schools on the basis of ideological orientation. Because of this fact, children who are in religious schools are not responsible for the fact that they are there rather than in a public school. Thus, the primary reason why denial of funding for religious schools is not an affront to the equal personhood of parents—namely, that they rightly bear the consequences for their own voluntary choices—simply does not apply when discussing fairness to children. As manifested in several Supreme Court decisions regarding denial of state benefits to children on the basis of "illegitimacy," our shared moral beliefs today are contrary to the proposition that children should suffer for the choices and actions of their parents.[19] Translating our collective moral outlook into legal terms, the Court stated in *Weber v. Aetna Casualty & Surety Company* that "imposing disabilities on the illegitimate child is contrary to the basic concept of our system that legal burdens should bear some relationship to individual responsibility or wrongdoing."[20] The same would be true of state action "imposing disabilities" or "burdens" on a child because of her parents' religious beliefs.

Children also are not responsible, of course, for the relative affluence of their parents, or for the relative affluence of the community in which they live, or for decisions local governments make about how much money to raise locally for the public schools. Thus, children who are suffering educational deprivation are doing so for reasons that are entirely beyond their control and that are certainly not of their choosing. The state therefore has no excuse tied to the moral responsibility of those denied a benefit for failing to fulfill its obligation to these children. The Supreme Court rejected this sort of rationale for using the federal Equal Protection Clause to compel school finance reform, in *San Antonio Independent School District v. Rodriguez*.[21] But the ostensible rationale for the Court's denial of an equal protection claim for more equitable spending on public schools in different school districts in *Rodriguez* had much to do with the traditional allocation of school financing responsibilities between a state and its political subunits, which is not relevant to the question here, and the Court certainly did not conclude that the children in poor public school districts were in fact responsible for their plight. In addition, advocates for interdistrict school finance reform have had considerable success using state constitutional provisions, including state equal protection rights in litigation.[22]

Thus, the proper baseline against which current state education funding practices should be evaluated is not making a state-operated service available equally to all who want it, as it was in connection with parents. Rather, the proper baseline is guaranteeing all children a good secular education without regard to the type of school in which their parents enroll them. The question, then, is whether vouchers are a necessary means to fulfilling the state's obligation. With respect to children now in bad public schools, the answer is "no," or at least not demonstrably "yes." As discussed in Chapter 4, the state could now fulfill its obligation to these children *either* by providing vouchers that would make it financially possible for their parents to send them to a good private school, if their parents wish to do so, *or* by doing whatever is necessary to transform the public schools. In fact, for children whose parents would not transfer them to a private school even if they could afford to do so, reforming the public schools is the only way to ensure them a good education. While some might claim that some public school systems are unreformable, there has not been sufficient commitment in the past to reforming the worst systems to warrant such a conclusion. And while it is true that the broader socioeconomic environment in which we allow many children to live makes it extremely difficult for schools to give them a real chance for a better life, states can and should at least make sure public schools are part of an attempted solution rather than part of the problem.

For children now in religious schools, however, the situation is very different. For some it might be the case that their education can be improved without state funding of religious schools. If a state improved its public schools dramatically, some parents who currently send their children to a type A religious school would likely be induced to transfer their children to the public schools, so that their children would receive a good secular education. But many parents would send their children to type A religious schools regardless of what the local public schools were like. Investment only in public schools cannot help those children. This is an important point that opponents of vouchers are missing. From a child-centered perspective, one must consider the situation of all children, and there are now many children who are attending struggling religious schools and who will remain in those schools no matter what. Those children have a right to a good education as much as any other children, and it is a dereliction of our moral and legal obligation to those children to shrug and say that it is their parents' fault, or that there are more children in struggling public schools. We owe those children an obligation to do what we can to improve their situation, and if we are not willing to force their parents to send them to a better school, then we must take steps to improve the schools they are in. If the reason their schools are doing poorly is that they lack resources, then we have an obligation to provide them with resources.

A voucher program, or some equivalent aid mechanism, is therefore a necessary means to fulfilling the state's moral and constitutional obligation to children in type A religious schools, and therefore is presumptively mandatory, as a right of these children. The current failure to allocate a share of state education funding for these children constitutes a prima facie violation of their moral right to equal treatment and their legal right to equal protection. The question then becomes whether the state can nevertheless justify this discriminatory treatment. The principal justification given above for the state's alleged discrimination among parents—responsibility for voluntary choice—is not available in this case. I consider below whether other justifications might be available.

What about children in type B religious schools? The educational deprivation (from the state's perspective) in those schools is not solely the result of inadequate resources, and in fact some such schools might have all the resources they could want. The most straightforward way for states to fulfill their obligation to children in these schools is, of course, simply to impose the regulations on them. But as indicated in the Introduction, there is no political will today to do this. In light of that reality, the only feasible mechanism the state has for attempting to ensure a good secular education for children in these schools is to create a large financial incentive for the schools to change their practices or for parents to transfer their children to a school that does strive to provide a good secular education. Here again, a child-centered perspective shows opposition to vouchers to be myopic. To the extent liberal opponents of vouchers focus on the welfare of children at all, it is only children whose parents place them in public schools. They fail to see the opportunity that vouchers present to have some positive effect on the education of children placed in schools whose mission is antithetical to the aims of liberal education. We have an obligation to those children to do whatever we can for them, and given political realities it appears that the most we can do for them is to create a strong incentive for their parents and schools voluntarily to accept secular, liberal standards of education. If we are unwilling to constrain the market for private education with involuntary regulation, we should attempt to channel it with financial incentives.

Thus, children in type B schools also have an equal protection right to a voucher program or other financing scheme. Importantly, however, the voucher program must be designed to insure that the money does in fact result in a better secular education, rather than bolstering the efforts of parents and school operators to deny children such an education. The regulatory strings are therefore essential. For this same reason, children who, after vouchers were in place, remained in type B schools unmoved by the financial incentive to change their practices would not have an equal protection objection to the denial of funding to their schools, because funding would not secure for them the good to which they are ultimately entitled, which is not money per se but a good secular education. For these children, unfortunately, there might simply be no politically (or judicially) feasible means of fulfilling our obligation to ensure them a good education. Our obligation to them would, sadly, continue to go unfulfilled.

In the real world, courts are generally resistant to upholding constitutional rights claims on behalf of children, especially when doing so would require conceptualizing children as persons distinct from their parents. The abortion context is unusual insofar as courts have ascribed rights to minors to do things presumably contrary to parents' wishes without interference by the state. There the minors involved are older, the activity in question is an adult activity, and the right at issue is viewed as a negative right—that is, a right to do something without interference by the state. While an equal protection right is not a positive basic right of the sort that is generally thought foreign to our adult-centered constitutional jurisprudence, the remedy that would be sought in the type of equal protection suit I am envisioning here would be ordering the state to provide a benefit rather than to forbear from imposing a restriction on conduct.

[163]

In addition, such a suit would probably have to be initiated by a representative of the children other than their parents, since it would be quite awkward for parents to charge that their children should not suffer for their (the parents') choices. Courts generally look askance at suits brought on behalf of children in intact families by persons other than their parents.[23] Parents, however, presumably would not object to such a suit, as they might to suits claiming rights for children that cut against parental preferences. And schools have been successful in the past in several contexts making rights claims on behalf of their students, so the religious schools themselves might be able to bring suit on the basis of children's equal protections rights.[24] In any event, we can assess the claim as a theoretical matter, and legislators might be persuaded by conclusions reached even if courts would not.

As discussed in connection with an equal protection claim on behalf of parents, an important threshold issue in judicial analysis would be what level of scrutiny to apply. In the cases cited above involving illegitimate children, the Court has applied a heightened level of scrutiny to the discriminatory laws because of special concerns that the state has acted on illicit bases. The Court has recognized that illegitimate children have been the target of much unwarranted antipathy and stigmatizing throughout our nation's history. The same cannot be said of a class of "children whose parents choose religious schools." A court would likely view that class as more like one based on political divisions of a state—that is, on where parents have chosen to live, a kind of class the Supreme Court has declined to afford special protection.[25] Based on the nature of the class, then, a court would likely apply only rational basis review, which is very deferential to legislatures, requiring only some legitimate state interest, however flimsy, to support the classification.[26] Avoiding the appearance of supporting religion might suffice in that case.

However, courts also apply more rigorous, or heightened, review under the Equal Protection Clause when the interest at stake for the class discriminated against is particularly important. Heightened scrutiny might be "intermediate," in which case the state is required to demonstrate that its action is substantially related to a state interest that is both legitimate and "important" or "substantial." Or it might be "strict," which requires the state to show that its action is necessary to achieve a compelling state interest, an exceedingly difficult burden for the state to bear. Strict scrutiny applies when the court deems the interest at stake "fundamental," which does not occur very often, especially in the Rehnquist Court era. Intermediate scrutiny has sometimes been said to apply when the interest at stake is "important," though the Court has been rather fuzzy and inconsistent in articulating the nature and basis for this level of review.[27]

The Supreme Court has declined to hold that education is a fundamental interest or right of children that triggers strict scrutiny. However, it has indicated on a few occasions that it regards education as an interest sufficiently important to require heightened scrutiny of state action that discriminates in distributing it.[28] In *Plyler v. Doe*,[29] for example, the Court applied heightened scrutiny to a Texas law that denied a free public school education to children of illegal aliens, in part because the benefit denied was a publicly funded education. The Court stated that education is not "merely some governmental 'benefit' indistinguishable from other forms of social welfare legislation." For the Court, education was important for equal protection purposes because it was necessary for "advancement on the basis of individual merit" and because it enabled an individual " 'to participate effectively and intelligently in our open political system.' " Education is the principal means by which a traditionally subordinate group "might raise the level of esteem in which it is held by the majority." As such, a law denying a quality education to a discrete class of children tends to create an underclass of persons unable to participate in and contribute to society, and thereby runs directly counter to the central purpose of the Equal Protection Clause. The Court elaborated:

> The inestimable toll of that deprivation on the social, economic, intellectual, and psychological well-being of the individual, and the obstacle it poses to individual achievement, make it most difficult to reconcile the cost or the principle of a status-based denial of basic education with the framework of equality embodied in the Equal Protection Clause.

On other occasions as well, the Supreme Court has affirmed the importance of education and the integral connection between education and the primary purpose of the Equal Protection Clause—to eliminate inequalities of opportunity in our society. In condemning racial segregation in schools in *Brown v. Board of Education*, the Court stated:

> Today, education is perhaps the most important function of state and local governments. Compulsory school attendance laws and the great expenditures for education both demonstrate our recognition of the importance of education to our democratic society. It is required in the performance of our most basic public responsibilities, even service in the armed forces. It is the very foundation of good citizenship. Today it is a principal instrument in awakening the child to cultural values, in preparing him for later professional training, and in helping him to adjust normally to his environment. In these days, it is doubtful that any child may reasonably be expected to succeed in life if he is denied the opportunity of an education.[30]

Of course, the state's failure to give some children a share of state funding on education does not result in their receiving no schooling whatsoever. They are still in some school. But that could have been true of the children in *Plyler*

[165]

as well; the state in that case had not prohibited children of illegal aliens from attending school, but rather refused to let them attend public school at public expense. Some might have attended private schools. Children in type A schools, at least, are thus in a very similar situation; the state does not preclude them from receiving any schooling whatsoever, but it does deny them any state funding for their education, based on something about their parents rather than about them. The only distinction between the two cases lies in what it was about parents that triggered the discrimination; illegal alien status in *Plyler,* choices parents have made here. The inclination one might have is to say the parents are to blame here, not the state, whereas in *Plyler* the parents presumably wanted a public school education for their children and it was entirely the state's choice to exclude them. But that ignores the state's obligation to these children as persons distinct from their parents, the principle constitutionalized in the illegitimacy cases that children should not be deprived of state-conferred benefits because of their parents' choices, and the fact that the state also bears responsibility for their being in a religious school, because it is the state that gives parents the power to put them there. The case is therefore strong for finding that heightened scrutiny should apply.

Two things distinguish a claim on behalf of children from a claim on behalf of parents, therefore. First, while there is arguably no discrimination among parents at all, since the state benefit is made available to all parents for them to accept or not as they choose, there clearly is discrimination among groups of children. Some children are denied a share of public money for education through no fault of their own. Second, if there were discrimination among parents, rational basis review would be appropriate, while heightened scrutiny should apply to the discrimination among children, because the children have such an important interest at stake. When subjected to heightened scrutiny, the failure of states to create a well-designed voucher program should be found unjustified.

The justifications offered to defeat a claim on behalf of parents would not be sufficient here. The justification for funding only public schools necessarily depended on parents' voluntary choice, and that would not apply to a claim on behalf of children. With respect to funding only nonreligious schools, one justification was that the state might wish to ensure that members of the public can obtain the service without having to get it from a religious institution. But that justification, too, ultimately leans on the premise of voluntary choice and so fails here. The result of funding only nonreligious schools is that some children fail to receive the service through no fault of their own. The second justification was that the state might wish to avoid ideological conflicts with its contractors. That justification applies here, but avoiding conflicts over regulation is not the sort of government interest the Supreme Court has found to be "important." It certainly pales in comparison with the interests of the children at stake, particularly given that regulations would be imposed voluntarily as a condition for accepting funding and thus would be less likely to give rise to pronounced conflicts. Finally, the justification based on avoiding the appearance of supporting religion would also apply here, but that too is not a state interest sufficiently important to justify discriminatory denial of such a large benefit to children. That states and the federal government themselves do not attribute much importance to concerns about conflicts over regulation or about creating the appearance of supporting religion is evidenced by the fact that they already provide many forms of aid to religious colleges, religious hospitals, and many other religious providers of social services, typically with significant regulatory strings attached.

In sum, the state owes an obligation to children in religious schools to do what it can to ensure them a good secular education, and to give them a fair share of state spending on education if that would in fact advance their educational interests. That obligation is not erased by choices the state empowers parents to make. And it is a very important obligation, because of the great importance of the interests those children have at stake. Failure to fulfill that obligation therefore requires strong justification, and the concerns opponents of vouchers raise with respect to funding of religious schools, however legitimate, are simply not compelling enough to override this obligation and to justify leaving children to suffer educational deprivation in underfunded religious schools.

Conclusion

We have come to the end of a rather exhaustive analysis of an idealized voucher program, having examined the normative status of such a program through four different lenses. Happily, all four ways of looking at the matter support the same conclusion. Here we find that application of the constitutional principle of equal personhood leads to the same conclusion reached by applying the two political morality approaches—a utilitarian weighting and balancing of interests and a rights-based analysis—to the voucher issue. A well-designed program of vouchers for private schools, including religious schools, is not only permissible but in fact mandatory. This is so not because of any right that parents or any other adults have. Rather, children enrolled in religious schools that strive to provide a good secular education but that suffer from lack of resources possess an equality-based constitutional right to a fair share of the state's expenditures on education. Coupled with their basic moral right, discussed in Chapter 4, to receive a good secular education, this constitutional right could well convince some legislators, judges, or both to guarantee state financial support for their education. In contrast, claims advanced on behalf of parents will always ring hollow, because parents properly suffer adverse consequences for their own voluntary choices.

Proponents of vouchers might do well to shift their focus from the supposed rights of parents to the rights of children, and in particular to the rights of children already in religious schools, if they want to present a compelling case for vouchers. To do so, though, they would need themselves to be able to conceptualize a parent and a child as two distinct persons with potentially conflicting interests. Probably most are unwilling to go down that road, because it might lead them to a world in which certain groups of parents would hold less power over their children's lives than they do today.

[7]

An Introduction to the Real World

We now turn to the real world, to see how the analysis of vouchers changes when a voucher program lacks the regulatory component that proved critical at many junctures of the analysis in previous chapters. Supporters of state aid to religious schools typically assume or imply that religious schools are academically superior and / or that states regulate and monitor private schools to ensure that they all provide at least an adequate secular education (in addition to any religious training they provide). Based on this assumption, they contend that there is no religion-neutral criterion on the basis of which the state could exclude religious schools from a program of education funding, particularly a funding program that includes nonreligious private schools.

That assumption is, however, patently false. The truth is that there is virtually no regulation of private schools in this country. And the available empirical evidence suggests that some of the more prevalent kinds of religious schools are in fact educationally deficient in important respects and engage in practices that, from the state's perspective, are harmful to children. Voucher supporters either refuse to address this evidence in a serious way or do not bother to investigate the literature on religious schools. They are instead content to seize upon any studies of test scores that appear to support their advocacy for religious schools, and to accuse of hostility to religion anyone who questions the methodologies or implications of the studies. But the fact is that reliance on such studies to draw sweeping conclusions about private schools is foolish.

First, existing standardized tests do not measure acquisition of most important cognitive skills. They test for the most rudimentary skills and for memorization of trivia. The current political emphasis on these tests is discouraging and dangerous.[1] As more and more schools "teach to the test," drilling students on how to answer multiple choice questions, children's educational interests are sacrificed. Voucher supporters' trumpeting of results on these tests contributes to the problem and hurts America's children. Second, even if the cited tests measured the right things, simplistic comparisons between the public and private school sectors would be meaningless. What policy decision could rationally turn on this comparison? Boosters of religious schools recognize when they discuss public schools that what matters is what each individual school is doing. They do not claim that studies show all public schools are bad. That would be demonstrably false, and not supported by the aggregate sector results, which they point out are very similar to those for the private sector. Instead they assert, correctly, that *some* public schools are bad. Why is it, then, that when they discuss private schools, they do not likewise acknowledge that some are good and some are bad, rather than pointing to the aggregate sector results and implying that all private schools are good? Clearly, they do not want to call attention to the bad private schools. Why not? Are the educational interests of children in those schools of no concern?

Third, even if the tests studied were meaningful, the studies do not include test results from all private schools. Some studies limit themselves to results for Catholic schools. Those studies tell us nothing, then, about non-Catholic private schools. Other studies purport to look at all private schools, but the fact is that not all private schools administer tests, even in states that nominally require all schools to do so. Many schools, particularly Fundamentalist Christian schools, simply refuse to comply, and state education officials do nothing about it. Finally, there are the more frequently discussed methodology problems. It is exceedingly difficult to eliminate all variables other than school effect. In particular, it is very difficult, perhaps impossible, to factor out family background as an influence on achievement. As indicated in Chapter 3, none of the studies conducted to date has done so. In any event, for the reasons given above, a perfect study showing that average test scores improved for voucher students would not give us any justified confidence that existing programs are well designed.

Having laid to rest the test score bugaboo, this chapter first provides below a description of one kind of religious school that exists in this country in substantial numbers, a kind of school the state must regard as anathema to children's well-being. It then explains how it is that such a school can not only exist but actually be funded by the state. It describes the regulatory environment in which religious schools generally operate and the requirements for participation in existing voucher programs. Chapters 8 and 9 then apply the same analytic approaches used in Chapters 3 through 6, to assess the morality and constitutionality of a voucher program that includes schools like the one I describe in this chapter.

A Religious School in the Real World

The school I describe here is a Fundamentalist Christian "self-paced curriculum," or "teacherless," school.[2] The "video school" in Cleveland mentioned in the Introduction likely resembles this sort of school, except that it substitutes videos for workbooks. Although there are no good estimates of how many children attend self-paced Fundamentalist schools, they may enroll as much as 8 percent of all children in religious schools in this country, or roughly a third of a million students.[3]

Picture a school that operates in one large room in the basement of a small church building. The school has thirty students, spread out over the thirteen grade levels of kindergarten through twelfth grade. The room contains thirty work carrels, and each student is assigned to one for her thirteen years of school. Each school day, after morning prayers, students sit at their carrels and remain there throughout the day, except for brief stretching periods on the hour and a lunch break. Only during the lunch break do students speak to each other. During the rest of the day, students complete workbooks. The school has purchased a large school kit from a Christian publishing house, containing a series of workbooks for each grade level. There is no oral instruction in this school. In fact, there is no teacher in the school.[4] An adult member of the church volunteers to sit in the church basement each day, to ensure that the students remain at their workstations, to verify that students have properly graded their worksheets using the answer key provided in the curriculum kit, and to authorize trips to the bathroom. All the instruction the children receive, therefore, comes from the workbooks in the kit. Of what does it consist?[5]

The workbooks are written by Bible college graduates, who shape the content in all subjects to fit religious doctrine and suffuse it with explicitly biblical teachings. Anything ordinarily taught in a nonsectarian school that is inconsistent or in tension with a Fundamentalist interpretation of the Bible does not appear, and in fact the workbooks are likely to teach that the opposite is true. For example, one workbook contains a photograph that "proves" that dinosaurs lived on the earth at the same time as humans, in order to make natural history conform to creationist beliefs. Another workbook characterizes the Civil War as a Christian holy war to protect God-given property rights and to preserve the biblically mandated separation of the races. Another describes as being poor writers, as well as spiritually misguided, great literary figures such as Emily Dickinson and Ernest Hemingway, whose writings are viewed as antithetical to a Fundamentalist worldview. The introduction to materials on American government and state history announces as an objective of the unit: "When you have successfully completed this [material], you should be able to recite the Ten Commandments and to recognize the facts related to the Biblical bases of government." Study of ancient world history is study of biblical history. This approach to curricular content is consistent with the overriding purpose of these schools, which is to provide not academic training but "Christian character training."

The workbooks also contain many explicit and implicit messages of hostility toward persons of other religious faiths, particularly Catholics and Jews. Catholicism—or "Romanism," as Fundamentalists are wont to call it—is "a perversion of biblical Christianity," its "false doctrines" the result of "infiltration" of the Church by Satan. In addition, students are told many times and in many ways that women are morally and socially inferior to men and should pursue no ambition other than service to men in the home. The children learn that they are insignificant, inherently wicked, and unworthy, that until they are "saved" they are the devil's children, and that they will suffer a horrible fate if they are not saved. They are warned against the perils of pursuing any ambition in life that would have them associate with nonbelievers. Only male students should go to college, and they should attend only conservative Christian Bible colleges.

Not only do students in these schools not have the opportunity to discuss what the workbooks teach, they are instructed not to question anything they are taught. To think for oneself is to manifest sinful pride. The truth is received, not discovered. The school's aim is to break the students' will, not to build confidence in their intellectual abilities. Independent and critical thinking is an impediment to producing true believers and so must be squelched. Rote learning is what is called for; what the school expects of students in all areas of study is acceptance, memorization, and repetition of what they are told is true.

Contrast this approach to schooling with the autonomy-fostering component of a liberal education, the kind of education the state in our liberal democracy necessarily values. Meira Levinson writes:

> [I]n order to develop and achieve autonomy, children should gain sufficient self-esteem and confidence to feel comfortable articulating their views in public and laying themselves and their views open to challenge—but also possess enough humility to take challenges to their positions seriously; learn to express themselves in terms others will understand and listen to others' responses; be imaginative, possessing the ability to step into other people's shoes and to see perspectives other than their own; be creative, observant, and sensitive to subtlety; learn to think critically and to use reason effectively, and judiciously; be willing to subject their own arguments and intuitions to the demands of proof; gain the skills and knowledge to put their beliefs and values into practice, including vocational and personal skills, manual and technical competency, and social skills, among others; be exposed to and interact with people from different backgrounds, and in different contexts. . . . [6]

Harry Brighouse argues that for children to become autonomous persons they must learn:

> [h]ow to identify various sorts of fallacious arguments, and how to distinguish among them, as well as between them and non-fallacious arguments. The autonomous person needs to be able to distinguish between appeals to authority and appeals to evidence, between inductive and deductive arguments, as well as to identify *ad hominem* arguments and other misleading rhetorical devices.[7]

And along the same lines, Michael Pritchard adopts as a description of the sort of critical thinker children should be educated to become someone who

> is habitually inquisitive, well-informed, trustful of reason, open-minded, flexible, fair-minded in evaluation, honest in facing personal biases, prudent in making judgments, willing to reconsider, clear about issues, orderly in complex matters, diligent in seeking relevant information, reasonable in the selection of criteria, focused in inquiry, and persistent in seeking results which are as precise as the subject and the circumstances of inquiry permit.[8]

The Fundamentalist school does not aim to foster these many important abilities and attributes. In fact, it aims to prevent them from developing in its students.

In short, the school I have described is clearly antithetical to what the state regards as proper aims for children's schooling.[9] It does not endeavor to provide a good secular education and so, unsurprisingly, does not. It does impart the most basic reading, writing, and math skills, but not the higher-order cognitive skills that are essential today if one is to have a broad range of life opportunities. It fails to provide students with the understanding of methods of inquiry in different disciplines and of mainstream views in different subject areas that is necessary for higher academic studies and entrance into many occupations.[10] In addition, it places severe restrictions on children's physical liberty, simply by confining them to workstations all day, but also by moral haranguing against interacting with members of the opposite sex, dancing, associating with non-Christian peers, and participating in non-Christian public events or entertainment (e.g., non-Christian movies, popular music concerts, etc.). It also places severe restrictions on children's freedom of thought and expression, particularly in relation to religious belief. It instills dogmatic and intolerant attitudes that will make it difficult for its graduates to function successfully in a religiously or ethnically diverse environment, and thereby further limits their opportunities for careers and for participation in political life.[11] It also undermines students' self-esteem, particularly that of female students, and induces great anxiety in children.[12]

Confronted with this reality, the state would have to conclude that this school fails to provide an adequate secular education and that many of its practices are harmful to children. The school thwarts development of the cognitive skills states believe essential to preparation for adult life and therefore aim to foster in public schools. And it treats students in ways that states prohibit in their public schools because such treatment would violate the rights of students and hinder what the state regards as healthy cognitive and social development. In other words, given the conclusions states have reached about the appropriate approaches to education and treatment of students in their own schools, as reflected in the extensive regulations imposed on public schools, and the reasons why they have reached those conclusions,[13] the states could not consistently conclude that the school described above is acceptable, let alone that it is a good alternative to public school for any child.

One might assume that a school of this sort could not exist, even if state laws did not prohibit it, because any private school would have to provide a secular education superior to that of public schools in order to attract parents. Yet this kind of school does exist. It exists in Milwaukee. It exists in Cleveland. It exists in Florida. A great number of parents who send their children to religious schools (though certainly not all) do so not because they believe such schools provide a superior secular education, but rather primarily or solely for religious reasons. They might view the public school environment and pedagogy as antithetical to their religious beliefs,[14] and want their children to be immersed in a religiously orthodox environment at all times. Or they might simply want their children to receive religious instruction on a daily basis, and are unconcerned about, inattentive to, or incapable of judging the nature and content of instruction in state-mandated subjects.

Moreover, the problems identified above with respect to Fundamentalist Christian self-paced curriculum schools are not confined to that kind of school. Other common types of religious schools share many of the troubling characteristics of the school just described, particularly other kinds of Fundamentalist Christian schools. In none of the jurisdictions where voucher programs are in place is it possible to say how many of what kind of school exist and to what extent they have any of these characteristics, because, as explained below, no one is overseeing religious schools to determine what they are doing. In all likelihood, the vast majority of religious schools in any of these jurisdictions engage to some degree in one or more of the practices described above that are, from the state's perspective, harmful to children. Catholic schools, which enroll half of all religious school pupils in this country, have a history of teaching sexism, fostering dogmatic attitudes, excessively restricting students' freedom of thought and expression, thwarting development of critical thinking skills, and generating high levels of anxiety in students.[15] There is no reason to believe those practices have disappeared from Catholic schools.

[174]

There is also no reason to believe that all or most voucher schools are academically inadequate. It might well be that most provide a better secular education than the public schools in their area, and provide a healthier environment than the public schools in many ways. Certainly many parents have chosen a religious school primarily or solely for academic reasons (as evidenced, for example, by the significant percentage of non-Catholic parents patronizing Catholic schools in poor urban areas), and are capable of evaluating schools on that basis. No doubt for some children who have transferred to a religious school as a result of vouchers, the move has made or will make a tremendous positive difference in their lives. But aside from anecdotal evidence, we simply do not know what schools are doing and how individual children are affected. And there appears to be little interest in finding out. Several researchers have studied aggregate test scores for voucher students (with ambiguous results), but these researchers ought to know that the tests used are very superficial measures of learning and that aggregate results mask wide divergences. From a child-centered perspective, this is simply not good enough. If "Leave No Child Behind" is more than a slogan, we should be attentive to how vouchers affect each and every child whose parents claim them, and we should look beyond performance on multiple-choice tests of rote learning. And we should do everything we can in advance to ensure that voucher schools are prepared to provide a high-quality secular education.

Regulation of Schools Participating in Existing Voucher Programs

What is the background regulatory environment against which vouchers operate? The reality is that there is virtually no regulation in this country of the content of instruction or treatment of students in private schools.[16] Assertions to the contrary by voucher supporters are simply irresponsible. A typical state's regulations require only that private schools operate in a safe building, provide the state with a list of the students they enroll, and attest that the school operates for at least a certain number of days per year and teaches certain core subjects. States generally do not require that private schools have teachers, let alone that they have teachers with any particular qualifications. States do not even attempt to control or oversee the nature or content of instruction in classes that ostensibly teach core subjects such as history, science, and literature. As long as the schools *say* they are teaching the state-mandated subjects, they satisfy state compulsory attendance laws. Some states require that private school students take standardized tests, but they attach no consequences to the results on the tests. State education officials have no legal authority to do anything to a "failing" private school. Moreover, states generally do not enforce what few regulations they do have against any religious groups that resist them.[17] As a result, many schools simply decline to report attendance or to administer tests, with the result that the state knows virtually nothing about them. There is, in sum, no obstacle in any state's general regulatory scheme to the operation of the school described above.

Do voucher programs add any significant requirements for instruction or treatment of students to this general regulatory scheme? They do not. It does appear that state education officials administering these programs are more inclined at present to enforce whatever regulations the programs do contain, because public attention is so high. The regulations, however, do nothing to ensure education quality. It is worth examining each program in some detail.

The Milwaukee Parental Choice Program

The general education statutes of Wisconsin set forth several requirements private schools must meet in order to satisfy the state's compulsory education law. The only requirements relating to the schools' operations are (1) that they provide at least 875 hours of instruction each school year and (2) that they provide "a sequentially progressive curriculum of fundamental instruction in reading, language arts, mathematics, social studies, science and health."[18] Neither state statutes nor regulations issued by the state's Department of Public Instruction prescribe what constitutes a "sequentially progressive curriculum." The statute actually states that private schools are not required to do anything with respect to curriculum that conflicts with their religious beliefs: "This subsection does not require the program to include in its curriculum any concept, topic or practice in conflict with the program's religious doctrines or to exclude from its curriculum any concept, topic or practice consistent with the program's religious doctrines."[19] Thus, the only real requirement a religious school must meet in order to satisfy the compulsory attendance law in Wisconsin is that the school provide 875 hours of instruction of whatever sort each school year.

The 1995 Wisconsin law creating the current voucher program imposes six requirements on private schools as conditions for participation.[20] The first five are that a participating school operate in a building that complies with health and safety laws; annually submit an independent financial audit; comply with a federal law prohibiting racial discrimination;[21] accept voucher students without regard to past academic performance or membership in a religious organization; and excuse students from religious activities at the school if their parents request this in writing.[22] These first five conditions are all salutary, though private schools' complete freedom to expel students weakens the last two. The sixth condition for participation, however, is the only one that potentially impacts the quality of instruction. It requires that a participating school satisfy *one* of the four following requirements: (1) 70 percent of voucher students advance one grade level each year; (2) voucher students have an average attendance of at least 90 percent; (3) at least 80 percent of voucher students "demonstrate significant academic progress"; *or* (4) at least 70 percent of voucher families "meet parent involvement criteria established by the private school."[23]

The State Department of Public Instruction regulations implementing the statute add various reporting requirements, principally reporting of the names of voucher students attending the school and reporting of information necessary to demonstrate compliance with the six conditions set forth above.[24] The implementing regulations also define what it means for a student to advance one grade level each year and what it means for a student to demonstrate significant academic progress. Grade level advancement is measured, at the school's election, by reference to either *(a)* any standardized achievement test *of the school's choosing* or *(b)* "instructional objectives" in reading, writing, and math *established by the school itself.* "Significant academic progress" means that a student *(a)* demonstrates *some* improvement in reading and math from one year to the next, and *(b)* demonstrates "satisfactory performance" on at least half of whatever instructional concepts in reading and math *the school chooses* to add in a given school year to its expectations for the student. Thus, both of these provisions relating to student performance leave it more or less entirely up to voucher schools themselves to define the objectives for their students' education. Moreover, these are the only provisions in the statutes or regulations concerning student achievement, they are limited to reading, writing, and arithmetic, and they are easily avoided simply by achieving a 90 percent attendance rate among voucher students or a 70 percent rate of parental participation (however the schools define that). In other words, as long as participating schools report that voucher students are regularly attending school or that most parents do something that the school considers "participation," the state of Wisconsin does not care what children who receive vouchers are learning or whether they are learning anything at all.

Thus, nothing in the laws of the state of Wisconsin precludes the school described above from participating in the Milwaukee voucher program. There are no real requirements for what participating schools teach, how they teach it, or how they treat their students. Religious schools funded by the state are not required to have teachers, let alone qualified teachers, and they are not required to administer any performance assessments, let alone assessments that measure important cognitive abilities. The only possible exception regarding treatment of students is the religious activity opt-out provision. But that provision is not designed to protect children from anything; it is designed to protect parental power over children's belief formation. That some liberal theorists seize on opt-out provisions as an important condition for state subsidies is, from a child welfare perspective, quite peculiar.

It is not surprising, therefore, that studies of the Milwaukee program have not shown a significant aggregate improvement in students' performance, even on standardized tests, as a result of switching from the public schools to private voucher schools. Given the lack of substantive requirements for participation, the state could not rationally have expected voucher schools on the whole to do better than the public schools at anything, since the state could have known nothing in advance about the quality of voucher schools (in fact, some participating schools have been newly created ones).[25] More to the point, however, the state could not rationally have assumed that no children would end up *worse off*, in terms of their education and other developmental interests, as a result of vouchers. Nothing prevents the state of Wisconsin from paying the tuition of a school that does not even aim to provide a good secular education and that treats students in ways the state regards as harmful. The state superintendent of public instruction has himself acknowledged this problem, and has complained on several occasions to the governor of Wisconsin and to the state legislature that the voucher law does nothing to ensure that participating schools are providing an adequate education, and does not even enable him to determine whether they are doing so. For example, in a letter dated February 14, 2001, addressed to the governor and the state senate and assembly (and posted on the Department of Public Instruction website), the superintendent pled for an amendment to the voucher laws that would add "accountability requirements." The superintendent stated:

> Under the current reporting requirement, it is not known which MPCP schools have been successful in providing quality education. . . . [T]he public has not had the information to judge whether taxpayer funds have been producing good academic results. The current MPCP standards provide almost no information on student achievement at participating schools.[26]

The Cleveland Program

The general education laws of Ohio create a two-track system of private schooling.[27] Private schools can elect to be "chartered" (i.e., licensed), making them eligible for certain forms of state aid, but also requiring their compliance with greater regulations than those applying to nonchartered schools. Nonchartered private schools need only submit an annual report to the state department of education identifying the pupils they instruct and certifying that they operate for 182 five-hour days each school year in a safe building, teach certain core subjects in whatever way they choose, and "follow regular procedures" for promoting students who satisfy their educational requirements, whatever those might be. State regulations also require that teachers and administrators in nonchartered schools have at least a bachelor's degree from a "recognized" college or university, but do not require that teachers or administrators have any training as teachers or administrators, or even that schools have any teachers at all. Thus, schools of the kind described at the beginning of this chapter are clearly permitted to operate in Ohio.

The Ohio law creating the Cleveland voucher program manifests an intention to direct vouchers primarily to schools meeting the requirements for chartered schools, so it is relevant to examine those requirements. However, that law also gives the state superintendent discretion to register nonchartered schools for participation,[28] and the superintendent has in fact registered nonchartered schools. These have included schools similar to the Fundamentalist school described above, as well as schools with other problems—for example, a school with a convicted murderer on staff and a dangerous building.[29] Nonchartered schools that wish to participate in the voucher program do have to abide by certain requirements included in the voucher law. They must (1) commit in writing to admit voucher students in accordance with certain priorities (e.g., students who attended the school in the past, students with siblings in the school, and students from low-income families); (2) not discriminate on the basis of race or religion in admissions; (3) enroll at least twenty-five students in the school as a whole; (4) refrain from advocating or fostering unlawful behavior or hatred of other racial or religious groups; (5) provide only accurate information about the school to the public; and (6) not charge poor families tuition, over and above the voucher, in an amount greater than 10 percent of the voucher amount.[30] Apart from the provision regarding fostering unlawful behavior or hatred, the voucher law imposes no restrictions on the nature or content of instruction in nonchartered schools receiving vouchers.

The state superintendent *could* choose to allow only chartered schools to receive vouchers. The current holder of that office expressed an intention, after stories of grossly inadequate schools participating in the program appeared in the news, to allow only chartered schools as new entrants to the program.[31] But she or a future superintendent could change that policy at any time. If all participating schools were charter schools, then all voucher schools in Cleveland, might be subject to more elaborate regulations. State regulations relating to chartered private schools contain lengthy descriptions of administrative procedures and practices, courses of study, and facilities.[32]

These regulations might require a school of the kind described earlier in this chapter to add many things to its program, nominally at least, and those additions might entail costs the school cannot bear. That would depend on how substantial the additions must be to satisfy the state superintendent—for example, whether a few books on a shelf could constitute a "library." None of these requirements, however, would prevent such a school from doing anything it was already doing. And while the lengthy list of curricular requirements might seem demanding, it is not clear that they require schools to do anything more than profess to be teaching certain subjects. The school I described could certainly continue to teach students core subjects using just

Christian curriculum packets, and might be able to satisfy the requirement to teach certain other subjects however they liked—for example, by having students read a few pages of the pastor's views on careers, citizenship, human relations, multiculturalism, and energy and resource conservation. Nor would these regulations require that a school hire any teachers, let alone teachers with any particular qualifications.

Most significantly, though, there appears to be an escape valve in state regulations for schools that want to be chartered but do not wish to comply with the requirements just discussed. The regulatory provision setting forth the basic rule for chartering private schools provides that such a school can assure the state that its students are receiving an adequate education *either* by fulfilling the requirements enumerated in the administrative code *or* by "[b]eing accredited by an association whose standards have been . . . approved by the state board of education."[33] There are several associations in this country that "accredit" conservative Christian schools , and they are generally successful in currying favor with state education authorities. If the school described above were accredited by an approved association, it could receive vouchers without complying with the regulations for chartered schools, even if the state superintendent elects to exclude schools that do not satisfy the requirements for charter schools. The only new burden the school would have to assume is a testing requirement for charter schools set out in state statutes. To remain chartered, schools must administer one round of tests in the areas of reading, writing, mathematics, science, and citizenship at some point in the high school years. It does not appear that students in the school must achieve a particular level of performance on the tests, however. It appears sufficient that the school simply not award a "high school diploma" to any of its students who does not score at or above the level the state department of education deems indicative of ninth-grade proficiency in those areas.[34]

The Florida Program

Private schools in Florida, in order to operate, need only comply with basic health and safety rules, report aggregate attendance data, maintain a register of individual student attendance, and operate for a certain number of days each year.[35] There are no general regulations concerning the content and methods of instruction in private schools. The voucher law imposes several additional requirements as a condition for participation.[36] Private schools seeking eligibility to receive vouchers must have been in operation for one year or must demonstrate fiscal soundness; must satisfy all applicable health and safety codes; must admit students on a racially nondiscriminatory basis and without regard to past academic performance; must conform to the standards of *some* private school accrediting body; must "be academically accountable to the parent"; must provide the state with a school profile that includes a statement of past student performance; must agree not to charge any tuition beyond the amount of the opportunity scholarship; and must adhere to whatever disciplinary procedures, if any, the school happens to have. None of those conditions would preclude a school of the kind I have described from receiving voucher money.[37] Three further requirements might appear to do so, but it is not clear that they do.

First, schools that receive voucher money in Florida must agree not to compel any voucher student "to profess a specific ideological belief, to pray, or to worship." The terms "compel" and "profess" are open to interpretation, and a school could represent to the state that it does not compel profession of any religious beliefs even though it punishes expression of views inconsistent with Fundamentalist Christian orthodoxy, and even though it deploys an arsenal of pedagogical weapons to convince students that they should profess certain views "voluntarily." It is exceedingly unlikely that state education officials will closely scrutinize internal practices of voucher schools in order to determine whether teachers are being too coercive with respect to religious belief.

Second, schools receiving vouchers must "[e]mploy or contract with teachers who hold a baccalaureate or higher degree, *or* have at least 3 years of teaching experience in public or private schools, *or* have special skills, knowledge, or expertise that qualifies them to provide instruction in subjects taught." I have described the Fundamentalist self-paced curriculum school as having no teachers, so this provision would appear to preclude such a school from eligibility. The operators of such schools, though, have no doctrinal objection to having "teachers" in their schools, and they could simply characterize the room supervisor in a school as a teacher in order to receive voucher money. As long as that person has been employed by that school or by any other school for at least three years, or has some unspecified "special skills, knowledge, or expertise," this provision would not preclude such a school from eligibility. Simply reading the instructions that come with the Fundamentalist curriculum package might be said to give one "special knowledge or expertise" relevant to the school's operation. Even if the state department of education were to interpret the provision relating to teachers as requiring that all participating schools employ someone to provide some oral instruction, nothing in the statute requires that any particular amount of oral instruction be given or that the instruction have any particular content. Thus, schools that differ only slightly from the one I have described would still be eligible for full funding by the state of Florida.

Finally, the voucher statute requires that all voucher students take all statewide assessment tests that public school students take. It imposes on parents the obligation to ensure that this happens. Other provisions in the Florida education code mandate that the education department develop tests that go beyond the traditional multiple choice tests, which principally measure rote learning, to measure the "problem-solving and higher-order skills" that enable students to "successfully compete at the highest levels nationally and internationally."[38] This is an important step in the right direction, and one might expect a school of the kind I have described, which not only fails to foster higher-order cognitive skills but in fact tries to thwart their development, to show very poor results on tests of that sort. However, nothing in the voucher law conditions eligibility for state funding on achieving any particular outcomes on any tests. The law confers no authority on the state's department of education to exclude a school from participation because tests show it to be doing a terrible job. Thus, the testing requirement would have no direct effect on any private school.[39]

In sum, while the voucher law in Florida requires schools to do several things in order to participate in the voucher program, none significantly affect the nature and content of instruction provided. The two requirements that appear to pose a problem for the sort of Fundamentalist school I have described—the agreement not to compel profession of religious beliefs and the mandate to hire a teacher—are of uncertain significance. Schools might easily evade them, particularly if the schools themselves are left to interpret "compel" and "teacher" as they see fit. At most, the criteria for participation in the Florida voucher program would require only minor modifications in the practices of schools of this kind.

Conclusion

Existing voucher programs allow religious schools to be fully or nearly fully state funded, while doing little or nothing to ensure that the schools provide any secular education, let alone a high-quality secular education. The general public inattention to this reality is astonishing. The content of the hundreds of voucher bills that state and federal elected officials have put forward in recent years suggests that voucher supporters are simply unconcerned about it, which reinforces the conclusion that improving education for children is not really their aim. Some bills would, in fact, have expressly forbidden state education officials from exercising any increased control or supervision over voucher schools.[40] From a child-centered perspective, this raises serious concerns. The final two chapters consider the morality and legality of the actual approach states are taking to vouchers.

[8]

A Moral Assessment of Existing Voucher Programs

The final two chapters of the book assess the normative status of voucher programs in light of the real world situation described in Chapter 7. They assess the moral and constitutional permissibility of voucher programs that include religious schools while in no way ensuring that recipient schools provide an adequate education and refrain from harmful practices, and where there is ample evidence that many schools eligible to receive vouchers do not pursue the secular aims that the state has established for schooling and / or treat students in ways the state deems harmful. In this chapter, I deploy the two moral theoretical approaches—a consequentialist balancing of interests and a rights-based analysis.

Do Existing Programs Do More Good Than Harm?

In Chapter 3, I identified and ranked ten groups of persons who might have interests at stake in the voucher controversy. Those same groups have the same interests at stake under the real world factual assumptions that inform the analysis in this chapter. Those interests might simply cut in a different direction as a result of the change in factual assumptions.

Children

I explained in Chapter 3 why vouchers themselves do not clearly affect the interests of children who would remain in public schools after vouchers are in place, despite the focus of many opponents of vouchers on the supposed consequences for public schools. The greatest concern is with lost funding, but a state's decision whether to adequately support the education of children in public schools is conceptually independent of its decision whether to fund education in private schools, just as it is conceptually independent of its decision whether to spend more money on highways. The fact that the legislation creating each of the existing voucher programs also contains a provision for reduction of public school funding by the amount spent on vouchers does not alter the fact that the reduction in funding is a conceptually distinct decision by legislators, and not an inherent feature of a voucher program. Legislators can and should be faulted for failing adequately to fund public schools, irrespective of their decision regarding vouchers.

The greatest difference between analyzing an ideal program and analyzing existing programs relates to the interests of children who receive vouchers. It is principally this difference that changes the ultimate conclusion about the permissibility of vouchers. No doubt there are many children who, from the state's perspective, benefit from existing voucher programs—namely, those who attend a "type A" religious school, a school that strives to provide the best possible secular education. These children should be experiencing an improvement in their secular education. However, it is at present impossible to determine for what percentage of children receiving vouchers this is true, because the states do not monitor voucher schools sufficiently to make that judgment.

In addition, existing programs probably make some indeterminate number of children *worse off.* Some children may have been transplanted from public schools that aim to provide a good secular education, and that succeed to some degree in doing so,[1] to "type B" religious schools—those that, because of their religious beliefs, do not pursue this aim or pursue it insufficiently. In addition, it is likely that most children moved from public schools to religious schools have been made worse off in at least *some* respects. The available evidence suggests that most religious schools engage, to some degree, in practices that are from the state's perspective harmful to children. These practices include suppression of independent thought and free expression, denial of freedom with respect to religious belief and practice, instilling of intolerant and / or dogmatic dispositions, gender discrimination and inculcation of gender stereotypes, and denigration or punishment of aspects of students' personality that school officials deem incompatible with religious principles (e.g., creativity, assertiveness in girls, homosexuality).[2]

Children, like adults, have an interest in intellectual freedom, in not being coerced in their beliefs about the world absent a compelling justification for such coercion. With respect to religious belief, there can be, from the state's perspective, no compelling justification for anyone to coerce children; such coercion is certainly not necessary in order to protect a child's temporal interests. Children therefore have an interest in being free to make up their own minds about religion, and about many other things, as they grow, and authoritarian indoctrination threatens this interest. They also have an interest in developing the ability to engage in reasoned and respectful discourse with persons of different races, religions, and backgrounds. And they have an interest in being respected as equal persons, regardless of their gender or their conformity to stereotypical roles and personality traits. If voucher schools threaten any of these interests, we should ask whether these schools provide compensating benefits, and whether a net gain should be deemed good enough, or whether the state should be required to eliminate these harmful practices anyway.

One might suppose that any children already in religious schools could not be made worse off by vouchers, because the effect of vouchers would simply be to enhance the resources of their schools and / or their families. Of course, vouchers might allow some parents to keep their children in religious schools when otherwise they would have to transfer them to public schools, and those children would be in the same position as those discussed above whose parents would use vouchers to transfer them from public to religious school. But even for some who would be in religious schools regardless of vouchers, there are costs.

First, the assumption at work in the earlier chapters that all schools and parents participating in the voucher program would use the increased resources to enhance children's secular education would not hold true for many who participate in existing programs. Schools and parents that assign little or no importance to secular education would likely use the increased resources instead to promote religious ends, some of which may be antithetical to the children's temporal well-being. Second, apart from how the additional resources would be used, the very fact of state financial support for these religious schools would reinforce the beliefs of parents and teachers that the kind of schooling they are providing is appropriate, even though, from the state's perspective, it really is not. By way of analogy, the Supreme Court held in *Norwood v. Harrison* that merely providing textbooks to private schools amounts to encouragement of all their practices, including any racially discriminatory admissions policies.[3] Providing large tuition subsidies even more clearly amounts to encouragement.

Currently, some religious schools—most notably, Fundamentalist schools—operate under a cloud of implicit state disapproval. This disapproval is not manifested in state interference with their operations, because state officials have largely given up on trying to overcome the schools' resistance to regulation. Fundamentalists are well aware of the disapproval nonetheless. It is precisely because they know that their schooling practices are inconsistent with the state's educational aims that Fundamentalists attempt to operate in secrecy and to avoid any interaction with state officials. From their perspective, it must seem remarkable that states that have appeared hostile to their mission in the past are now offering financial support for their mission, with (at present) no attendant regulation of their instruction.

Some religious school operators actually view vouchers as a kind of Trojan horse, a way for the state to get inside their walls so it can later launch a regulatory attack, and are leery of vouchers for that reason. But many might conclude that the state has turned around and come to acknowledge the validity of their child-rearing practices, seeing in more recent Supreme Court decisions and in the recent wave of religious freedom legislative initiatives a new attitude toward conservative religious groups among government officials. This perception might in turn lead them to *intensify* those aspects of their schooling that are antithetical to their pupils' secular interests. Because they no longer fear state education departments, they might suppress children's independent and critical thought more vehemently, distort the content of core courses even more to serve religious ends, impose even more pressure on students toward conformity of beliefs, and reinforce more strenuously beliefs about gender roles and separation of races and religions.

Finally, the category of children in "nonqualifying" schools (and that of their parents) drops out of the calculus. They are not really affected by existing programs. Because schools need not provide education of any quality in order to qualify, the programs do not create an incentive for any private schools to provide a better education. In the context of existing programs, it makes more sense to speak of schools that do not wish to participate rather than schools that do not qualify. It is conceivable that some schools today decline to participate even though they would provide a better secular education if they received state support, but children in those schools are not made worse off by the state's providing financial support for other schools.

In sum, existing voucher programs likely advance some educational interests of some children, but they likely also harm educational and other interests of other children. State officials have no way of knowing how many children they are helping and how many they are hurting, because they do not exercise the kind of oversight that would be necessary for them to know what is actually going on in voucher schools. I consider below what the state should conclude in the face of this uncertainty, after considering how existing programs might affect the interests of other groups.

Teachers

Public school teachers have at stake under programs like those now in place the same important but nonfundamental interests in retaining their jobs that might be impacted by a well-designed program. Existing programs put that interest at risk for more of them insofar as the absence of meaningful requirements for eligibility to receive vouchers enables more private schools to qualify. The greater the number and diversity of private schools available, the more parents are likely to transfer their children from the public schools to private schools. With a greater exodus from public schools, there is a greater likelihood that public school teachers will be laid off. On the other hand, existing programs have other features that limit the number of students who can receive vouchers—principally, limiting eligibility to children from poorer families (as in Milwaukee) or to children in the very worst public schools (as in Florida), although most voucher supporters hope to have those limitations eventually removed. In any event, it would be difficult to determine whether and how many teaching positions are eliminated (or not created) because of vouchers per se rather than because of some other cause, including unwarranted cuts in public school funding. And again, we would expect a corresponding increase in positions in the private school sector, which some public school teachers might be willing and able to fill.

The effects of existing programs on teachers who do or have wanted to teach in religious schools should also be the same as under the ideal program. Teachers in some voucher schools might have received an increase in salary or other benefits, and some teachers who previously wanted to teach in religious schools but were unable might now be able to do so. Among these teachers, too, a greater number would be affected under existing programs insofar as the lack of meaningful regulation translates into a larger exodus of students from public to private schools. As discussed in Chapter 3, though, the affected interests of these teachers are not particularly compelling.

Parents

The effect on various groups of parents is also more or less the same under existing programs as under the idealized program. Existing programs undoubtedly give parents who prefer to send their children to a religious school enhanced satisfaction regarding their children's education, possibly also an increase in family resources, and relief from a perception of being treated unfairly. Satisfaction regarding their children's education might be greater for some parents under existing programs than it would be under the idealized program, if the lack of regulation allows them to use vouchers at schools that would not otherwise be eligible. On the other hand, a possibility that commentators all overlook is that there might be some parents who want to send their children to a religious school, but who actually would prefer that their children's school be required to meet robust standards of educational quality and treatment of students. These parents might experience *less* satisfaction than they would under a well-designed program. They might wish that the state imposed stringent conditions on vouchers, as an inducement to the religious schools in their area to improve in certain ways. It seems fair to assume that, just as is true with parents who send their children to public schools, a significant percentage of parents who send their children to religious schools believe the school could be doing better academically and so might welcome state action that causes such improvement to occur. A fallacy underlying all the public commentary on private school choice is the assumption that all parents who send their children to religious schools are perfectly happy with everything the schools do, but that is far from the truth. It is also false to assume that all religious schools are highly responsive to parental concerns and demands. Parents choose private schools simply because they believe those schools are *better* in some respects than the local public school, not because they think those schools are perfect. Undoubtedly, many would welcome an external stimulus for the private schools to improve academically, or would at least applaud the result after the fact.

Parents of children who remain in failing public schools in Milwaukee, Cleveland, and Florida today have the same concerns about their children's education but, again, cannot rationally blame the poor quality of public school education on state support for private schools, any more than they can blame state funding of road construction. As with their children, the interests these parents have in the quality of public school education should not enter into the balancing of interests in an assessment of existing programs. Their complaint lies with the state's failure adequately to fund public schools, period. It does not lie with the state's conceptually independent decision to direct some funds to other schools or to pay for any other public program. The question should be put directly to legislatures why they think it appropriate to cut funding for public schools simply because enrollment drops, or in other words why they wish to maintain per-pupil spending at inadequate levels. Therefore, the only parental interests the state could take into account in a utilitarian evaluation of existing programs are the nonfundamental interests of parents who receive vouchers in being able to satisfy their preferences regarding schools and / or in having more money for other family purposes.

Bystanders

The effect of existing programs on citizen / taxpayer opponents of vouchers is greater than would be the effect of the program I outlined in Chapter 3, and this might justify ranking them higher than public school teachers and possibly even parents receiving vouchers in the real world context. Because Wisconsin, Ohio, and Florida cannot plausibly explain their financial support for religious schools by reference to secular public purposes, secularists have much sounder reasons for viewing vouchers as state endorsement for religion and for therefore experiencing offense and a sense of exclusion or second-class status. In an environment where public officials are espousing aid for religious schools without taking any significant steps to ensure that those schools provide a good secular education, and are funding schools of the kind described in Chapter 7, one can reasonably conclude that public officials are not really motivated by a desire to secure a better education for children, but rather simply wish to subsidize the religious preferences of parents and to placate religious groups. Inclusion in existing programs of a significant (though less than proportionate) number of nonreligious private schools, whose quality is also unknown to the state, might mute to some degree the impact on secularists, insofar as it suggests the state's aim is more to subsidize parental choice generally than subsidize religious choices per se or religious proselytizing.

I would still hesitate to conclude, however, that secularist bystanders have a fundamental interest at stake, or that any fundamentalist interest they have is significantly impacted. The offense or slight we secularists might feel as a result of this form of state support for religion is not so great as truly to undermine our psychological well-being or coerce our beliefs about religion. It is annoying, perhaps even infuriating for some of us, but so are unwarranted parking tickets. The situation might be different if a state attempted to eliminate nonreligious alternatives in the educational realm or in other aspects of life. Then the threat to our religious freedom and sense of belonging and equal citizenship might be great enough to say that fundamental interests are at stake. But merely subsidizing any and all private alternatives to the still predominant public school system, using our tax money, however wrong that might be, still implicates only nonfundamental interests of secularist bystanders, interests far less important than those of the children whose education is at stake.

Existing programs have a modest positive effect on bystanders who want the state to support religious schools, either because they belong to a religious organization that operates schools or because they believe (falsely) that religious schools do a better job across the board of educating children. They experience simply a sense of satisfaction with states of affairs. One could argue that it is not in a person's interests to satisfy desires that are based upon false beliefs, when the person might well have an opposite desire if the truth were known, but I will put that issue aside.

Balancing Interests in the Real World

How do all these interests cash out in the real world? Children who remain in public schools and their parents again drop out of the equation. The important but nonfundamental interests of public school teachers and the interests of secularist opponents of vouchers might be somewhat weightier in the real world than in the hypothetical situation, either because their membership is larger or because their interests are more threatened, and their interests count against existing programs. On the other hand, the nonfundamental interests of voucher parents, religious school teachers, and bystander proponents of vouchers count in favor of vouchers more or less to the same degree that they did in an assessment of the idealized voucher program. It is difficult to say what a balancing of just the interests of those groups would yield. Existing programs might harm public school teachers and secularists more than they benefit individuals in the other three groups, but they might be much fewer in number than the combined membership of those other groups.

It still might be possible to have confidence in a moral conclusion one way or the other if we knew how many children benefit on the whole from existing programs and how many are worse off, and in each case to what degree. If the great majority of children in the program are receiving a much better education as a result, then that might decide the interest balancing, given that children's educational interests are so important. Voucher supporters will say that of course that is the case. But the fact is that we simply do not know that, as the Wisconsin superintendent of public instruction has acknowledged with respect to the Milwaukee program, and we should be very reluctant to rely on speculation. The appropriate conclusion to this analysis might well be that we just do not know whether existing programs do more harm than good. The only thing that is clear is that the utilitarian analysis is less favorable for existing voucher programs than it was for a program with adequate regulations attached.

Let us assume for a moment, though, that a reasonable legislator could come to the conclusion that, given what information the state now has at its disposal, current voucher programs, even though they contain no assurances regarding the quality of the private schools at which vouchers are used, nevertheless are probably doing more good than harm. That is, she could safely assume that they create benefits for at least some people, and that those benefits probably outweigh the harms they cause to other people, including some of the children whose parents would receive vouchers. Assume also that there are no distributional constraints on a legislator's consequentialist reasoning, so that inequitable effects among children would not trouble her. The legislator might then feel justified, from a utilitarian perspective, in voting for current voucher plans, and in concluding that these plans are morally permissible.

This raises at least two questions. The first question is whether state officials have an obligation to secure better information about what they are funding before they set about doing it, particularly when children's fundamental interests are at stake, so that they have greater confidence in their judgments about the likely effects on those the program would affect. Currently, state legislators and education officials at best know enrollment figures and test scores for many schools in their states. Other schools they know absolutely nothing about—namely, those that refuse to report any information to the state or to administer standardized tests. Moreover, there have been several ethnographic studies of individual religious schools published, and these give legislators and state education department officials reason for great concern about particular types of schools. In this situation, legislative decisions on voucher plans are simply irresponsible. The state is essentially contracting out children's education and making no inquiry into the qualifications of the school operators with which it contracts. States probably take greater care in contracting for plumbing service in state office buildings. One might reasonably conclude, then, that it is morally impermissible for states to enact voucher programs unless and until they investigate private schools (something states should do anyway, regardless of whether they elect to fund private schools), to see what kind of schooling they are providing and how they treat students, and on that basis determine that vouchers would improve the education children in the aggregate receive.

A second question is whether, when a program might help some people while harming others, the state may undertake the program because it slightly raises overall well-being, or whether the state should instead take another approach, if one is available, that will have the *best* overall outcome. In other words, if the state is faced with a choice between two alternative approaches to a program, does it have an obligation to choose the one that is *more* utility promoting, to strive to *maximize* overall well-being, rather than being content simply to do more good than harm? In the voucher context, the question would be whether states may implement voucher programs without attendant regulations, based on a hunch that such a program would do somewhat more good than harm, or whether instead states are morally obligated to implement a voucher program with real accountability, if this would achieve a better overall outcome by ensuring that *all* participants benefit and none are harmed.

Sometimes, of course, states must decline to undertake the most ambitious form of a program, because the costs it would entail would be excessive. But that is really an argument that a more ambitious undertaking is really not the optimal course to take, all things considered. It is difficult to imagine a good argument, on the other hand, for the position that states may choose to pursue a worse approach to advancing the public good when a better approach, all things considered, is readily available. And in the context of vouchers, a better approach *is* readily available—namely, to tie vouchers to robust standards for and oversight of the content of instruction and treatment of children in recipient schools. The costs for states doing so need not be great. I discuss some details of implementation in the Conclusion, and here will just point out that much of the quality control can be done through testing—of the right kind—rather than on-site supervision. The cost of doing this would be greater than the cost of current oversight, no doubt, but this cost would likely be outweighed by benefits states would receive, particularly the greater educational benefit realized from the money they commit to private education, not to mention the satisfaction of fulfilling their moral obligation to children.

Some will raise at this point the "not another layer of bureaucracy" objection. Many prefer that the state throw out money for parents to use however they wish, without state oversight. They contend that parental concern ensures that all children end up in the best available school. But the available empirical evidence regarding religious schools belies that contention, because it reveals that many parents make schooling choices for their children that the state should not even tolerate, let alone subsidize. Some parents simply are not motivated to secure a good secular education for their children; their highest priority is ensuring that their children remain believers, and everything else is secondary or unimportant. So reliance by the state on unconstrained parental choice is a mistake. There is no legitimate reason for the state to give parents money for private schooling unless and until the state ensures that they will use the money for something the state deems good for children, and that is simply not possible without meaningful requirements for schools' eligibility to participate.

In the real world, then, a utilitarian analysis yields the conclusion that current voucher plans are not morally required, and in fact are morally impermissible. States have an obligation to *(a)* gather sufficient information about private schools, prior to subsidizing them, to ensure that the program of aid would, on the whole, benefit children, and *(b)* adopt a plan only if it is the best feasible approach to promoting the education of children. Wisconsin, Ohio, and Florida have done neither of these things.

A Rights-Based Assessment

A rights-based analysis makes even clearer the moral impermissibility of current voucher plans. As with the consequentialist analysis, the principal difference in applying the rights-based framework to the real world lies in the implications for the children who receive vouchers. Because, as explained above, children whose parents choose to keep them in public schools still have no stake in the voucher issue per se, they have no rights that vouchers implicate. And as discussed above, the interests of teachers and of parents who receive vouchers are more or less the same in connection with existing programs as they were in connection with the ideal program, and insufficient to generate rights in this context as well.

Rights of Children

In Chapter 4, I considered separately two classes of children that might receive vouchers. I concluded that children who attend religious schools have a right to state funding of their education if their schools would use the money only to improve their secular education. On the other hand, vouchers would simply be one possible means of satisfying the right of some children in bad public schools—those whose parents would take advantage of the vouchers—

to receive a good education. In the real world, however, the paucity of information about what goes on in religious schools, the troubling nature of what information is available, and the consequent likelihood that many children are actually harmed by the state's facilitating their attendance at religious schools make it utterly implausible to say that vouchers are an entitlement of either of these two groups of children. Children in bad public or private schools have a right to a better education, but it is not possible to translate this right into a right to vouchers for any of those children in the absence of assurance that the vouchers would actually result in their receiving a better education.

In fact, it seems correct to say that many children have a right that their parents *not* receive state support for the parents' choice of a religious school, because that support would worsen their situation. If the state has a duty to children in general to ensure that they receive a good secular education and a duty to promote their developmental interests in other ways as well, then it must certainly also have a duty not to cause any children to receive a worse education or to be subjected to harmful practices. Support for unregulated religious schools, such as the kind of school I described in Chapter 7, has the effect of facilitating and encouraging schooling practices that undermine many of children's fundamental interests—not only their interest in receiving a good secular education, but also their interests in free thought and expression, in being treated as equal persons (i.e., in not being discriminated against on the basis of personal characteristics such as gender), in being treated with respect, and in developing attitudes and interpersonal skills that will allow them to function successfully in a heterogeneous society. In Chapter 3, I emphasized the importance of a good secular education and said little about children's interests in how they are treated in schools, because schools participating in a well-designed voucher program would pose no threat to the latter interest. I want to say more now about treatment of students, in anticipation of the charge that I am proposing that states impose a radical child liberationist ideology on religious and other private schools.

In the case of adults, interests in intellectual freedom and in nondiscrimination are treated as sufficiently important to give rise to a right for them. Indeed the principal arguments voucher proponents advance are that parents' rights to religious freedom and equal treatment require that they receive state funding for their choice of schools for their children. To coerce the religious beliefs of these parents in any way or to treat them less favorably than other parents is said to be a great injustice. What voucher proponents fail to appreciate is that these interests are also sufficiently important for children to give rise to a right for them, that this right is more commanding than any right parents have, and that it requires that regulatory strings attach to vouchers.

Courts and legislatures have recognized the importance of children's interest in nondiscrimination on many occasions. *Brown v. Board of Education,* condemning racially segregated schooling, and the federal Title IX and its state

[193]

analogues, prohibiting gender discrimination in schools receiving government aid, are clear evidence of that. In addition, there is a mountain of academic literature demonstrating the harm to girls' life prospects from sexist treatment in school. In particular, numerous studies have shown that female students in certain types of religious schools have diminished career ambitions and greater reluctance to enter traditionally male-dominated fields relative to female students in secular schools.[4]

With respect to intellectual freedom, my point is not that children should never be subjected to greater restrictions on their freedom of thought and expression than adults are. There are valid paternalistic reasons for imposing greater restrictions on children in some contexts.[5] But children's interest in having a substantial measure of freedom to form their own ideas and to reason independently of authority is nevertheless, from a secular perspective, of vital importance to them both as children and as future adults. All schools must place some restrictions on student expression—the sort of "time, place, and manner" restrictions that make it possible for an educational institution to operate. And it may be that imposing some additional restrictions on children's freedom of thought and expression beyond what is needed for the orderly operation of the school is conducive to their well-being—for example, discouraging ways of thinking that are self-destructive or antisocial. Even so, children have an important interest, like adults, in being free to develop their own ideas about the world and to express those ideas. Such freedom is an important part of children's happiness as children and also important to their cognitive development and preparation for adult life, when they will fare better if they are creative and independent thinkers and good communicators, and if they are able to order their lives in accordance with self-chosen ends.

This interest children have in free thought and expression is sufficiently important that school practices unduly repressive of children's thought and expression—that is, restrictions beyond those necessary for the orderly operation of the school and for protection of children's temporal well-being—should be deemed violations of students' rights. There can be reasonable disagreement about precisely where the line between necessary and unnecessary restrictions lies, but one can easily imagine restrictions that are clearly unnecessary from a secular perspective but that a particular religious outlook might require. For example, there can be no justification, from a secular perspective, for forbidding children to express the view that men and women are equal or to express skepticism about the literal truth of the Bible. Yet the school described in Chapter 7 does just that. And if the state promotes such treatment of children, by giving substantial financial assistance to such a school, then it violates the rights of students in those schools just as much as if state officials themselves treated children in that way. As the Supreme Court stated in *Norwood,* "a state may not induce, encourage or promote private persons to accomplish what it is constitutionally forbidden to accomplish."[6]

Interests in being treated with respect and in developing traits conducive to successful social relations, including tolerance and open-mindedness, are also extremely important. Schools that routinely denigrate children as sinful and worthless except insofar as they serve God, or that communicate to girls that they are inferior, less capable human beings, threaten children's basic sense of self worth and value. Self-esteem is a primary good; without a sense of self-worth, a person is greatly handicapped in developing and furthering a fulfilling life plan. The importance of self-esteem is reflected in the now universal recognition of emotional abuse in states' child protection laws. It is also essential, from a secular child welfare perspective, that children develop the ability to cooperate with and engage in respectful and rational dialogue with persons much different from themselves—in other words, the capacity and disposition for reasonableness.[7] Without that ability, a person will find it very difficult to realize higher ambitions in mainstream society. Being intolerant of persons with different worldviews and being dogmatic about one's own views severely limit the kinds of occupations one can pursue, the places one can peacefully live, one's effectiveness in the political arena, and one's ability to learn about and enjoy the larger world. Typically we bemoan intolerance and dogmatism only because of the harm they cause others, but this is just moral blindness. The intolerant and dogmatic person also suffers for his intolerance and dogmatism, even if he is not likely to complain about it, in part because of the internal states attendant upon such dispositions and in part because of the reciprocal hostility such a person is likely to incur. For children to develop the capacity and disposition for reasonableness requires, from an early age, practice in analytical, synthetic, and creative thinking, regular opportunity for expression of one's ideas, intellectual empowerment, exercises in active listening and dialogue, emphasis on understanding the point of view of others who think differently and being open to revising one's own beliefs if they prove less rationally justifiable that alternative beliefs, testing of students' ability to muster evidentiary support for a position and to distinguish good and bad arguments, and encouragement of curiosity and inquisitiveness.[8]

In sum, children have many fundamental interests at stake in connection with their education, and these are sufficient to generate rights to both a good secular education and to appropriate treatment by authority figures. Vouchers without attendant regulations violate those rights with respect to an unknown, but undoubtedly substantial, number of children, by facilitating and encouraging educational deprivation and maltreatment. With respect to existing voucher programs, then, there is a conflict of rights as between groups of children. Vouchers fulfill the rights of some—those who use them at a religious school that strives to provide a good secular education and to treat students with respect. But they violate the rights of others—those who use them at a religious school resembling the one described in Chapter 7. The proper resolution of this conflict is clear. States can effectuate the rights of all children by creating voucher programs but discriminating in awarding vouchers between private schools that are, from its perspective, good and those that are bad, just as it would discriminate between private providers of other services based on the quality of the service they provide.

Rights of Adults

If parents in general do not have a right to vouchers when vouchers would clearly benefit their children, as was true with the idealized voucher program, then they certainly do not have a right to vouchers when vouchers might well harm their children. So, too, with religious school teachers and citizens who support vouchers. Quite simply, no one is entitled to state support of the sort of anti-intellectual, sexist, racist indoctrinating that goes on in many religious schools, regardless of any incidental benefit such support might have for certain adults (e.g., higher salaries for teachers and preference satisfaction for parents and other religious community members). In fact, the negative externalities such schooling generates would support an additional *taxing* of the parents, religious leaders, and school administrators who propagate it.

There are undoubtedly some religious schools in the real world that resemble those that would qualify for the idealized voucher program, and many parents who wish to send their children to such schools. Their claim to be entitled to vouchers, though, is still no stronger in the real world context than Chapter 4 found it to be in the context of a well-designed program. In fact, their claim might even be weaker in the real world context, because in the existing regulatory regime *there is no mechanism* for them to *demonstrate* that the schools at which they would use vouchers do in fact serve the secular aims the state has set for children's education. They would be claiming a right that the state act on blind faith that their representations about their intentions and about the schools they would choose are accurate. That is not a compelling claim.

On the other hand, secularist citizens and taxpayers have an argument that existing programs violate a right of theirs that is stronger than such an argument in connection with a well-designed program. I concluded in Chapter 4 that individuals have a right against state action that substantially threatens their sense of belonging in the community or their intellectual freedom. I determined there that a properly designed voucher program would not pose such a threat, because it would be justifiable on secular grounds and could not reasonably be interpreted as state endorsement of religion. Existing programs, however, because they provide state funding to religious schools with no assurance that any of the money will be used to improve secular instruction, can reasonably be viewed as endorsement of religion and therefore as posing some threat to nonreligious persons' sense of belonging and equal citizenship. It is clear that existing programs do pay for religious instruction per se, even from the economic perspective endorsed in chapter 5, and it is likely that in some instances *all* that state funding is accomplishing is greater religious indoctrination. Thus, under existing programs, citizens are clearly being taxed to support religious indoctrination, and arguably they have a right not to be. This is not a right of such strength that it would necessarily override any other rights, such as a child's right to education. But in this context, too, there is no conflict between the right of taxpayer objectors and the rights of children, because children do not have a right to state support for any religious instruction they receive. Nor do any other adults have rights that conflict with this arguable right of taxpayer objectors not to be tithed. In the absence of competing rights, this right would itself be sufficient to invalidate existing voucher programs.

Conclusion

A rights-based theoretical analysis therefore yields the same conclusion reached by the utilitarian assessment in the first half of this chapter—that is, that current voucher plans in the real world are morally impermissible. This is contrary to the conclusion reached with respect to a voucher program that contains assurances that all participating schools provide a high-quality secular education and do not mistreat students and that voucher money supports only the secular component of participating schools' curriculum. The difference in outcome suggests that, from a moral standpoint, voucher plans in the real world can be "fixed" by adding provisions to the governing laws that would ensure that all recipient schools look more like the schools described in Chapter 3—that is, by adding robust requirements for the content of instruction and the treatment of children, and by limiting payments to religious schools to amounts matching the portion of their budgets dedicated to secular instruction.

[9]

Applying Constitutional Principles
to Vouchers in the Real World

As noted earlier, analyzing the constitutionality of vouchers solely by applying Supreme Court doctrine on aid to religious schools is futile and inappropriate. That doctrine has too little coherence and rationality to serve predictive or prescriptive purposes. In addition, it unjustifiably subordinates all competing considerations to antiestablishment values, and entirely ignores the interests and rights of the children whose education is at stake. For these reasons, I have eschewed doctrinal analysis in favor of an analysis that makes antiestablishment values just one consideration, secondary in importance to the fundamental interests and rights of the children whose education is at stake, including the rights of children embedded in other constitutional provisions such as the Fourteenth Amendment Equal Protection Clause. In the early chapters, the fact that antiestablishment values and children's rights were not of equal importance was inconsequential, since both supported the constitutionality of a well-designed voucher program. In this final chapter, I explore the implications of antiestablishment and equal protection values for existing voucher programs.

Permissibility under the Establishment Clause

In assessing the implications of antiestablishment values for vouchers, I looked in Chapter 5 to underlying First Amendment principles for guidance in developing the best rule for effectuating those values. I arrived at a position whereby states may provide financial or in-kind aid to religious institutions to support secular activities that generate secular benefits, but may not give such institutions assistance for their essentially religious activities. Thus states could provide vouchers to religious schools under the program I outlined because they ensured that all recipient schools primarily provided secular instruction in core areas; states simply had to limit the dollar value of the vouchers to reflect the portion of schools' operations devoted to secular education.

Existing voucher programs violate this principle simply because they do not tie the dollar value of vouchers to secular education. Under the Milwaukee and Florida programs, the state can pay the entire operating budget of religious schools, even if part of that budget is devoted to purely religious instruction. Under the Cleveland program, the state of Ohio can pay up to 90 percent of a religious school's operating budget, regardless of what portion of the school's budget is devoted to secular instruction. Existing programs provide no mechanism for state education departments to determine how much of a school's resources are devoted to secular education and to restrict funding to that amount. In fact, education departments do not monitor voucher schools sufficiently to determine whether they are providing *any* significant secular education, or are instead like the school I described in Chapter 7 and therefore not using the state money to serve the purported public purpose of the voucher programs. Thus, there is no way to "cure" the Establishment Clause problem within the parameters of existing programs; a change in the basic structure of the programs is necessary. Below I elaborate on specific problems presented by existing programs.

Inclusion of "Pervasively Sectarian" Schools

In the real world context, the term "pervasively sectarian" aptly characterizes many of the schools eligible for vouchers. The Establishment Clause certainly requires that the state treat schools of the sort described in Chapter 7 differently from the schools of the sort described in Chapter 3. A school that rejects the state's goal of providing a good secular education; that does not aim to foster higher-order cognitive skills, teach standard methods of inquiry in a variety of disciplines, or impart mainstream views in core subjects; that strives to confine children's minds so that they are never able to question or disagree with religiously orthodox views or leave the religious community; and that engages in numerous practices the state deems harmful to children, such as sexist and racist teaching, denying students intellectual freedom, confining students to individual workstations and permitting very little interaction with other students, instilling intolerant and dogmatic attitudes, and threatening children's self-esteem and psychological well-being with constant reminders of their sinfulness and admonitions about the tragic consequences of not conforming to religious precepts—such a school, quite simply, *must not receive financial support from our government*. There can be no secular purpose to doing so. An "as-applied" challenge to inclusion of particular schools of that sort in existing voucher programs will therefore necessarily succeed, even if the first-round facial challenges do not.

Moreover, even if the state could provide *some* funding for the Fundamentalist school described in Chapter 7, to support what little secular value it produces—e.g., fostering just the most basic skills and imparting just the most basic useful information in a few subject areas—the antiestablishment rule would require that the state provide much less to this school than it provides to the sort of religious school that would qualify under a well-designed program. The state might be justified in funding 90 percent of the operation of the school described in Chapter 3, but surely could not pay for 90 percent of the operating costs of this Fundamentalist school. It is not satisfactory under the Establishment Clause for the state to create a program of state aid that simply serves secular aims to some degree, if it also promotes religion to a substantial degree, at least where it is possible to do the former without doing the latter. For the same reason, existing programs should not be deemed consistent with antiestablishment strictures simply on the basis of a showing that there are more type A religious schools than there are type B religious schools. To the extent that the state can, with proper screening and oversight, distinguish between schools that are pervasively sectarian in the proper sense and schools that are more like a nonsectarian school, but with segregated religious components, the state *must* identify the pervasively sectarian schools and exclude them from the program. If the state *can* restrict its funding to the schools that serve its legitimate, secular aim, then it must.[1]

Defenders of religious schooling will object that this amounts to viewpoint discrimination, because the state would effectively be discriminating among schools based on the beliefs of the religious organizations that operate them. However, if one regards it as viewpoint discrimination any time the state prohibits private conduct it deems harmful to others, because some people want to engage in that conduct for religious reasons, then the state engages in viewpoint discrimination all the time in innumerable ways, and its doing so must be legitimate if we are to live by any common norms. For example, laws against discriminatory treatment of adults on the basis of gender (e.g., in universities and workplaces) constitute viewpoint discrimination in this same way, yet few would contend that such laws are illegitimate for that reason. In fact, for nearly every significant legal restriction on private conduct, including those less value-laden than laws against gender discrimination, there is likely to be someone somewhere whose personal beliefs conflict with it. Yet even laws designed largely to protect people from harming themselves (e.g., laws against drug use), which may conflict with the religious beliefs of many people, are generally regarded as legitimate. It is a peculiarity of debates about state regulation of child rearing that many people express fierce resistance to the idea of imposing majoritarian norms. From an objective standpoint, one would expect there to be greater opposition to imposing majoritarian norms regarding treatment of other adults, who are more capable of self-protection than are children, or regarding conduct affecting only oneself, than to norms regarding appropriate treatment of children.

Intermediate Cases and Hybrid Activities

The general rule for aid to religious institutions I have arrived at leaves open difficult questions about schools that lie between the two extremes, in terms of commitment to secular education and treatment of students; about particular activities in religious schools that have inseparable religious and secular dimensions; and about how the state can implement a voucher program true to the antiestablishment rule in the face of such diversity and complexity. I look first at activities that might be termed "hybrid" activities, as to which it is not possible to segregate religious and secular aspects. May the state fund essentially religious activities that have incidental, positive temporal consequences, or essentially secular activities that have a religious "flavor"?

An example of the former kind of activity in a nonschool setting might be administering Holy Communion to a crime victim who is Catholic. This might have the temporal consequence of advancing the psychological healing process for that person. Healing the psychological harms caused by crime is part of the good the state legitimately aims at in supporting services for crime victims. May the state therefore pay for Holy Communion? I suspect that even proponents of evenhanded funding would say this goes too far, and they would probably give at least the following two reasons: First, the impression of church-state unity or state endorsement of religion is just too strong when the state funds quintessentially religious activities such as administering Holy Communion, even if that impression is not entirely accurate (i.e., because the actual purpose of the funding is to induce the positive secular consequences). Second, there is too great a danger that the state will fabricate secular purposes in order to allow it to pursue an agenda of supporting religious practices. Coupled with the fact that religious service providers may have available alternative means of securing the secular good, and might receive state aid for pursuing those other means, these appear sufficient reasons for limiting state financial support to essentially secular activities. This would rule out state support for some components of religious schools' activities, particularly religious services and prayers, even if these generate some incidental secular benefits such as improved reading skills, which can be provided by other means.

An example of the second kind of hybrid, where an essentially secular activity has a religious flavor, would be a literature course incorporating study of literary texts that are of special importance to the sponsoring religious group.

Michael McConnell imagines a teacher in a religious school using *The Pilgrim's Progress* and George Herbert poems instead of *Studs Lonigan* and Emily Dickinson poems in a literature course.[2] One could also imagine the teacher of a civics class in a Catholic school discussing with students the extent to which their legal obligations converge with or diverge from their religious obligations as Catholics. McConnell argues that the state should be able to pay for hybrid instruction of these sorts, because the secular purpose to which the funding is aimed can still be accomplished, and taxpayers should be indifferent to whether some religious education is accomplished at the same time. McConnell couches his argument in economic terms, asking whether aid for that kind of instruction would constitute a subsidy for religion. He contends that the incidental religious dimension does not increase the costs to taxpayers or reduce the secular value received by the public from the instruction. Rather, it simply lowers the cost to the school of providing religious education, since some religious education is accomplished as an incident of secular education.

This is a legitimate way of looking at the situation,[3] and it might support a conclusion that aid for that portion of the curriculum is *permissible,* at least if one assumes that the secular education is still taking place—for example, that students in the literature course are being taught how to analyze and critique the texts they read, using the same standards they would apply to *Studs Lonigan* and Emily Dickinson, rather than reading works simply to receive the religious truths they impart. However, one could just as plausibly say that intermingling religious and secular instruction reduces the cost of *secular* instruction, because instruction in literature is accomplished as an incident of communicating religious content, which the religious organization would do anyway. One might then conclude that the state *may* elect *not* to pay for that portion of the curriculum, even though it pays for literature classes in other private schools.

In fact, one could argue that the state *must* not pay for such instruction, because there is no incremental secular value secured as a result of paying for that portion of the curriculum. And as the religious component comes to dominate the instruction, the latter view becomes more plausible. For example, if in the context of what is clearly a catechism class, the teacher throws in an occasional math problem (e.g., 7 mortal sins + 7 venial sins = ?), the instruction is still essentially religious, and the addition of a trivial amount of secular instruction should not authorize the state to pay for the class. Or if a school substantially distorts the content of what it teaches in state-mandated subjects to make it conform to religious beliefs, it is difficult to say that the religious dimension is merely incidental, because the secular essence of the course is eroded. In these instances, the instruction appears more like an essentially religious activity that incidentally produces modest positive secular consequences.

I will assume that the economic argument can support the conclusion that aid for portions of a religious school's instruction that intermingle secular and religious education is permissible so long as the secular component predominates. This would appear consistent with the notion that state aid should have the "primary effect" of furthering secular purposes, or in other words must directly promote secular ends and may support religion, if that is unavoidable, only incidentally. It might also be consistent with a proper balancing of the interests at stake, of the kind undertaken in Chapters 3 and 8. If aid supports an essentially religious activity that has only a slight and incidental secular benefit for students, it might be that the adverse effect on secularist citizens / taxpayers outweighs the positive effect on students.

However, even if the state may, as a general matter, pay for instruction in core subjects in religious schools, despite the fact that instruction has some incidental religious aspects to it, an additional problem arises if the religious aspects are, from the state's perspective, harmful to students or antithetical to the state's purposes. For example, a teacher might convey a math lesson to first graders by enumerating the sins each student committed the previous day and then multiplying the number of their sins by 100 to arrive at the number of years the student will spend burning in hell if he or she is not "saved." From a secular perspective, this would be harmful to children because of the likely psychological consequences—humiliation and terror. If something comparable were done in a nonreligious context, we would call it psychological abuse. State funding for a class like that has implications for the state's obligations to respect the equal personhood of children, and I discuss these implications in the second half of this chapter. But it also raises antiestablishment concerns, because the state cannot have a secular purpose for funding activities of religious institutions that the state believes generate more harm than good. And in calculating the harm, the state should take into account that its financial support can send a strong message of encouragement to school operators, and so could cause schools to intensify the harmful aspects of instruction.

In addition, even if a particular class or other activity in a religious school provides secular benefits that arguably outweigh the harm, the antiestablishment rule ideally would require, at a minimum, reducing the amount of funding for that activity to reflect the diminished secular value from inclusion of practices contrary to the state's secular aims. This would be true as well of the school as a whole; if the school has essentially religious activities that cause harm to children—for example, prayer or worship services that have the same sort of psychological effect as the math class described above—the state should, in theory, not only refuse to fund that activity, but also reduce the amount of aid it would otherwise provide for essentially secular activities, to reflect the fact that the religious activity detracts from the net secular value the school provides.

Chapter 9

This is all theoretical nicety, of course. Making such calculations would be virtually impossible in practice, and so I consider in the next section feasible means of implementing the theoretical conclusions.

Implementation

The foregoing analysis suggests the following refinement of the antiestablishment rule derived from the best interpretations of the no-aid and neutrality positions: As a general rule, the state *may* fund aspects of a private school that promote the kind of child development the state values—for example, development of critical cognitive skills and acquisition of core secular knowledge. This includes essentially secular instruction that has a religious flavor added to it. On the other hand, the state may *not* fund inherently religious activities such as a worship service or instruction that is essentially or predominantly religious. In addition, if essentially religious activities or religious aspects of essentially secular instruction in a school are harmful to children, then the state should reduce the amount of aid to that school to reflect the net secular value the school provides.

The approach I suggest might seem to require intensive investigation by state education officials into the activities of any school that applies for participation in a voucher program, with close scrutiny of each class offered, and continual monitoring of the content of instruction and interactions between adults in the school and students. That would create a great administrative burden for the state, and also raise concern that excessive state intrusion would hinder operation of private schools to the detriment of students, and that the state is making decisions as to what is religious and what is not. There may be an alternative way, however, for states to accomplish the necessary discrimination among schools.

To ensure that they are funding only secular education, states might create a voucher program that includes stringent academic criteria for participation, and put the burden on the schools to demonstrate that they satisfy the criteria, or for new participants that they have a plan in place to meet those criteria within a reasonable time. Such demonstration could be made on the basis of student performance on meaningful assessment tools.[4] States could act on the basis of a rough estimate of what portion of a school's operations would, as a matter of practical necessity, have to be essentially secular in order for the school to satisfy certain standards of education outcomes. In other words, a state could assume that any school able to demonstrate that its students are advancing steadily in developing critical cognitive skills, learning methods of investigation in different disciplines, and acquiring core knowledge in a variety of secular subjects must be devoting most of its resources (say, for example, 80 percent) to essentially secular instruction. Without such a commitment to

[204]

secular learning, a school could not possibly meet the state's standards.[5] States could then limit the amount of vouchers for all religious schools to 80 percent of operating costs. Courts reviewing the constitutionality of voucher programs could accept from a state a reasonable estimate of what portion of a school's operating budget must be devoted to secular instruction in order to satisfy the state's performance standards, and would need only to scrutinize a state's performance standards to determine whether they are sufficiently demanding to support the state's estimate. This would avoid the intensive scrutiny that no one wants to do or have done to them.

Setting academic standards does not, however, enable the state to respond properly to harmful practices; it does not necessarily capture, for example, psychological harms children might incur in some schools. Some investigation and monitoring of voucher schools would therefore be unavoidable. This might be done, however, by relatively unobtrusive means. For example, it might suffice to require, as a condition for participation in the voucher program, that schools sign a pledge to avoid certain practices and distribute to all parents a mission statement that expresses a commitment to avoiding those practices. The state might also create a mechanism for violations to be reported by anyone who observes them, and impose financial penalties on schools found to have violated the pledge. As discussed in Chapter 5, such oversight of religious schools should not be regarded as an "excessive entanglement" of the state in the affairs of religious institutions, and so should not pose an obstacle to creating a voucher program.

Equal Protection Principles

The fact that states know so little about religious schools within their borders has not kept parents from claiming that states have an obligation to fund religious schools, as a matter of parents' right to equal treatment. In this final part of the book, I assess the viability of that claim. I also assess whether an equal treatment claim on behalf of children in religious schools has the same force in the real world as it had in relation to a well-designed voucher program.

Equal Treatment of Parents

An equal protection claim on behalf of parents is even weaker in connection with voucher programs of the type actually in place than it was in relation to the idealized program. In the latter case, the claim had some superficial appeal for parents who chose schools that would qualify, because those schools provided the same public good to which state education funding is directed. Even in that context, however, I concluded that a parental equal protection claim must fail, because the state would treat all parents equally by offering them all the benefit of a public school education. Any parents' failure to receive benefits from the state would therefore result from their voluntary choice to forgo that benefit in favor of a private alternative. In addition, there are legitimate reasons for the state's funding only schools it operates or for funding only private schools that most closely resemble public schools, and no right of parents precludes the state from acting on the basis of those reasons.

An equal treatment claim on behalf of parents against funding only public schools has not even superficial appeal under current circumstances. States have no reason to believe any religious schools that might claim vouchers provide, or even strive to provide, the secular good that state education funding is intended to generate—that is, a good secular education. The states oversee public schools (albeit imperfectly), and so a mechanism is in place for ensuring that those schools are striving to provide that good, but they do not oversee private schools at all. So parents cannot even claim that the state is refusing to fund a private analogue to a publicly provided service, because the state does not have the information it would need to determine whether a private institution is actually providing an analogous service.

Some might think a parental equal protection claim is actually made stronger by the great difference between public schools and many religious schools with respect to the content of instruction, because this means that privileging public schooling has potentially greater consequences for children's belief formation. Many parents, because of their personal beliefs, religious or otherwise, reject mainstream views in core subject areas—for example, in science, history, and social studies—and reject the secular aims of fostering critical and analytical thinking and creativity. And they want to prevent their children from adopting mainstream views or becoming critical thinkers. They can accomplish their overriding aims only in a religious school, and so are harmed more by state policies making it difficult for them to send their children to a religious school, than are parents who value secular liberal education.

The fact that some private alternatives are radically different from a public program, does not however, get the fairness claim past the difficulties identified in Chapter 6. The state does not incur a greater moral obligation to fund private analogues to public services—such as police protection, welfare benefits, and museums—the less the private analogue resembles the public agency. And persons do not become less responsible for their personal choices when they have views more radically divergent from the mainstream. This is even more true when the more radically different service a person chooses is not for himself but for another person under his care.

The only way those who advance this sort of fairness claim in the real world can get any purchase for it is by asserting that parents have a fundamental right at stake. In effect, they assert that parents have a right to substitute for their children what from the state's perspective is a *noneducation,* and to receive state financial support for doing so. As explained in Chapter 6, such an entitlement has no basis in legal doctrine or in the principle of equal personhood. The law and widely held moral beliefs support the right of individuals to refuse public services *for themselves* if they object to the values and beliefs reflected in the nature of the services. The state must confer that self-determining right equally on all autonomous persons. Even in cases of self-determination, though, the state has no obligation to fund a private alternative. In addition, established general principles of law and morality do not support a right to decide that *someone else* will not receive a certain state-guaranteed benefit. As such, they certainly cannot support a right to state financial support for a decision to deny someone else what the state believes to be an important benefit or for doing to someone else what the state believes to be harmful. It is bad enough that we permit parents to deny their children a good secular education; it is ridiculous for parents to assert that they are entitled to state support in doing so.

All that said, there should be a mechanism for parents and other concerned private parties to challenge in a neutral forum the state's judgment as to what sort of education children should receive. If the state's judgment is mistaken, in terms of the kinds of interests the state can permissibly assume children to have (i.e., temporal interests), then it is best for children that the state's judgment be susceptible to review by the courts or an adequate administrative tribunal, and that their parents be among those authorized to trigger such review. Such a challenge to the state's judgment, though, would be in the nature of a claim that the state misused its power to decide these matters, rather than a fairness-to-parents claim.

Equal Treatment of Children

We come finally to the question whether existing voucher programs are consistent with a proper respect for the equal personhood of all children. I concluded in Chapter 6, that children's equal personhood requires that children attending religious schools receive a fair share of state funding for education, under a properly designed voucher program. This conclusion rested in large part on the fact that those children are not responsible for their being in a religious school rather than a public school or nonsectarian private school. They have not chosen to forgo a public school education and should not bear the cost of their parents' choices. One might think existing voucher programs likewise justifiable because they fulfill the equal protection right of children in religious schools to receive a fair share of education spending.

Receiving a share of state education spending was, however, just a means to the real benefit to which children in religious schools are entitled. The real benefit the state aims to secure for children in public schools by funding their schooling is a good secular education. And *that* is the benefit to which children in religious schools are also entitled. Children in religious schools are entitled to a share of funding only derivatively, to the extent this will facilitate their receiving the ultimate benefit of a good secular education. If funding will not promote their secular education, then respect for their equal personhood does not require that they receive it. Children do not benefit simply by third parties' receiving money from the state to be used in connection with their upbringing, irrespective of how the third parties will use the money. Children in religious schools benefit from vouchers only if their schools use the additional resources to enhance the secular curriculum.

Assume again the role of legislator. You look out on society, perceive the critical importance to all children of a good secular education, and are troubled by the fact that your state strives to ensure that only some children, not all, receive such an education. You are also troubled by the fact that the state is failing in some places in its efforts to ensure children in public schools a good education, and you commit to devoting whatever resources and enacting whatever reforms are necessary to achieve success in those schools. But your concern is not limited to those children whose parents have chosen (or been financially constrained) to accept a state-provided education. You believe you have an obligation to all children, wherever they might be receiving their schooling, to provide whatever state assistance is needed to ensure them a good secular education. You are very receptive, then, to parents and religious leaders who come to you and ask for a share of state education funding, not because you feel any obligation to them, but because you feel an obligation to the children under their care.

You face a dilemma, however. You have no idea how private schools would use state funding if you provided it. You assume it must be the case that *some* of them would put it to precisely the purpose that would motivate you to provide it—that is, to enhancing the secular instruction they provide. But you have no idea of which schools this is true, or of how many schools it is true. You might conclude that it is permissible for your state to provide the funding to all takers, since this would likely benefit many children and effectuate their right to equal treatment. And if funding would have no effect on other children, but rather just constitute waste as far as the state is concerned, then you might be right. You would still owe an obligation to those other children, to *somehow* secure for them the same benefit of a good secular education, but the fact that a particular measure will not fulfill your obligation to all children should not prevent you from taking that measure in order to fulfill your obligation to some.

The problem though, is that the effect of funding on schools that would not use it to provide a better secular education is not entirely benign. It is not simply a waste; it is in many cases counterproductive. Some religious schools not only fail to provide a good secular education, but in fact provide what from the state's perspective is anti-education, and they inflict on children what from the state's perspective are harms. If those schools receive state funding, they are likely to use it to intensify their anti-educational and harm-causing efforts, and so to make the children who attend them *worse off*. In making vouchers available without regard to the character of recipient schools, therefore, you would be benefiting some children, effectively according them equal treatment, but harming others and exacerbating the offense to their equal personhood. Surely the children in those schools have a right that you not do that, a right that you not subsidize and implicitly encourage their parents and schools in thwarting their intellectual development and in assaulting their personality and well-being. You have a duty to the children in the Fundamentalist school I described in Chapter 7, at the very minimum, to refrain from reinforcing and perpetuating the kind of instruction and treatment they are receiving.

The clearest case for this conclusion, at least for those familiar with constitutional law, is with respect to sexist teaching and treatment in Fundamentalist schools, because of existing doctrine concerning state support for invidious discrimination. These schools are unapologetic about imposing on children their conviction that women are not equal to men, that "sexual equality denies God's word."[6] They explicitly instruct girls that their role in life is to serve men and that they should not develop ambitions for any role in life other than that of wife and mother. They are preparing girls for lives of subordination, denying them equality of opportunity in education and in life, and shaping their self-conception so that they see themselves as inferior and less competent. Thirteen years of this treatment is undoubtedly much more harmful to the girls in these schools than denying admission is to a child of minority race. Surely, if the Equal Protection Clause prohibits states from lending textbooks to schools that have racially discriminatory admissions policies, it also prohibits states from paying the entire operating budget of schools that engage in sexist teaching and sexist treatment of female students.[7] It is just a matter of time before someone files suit to extend the *Norwood* holding, which prohibited aid to racist schools, to also prohibit aid to sexist schools.

This analysis suggests that the state may not allow *any* amount of state funds to be used at schools that engage in practices it deems significantly harmful, and so must exclude such schools from a voucher program entirely, to avoid exacerbating the harm and to send a message of disapproval to the school. I would add one qualification, however. The state's ultimate aims are for every child to receive a good secular education and for all schools to eliminate harmful practices. Denying aid to any school that is any respect sexist or overly authoritarian would mean sacrificing the first aim to serve the second. It would certainly be preferable to use vouchers to advance both aims if possible. And this would be possible if states were to require, not that schools be completely sanitized of all practices the states deem harmful before they can receive any aid (which would make funding of many public schools problematic), but rather simply that schools demonstrate a commitment to eradicating such practices in order to receive vouchers. In other words, the state could, and should, condition aid to private schools on their providing a good secular education and on their being committed to eradicating any practices that are, from a secular perspective, inimical to children's welfare. Schools could demonstrate such a commitment by expressing it in their mission statement and making all parents aware of it, having their teachers go through a program that trains them to avoid those practices, and revising their curricular materials to eliminate sexist and other harmful messages. For a majority of schools, this should be unproblematic; many Catholic educators, for example, have recognized the problem of sexism in Catholic schools in the past and have expressed an intention to eliminate it.

The prospect of the state's conditioning aid in this way will trouble some people, because it suggests the state may use the awesome power of its purse to coerce belief and to impose majoritarian, secular norms and views of child welfare on everyone. The concern is misplaced. First, once again, we are discussing state *funding* for private activities, not universal prohibitions imposed regardless of aid received. If the state is going to fund a particular private activity, it must have a legitimate purpose in doing so. It cannot have such a purpose if state officials are confident in *their* judgment, as state actors, that the activity is harmful. The state cannot say: "We believe X is harmful to children, and for that reason prohibit it in public schools, but some private individuals think X is good and for that reason it is all right for us to pay for X." Second, the state will not be prohibiting any adults from believing whatever they want; it will simply be prohibiting all adults from causing certain harms to children through any form of instruction, religious or nonreligious, that the state subsidizes.

Your obligation as legislator should therefore be clear. You may not allow vouchers to be used at a school of the kind described in Chapter 7. At the same time, you have an obligation to advance the secular education of children in religious schools. To fulfill both of these obligations, you must attach stringent regulations to state aid to religious schools. You must ensure that vouchers go only to schools that will use them to improve their secular education and that are demonstrably committed to eliminating sexist and other harmful practices. In doing so, you will create a strong incentive for all religious schools to become more like the school described in Chapter 3. You will therefore benefit a great number of children in religious schools while harming none. You will still have an unfulfilled obligation to children in schools that refuse state aid because they are unwilling to conform to state standards for education and treatment of children, an obligation that ultimately can be fulfilled only by imposing regulations on them involuntarily or shutting them down. But that unfulfilled obligation should not prevent you from acting now to benefit the children you can by using vouchers with the necessary strings attached.

Conclusion

Reorienting our moral compass to focus first and foremost on the developmental needs of all children points us in a new policy and legal direction in the voucher context, as it would in many other areas of child-rearing law and policy. Here it has led to a conclusion that will strike many as counterintuitive and most will find hard to accept—namely, that states have a moral and constitutional obligation to children already in private schools to establish a voucher program that includes religious schools but that restricts participation to schools that comply with robust regulations regarding academic quality and treatment of students. From an adult-centered perspective, this conclusion makes little sense. The challenge I hope this book has sufficiently laid down, for those instinctively inclined to disagree with the outcome, is either to demonstrate that a child-centered approach to state child-rearing policy is not the correct approach or to show that I have misapplied such an approach.

I have considered a number of theoretical and constitutional objections along the way, but have not said much about practical issues of implementation. As noted in the Introduction, questions of implementation are best left to persons with expertise in administering schools and delivering education to children. I will address here just a few of the concerns that would likely arise. First, there is the concern that once a voucher program of the sort I propose is in place, and after public attention has waned, opponents of regulation will amass their tremendous political influence to get new legislation passed that weakens or eliminates the conditions I have argued must be attached to a voucher program. One might also think I have placed too much faith in the commitment and ability of legislators and state education departments to get it right in the first place, let alone to stand up to intense lobbying efforts by the religious right in the long run. These are, after all, the same people who created the current systems of public school governance and of unregulated private schooling, and the same people responsible for the destructive obsession with standardized tests.

There is much validity to these concerns. However, I do not believe them sufficient to justify abandoning the idea of a well-designed voucher program. First, a voucher program is necessarily bounded by federal (and generally state as well) constitutional restrictions. The courts, and private organizations and individuals motivated to challenge voucher programs, can therefore play a much stronger policing function than they can in the context of public school improvement. Were legislators or state departments of education to whittle away at the regulations attached to vouchers, they could expect quickly to be hauled into court by the same groups that have been advancing legal challenges to existing voucher programs.

Second, children deserve better than for us to shrug our shoulders and abandon ideas to improve their education at the first sign of difficulty. It is not good enough to say X might be a problem and therefore there is no point in trying. The alternative is simply continuing to abandon large numbers of children now in religious schools, and we should make every effort to avoid that. Being child centered means that we should think seriously about the likelihood of a problem and what steps might be taken to avoid it, and then, if it appears inevitable, that we think first about whether and how it will affect the children, and whether any unavoidable costs for them exceed the benefits. Only after we determine whether the program would still be good for children, taking into account practical difficulties, should we adults worry about how the difficulties affect our own interests. And we should presume, until proven otherwise, that the effects on us are less important than are the benefits the program would create for children.

From the other side there will be objections about interference by state bureaucracies in market experiments. Why not let states go forward with programs that leave maximum freedom for private actors, and see what develops? We have had some good results with charter schools by reducing regulation, which suggests that states get the best results when they get out of the way. For several reasons, this objection is unconvincing. First, children are not rats in a laboratory. Experimentation is a wonderful thing in the abstract, but it is not so wonderful when in practice the failures harm persons' fundamental interests. Those who tout it are those who look at national test score averages to determine whether all is well, who are content if the next generation as a whole is not doing so badly, not caring whether any particular individual child is receiving a good education. While there have been successes with charter schools, there have also been failures and abuses, and states have had to shut some down.[1] This has been true of the Milwaukee and Cleveland voucher programs as well.[2] Is anyone concerned about what the effects of those failures were on the children placed in the schools? When experiments are made with children's education, they must be carefully controlled to make sure no children suffer substantially when mistakes are made, as they inevitably will be. That means regulation and oversight.

Second, and relatedly, consumer choices cannot play the same role in private schooling as they play in markets for goods like cars or beer, in which the purchaser is the consumer and the test of quality is principally whether the consumer likes the product. In the schooling context, the purchaser and the consumer are two different people, and a unity of interests between the two parties should not be assumed. When religious schools are thrown into the mix, which is true of voucher programs but (so far) not charter school programs, there is the problem that a substantial percentage of purchasers (parents) operate on the basis of purchasing criteria that are very different from, and in fact are diametrically opposed to, the general criteria that characterize the good that the state—whose decision to subsidize purchases is at issue—is necessarily seeking to promote for the consumers of the good (children). (In contrast, this is not true of the market for cars; no one goes looking for a car that the wheels will fall off of.)

Moreover, in the market for schools, there is, even with respect to purchasers who have the same ultimate good in mind that the state does, the problem that the good being purchased is a very complex one that few purchasers know much about. (This is true to a lesser extent of cars, and helps explain why so many poor-quality cars continue to be manufactured.) Most parents, if they investigate schools in advance at all, rely principally or solely on standardized test scores, not knowing what those scores signify or that high scores might actually be indicative of a bad education, because schools are jettisoning good education in favor of teaching children how to take multiple choice tests.

Finally, a well-designed voucher program need not entail micromanaging schools. The program I outlined in Chapter 3 identified general aims, and I have suggested that satisfaction of academic aims could be gauged primarily, if not exclusively, by appropriate testing instruments. Determining compliance with general guidelines for treatment of students might require some on-site monitoring, but might instead be accomplished sufficiently simply by requiring express commitments to compliance in schools' mission statements and by creating mechanisms for reporting of problems. Within the parameters set by the general aims and guidelines, private schools would remain free to pursue different strategies for accomplishing academic goals, to experiment with different approaches to the secular curriculum, to critique mainstream views in any subject area, and to enforce rules of decorum and respect for others. For many schools, including many religious schools, substantial change in policies and practices would not be required. And, of course, a voucher program of this nature would not diminish parents' freedom to teach and practice their faith with their children in the great majority of children's time that is spent outside of school.

That said, a well-designed voucher program has the potential to dramatically alter the private school landscape and to change schooling as a whole in our society. Such a program would likely move many existing schools in a liberal direction—that is, toward greater emphasis on intellectual autonomy and on preparing our youth to pursue a wide range of careers and ways of life in a diverse society. It would also cause many new liberal private schools to come into existence. Most parents, I think, would find this type of school perfectly acceptable, and many would find it preferable to a public school in which religious instruction and worship are entirely absent. Schools of this kind might draw many students away from the more pervasively sectarian and oppressive religious schools, which would not be eligible for vouchers. We would then move toward a dual system of public and private schooling where the alternatives would not be as far apart as they now are. From an adult-centered perspective, this might sound like a bad thing. From a child-centered perspective, it would be a good thing. Joseph Viteritti writes of public school choice programs:

> As far as the market is concerned, if choice is to function as an instrument to improve the educational product available to the public, then it must include a mechanism to replace under-achieving institutions with new ones that are more responsive to students' needs. Protecting failing schools is counterproductive.[3]

This statement applies equally to choice among the full range of schooling options, public and private. A well-designed voucher program would be such a mechanism. Current voucher programs are just the opposite; they protect failing private schools by giving financial support to any and all schools that care to claim it, while demanding nothing in return.

The great promise of school vouchers is that they provide a mechanism for accomplishing what some states once tried to do but ultimately found required more effort and resolve than they were willing to expend—namely, to rein in the practices of the worst religious schools, whose operators and parent clients vehemently and forcefully resist involuntary imposition of regulations.[4] A well-designed voucher program should not lead to the same sort of violent stand-offs; it would not require state officials to padlock doors or to jail parents. States would instead need only to refrain from writing a check to any school that does not meet proper standards. Such schools might then close by force of market rather than force of state, as parents take their children to another school where they can use vouchers. Many children would thereby have their educational interests protected without serious disruption in their family life. And states would then need to worry only about those children whose parents cannot be induced by financial incentives to accept an education for them that is within acceptable bounds. Those children, too, should not be forgotten, but until we figure out a way to reach all children, we should at least take this step of reaching more than we do now.

Notes

Introduction

1. *Boy Scouts of America v. Dale*, 530 U.S. 640 (2000).

2. Several professors of education at the University of Wisconsin reached this conclusion from observing the political maneuvering surrounding the Milwaukee program. See Alex Molnar, Walter C. Farrell Jr., James H. Johnson Jr., and Marty Sapp, "Research, Politics, and the School Choice Agenda," *Phi Delta Kappan* (November 1996): 240–43.

3. Milton Friedman, "On School Vouchers," *St. Croix Review* 32 (1999): 24.

4. For a description of the horrendous circumstances great numbers of children live in, see Jonathan Kozol, *Amazing Grace: The Lives of Children and the Conscience of a Nation* (New York, 1996). For examples of studies quantifying the effects of poverty on children's development, see Greg J. Duncan and Jeanne Brooks-Gunn, eds., *Consequences of Growing Up Poor* (New York, 1999).

5. See Joseph P. Viteritti, *Choosing Equality: School Choice, the Constitution, and Civil Society* (Washington, D.C., 1999), 5 ("Respected research on both public and private choice programs suggests that parents who take advantage of school choice tend to be better educated and more astute than those who do not").

6. I have elsewhere challenged the treatment of this authority by courts and commentators as an entitlement *of parents*. See James G. Dwyer, "Parents' Religion and Children's Welfare: Debunking the Doctrine of Parents' Rights," *California Law Review* 82 (1994): 1371–1447. However, this aspect of parental authority—that is, the authority simply to choose a nonpublic school from among available alternatives—is also justifiable on the basis of the interests and rights of children. The interests and rights of children do require that the range of available alternatives be more constricted than it is at present, and the analysis below considers what the implications for vouchers would be of taking that step. But children's interests do not require eliminating the option of private schooling. In any event, I treat the basic authority of parents to choose a private school for their children as a "fixed point" in the discussion below, because it is now an immutable feature of our legal and political culture. See *Committee for Public Education & Religious Liberty v. Nyquist*, 413 U.S. 756, 788 (1973) (recognizing that a state cannot prevent a parent from sending a child to a religious school); *Pierce v. Society of Sisters*, 268 U.S. 510 (1925) (holding that a state may not mandate that all children attend a public school rather than a private school).

7. It is important to distinguish between a secular education and a secularist education. The former entails fostering in children fundamental cognitive skills, such as critical and creative thinking and basic scientific methods, and imparting prevailing secular views in core subjects such as history and math. Members of some religious groups might regard that sort of education as a threat to their children's remaining true believers, but a secular education does not aim to instill in children any normative judgments about religion in general or about a particular religion, for or against. Its aim is rather to prepare children for a self-determined life within a broad range of life possibilities, and any effect on religious faith is incidental. A secularist education, in contrast, would be one that took direct aim at religious belief in general and attempted to persuade students that all religious beliefs are false or irrational and should be rejected. No reputable scholars of education law or constitutional law, and no state education officials, advocate for a secularist education.

8. See Scott Stephens and Mark Vosburgh, "Voucher School Relies on Videos as Teachers," *Cleveland Plain Dealer,* July 10, 1999, 1A. The state superintendent apparently learned about this situation only through the newspaper report. She ultimately decided that this school would no longer be eligible for vouchers, but not because of the nature of the instruction. Rather, she discovered that the school also lacked criminal background checks for its staff, a fire certificate, and environmental and health certificates, and failed to have files for all its students on school premises, and based her decision to expel the school from the program on those noncurricular deficiencies. See In the Matter of the Superintendent of Public Instruction's Intent to Revoke Registration of the Golden Christian Academy from Participation in the Cleveland Scholarship and Tutoring Program, (Decision of Ohio Superintendent of Public Instruction) September 28, 1999.

9. For a summary of this literature, see James G. Dwyer, *Religious Schools v. Children's Rights* (Ithaca, 1998), chap. 1.

10. Ibid.

Chapter 1. Vouchers and Adult-Centered Legal Reasoning

1. I include in the term "voucher" checks made out to parents that must be presented at a private school, tuition reimbursements, and direct state payments to private schools to cover all or part of the cost of educating particular individual children. Some states also assist parents in paying for private schooling by granting tuition tax credits or deductions. Analysis of such tax measures would differ in certain respects from analysis of vouchers.

2. The current program operates pursuant to state statute, Wis. Stat. § 119.23 (2001), and regulations of the Wisconsin Department of Public Instruction, Wis. Admin. Code, chap. PI 35 (2001). The quoted passage appears in the statute.

3. The Cleveland program operates pursuant to state statute, Ohio Revised Code §§ 3313.974–3313.979 (2001).

4. The Florida program operates pursuant to state statute, Fla. Statutes § 229.0537 (2001).

5. See James G. Dwyer, "School Vouchers: Inviting the Public into the Religious Square," *William and Mary Law Review* 42 (2001): 964.

6. See, e.g., L.B. 483, 1999 Regular Leg. Sess. (Neb. 1999); H.B. 5, 21st Leg. (Alaska 1999); H.B. 701, 156th Leg. Sess. (N.H. 1999); S.B. 866, 1999 Leg. Sess. (Va. 1999). The reimbursement these plans would provide for home school parents might actually exceed the monetary amount these parents pay for schooling expenses, because the amount would be determined by applying some percentage to the amount provided for regular private schools or to the state's per pupil expenditures in public schools. See, e.g., L.B. 483, 1999 Regular Leg. Sess. (Neb. 1999), sec. 5(2) (reimbursement for home-schooled children to be 50 percent of the per pupil expenditure for public schools). State support above and beyond parents' monetary outlays could be construed, however, as reimbursement for parents' labor expenses. I do not discuss home schools in this book.

7. 403 U.S. 602, 612–13 (1971).

8. See *Agostini v. Felton,* 521 U.S. 203, 234 (1997). See also *Mitchell v. Helms,* 120 S.Ct. 2530, 2540 (2000).

9. For an explication of the notion of lexical priority, see John Rawls, *A Theory of Justice* (Cambridge, Mass., 1971), 42–45.

10. The Supreme Court has on occasion suggested a kind of balancing, as have some commentators, but typically a balancing against just the free exercise rights of parents, not against state interest in meeting the educational needs of children. See, e.g., *Everson v. Board of Education,* 330 U.S. 1, 16 (1947); Joseph P. Viteritti, "Choosing Equality: Religious Freedom and Educational Opportunity under Constitutional Federalism," *Yale Law and Policy Review* 15 (1996): 142 (contending that parental religious freedom interests should outweigh Establishment Clause concerns in the context of aid to religious schools).

11. Strout v. Commissioner, Maine Department of Education, 13 F.Supp.2d 112, 114 (D.Me. 1998).

12. 178 F.3d 57 (1st Cir. 1999), *cert. denied,* 120 S.Ct. 329 (1999).

13. 728 A.2d 127 (Me. 1999), *cert. denied* 120 S.Ct. 364 (1999).

14. 641 A.2d 352 (1994).

15. 738 A.2d 539 (1999), *cert. denied* 120 S.Ct. 626 (1999).

16. 878 F.Supp. 1209, 1211 (E.D. Wis. 1995).

17. See *Jackson v. Benson,* 578 N.W.2d 602, 609 (Wis.), *cert. denied,* 119 S.Ct. 466 (1998).

18. *Goff v. Harris,* 1996 WL 466499 (Ct. Comm. Pleas 1996), °8.

19. *Simmons-Harris v. Goff,* 1997 WL 217583 (Ohio App. 10 Dist. 1997), °4.

20. *Simmons-Harris v. Goff,* 711 N.E.2d 203, 208 (1999).

21. *Simmons-Harris v. Zelman,* 72 F.Supp.2d 834 (N.D. Ohio 1999).

22. Id. at 843 (quoting Jefferson's *Statute of Religious Liberty*).

23. Id. at 842 (quoting Madison's *Memorial and Remonstrance,* June 20, 1785).

24. 234 F.3d 945 (6th Cir. 2000) (request for rehearing en banc denied).

25. *Holmes v. Bush,* 2000 WL 526364 °1 (Fla. Cir. Ct. 2000).

26. 767 So.2d 668 (Ct. App. Fla. 2000).

27. See, e.g., Clint Bolick, "Blocking the Exits," *Policy Review* 89 (June 1, 1998): 42 (arguing that opposition to school vouchers is an attack on parental freedom); Viteritti, "Choosing Equality," 117 (arguing that exclusion of religious schools from voucher programs "places an unfair burden on poor parents who desire to incorporate religious values into the education of their children or who seek to improve their educational opportunities beyond those available in public schools"); Joseph Spoerl, "Justice and the Case for School Vouchers," *Public Affairs Quarterly* 9, no. 1 (1995): 75 (arguing that state funding only for public schools unfairly restricts parental freedom).

28. See, e.g., Steffen N. Johnson, "A Civil Libertarian Case for the Constitutionality of School Choice," *George Mason University Civil Rights Law Journal* 10 (2000): 42 ("it must be remembered that religious schools, like their secular counterparts, are already subject to a host of state regulations even in the absence of state aid"); Michael A. Vaccari, "Public Purpose and the Public Funding of Sectarian Education Institutions: A More Rational Approach after *Rosenberger* and *Agostini,*" *Marquette Law Review* 82 (1998): 8 ("[t]he overall success of the sectarian schools and the inadequacy of many public schools have given rise to a movement for parental choice in education," religious schools "serve community and nation by performing essential secular educational functions"); Stephen L. Carter, "Parents, Religion, and Schools: Reflections on *Pierce,* Seventy Years Later," *Seton Hall Law Review* 27 (1997): 1218; Michael W. McConnell and Richard A. Posner, "An Economic Approach to Issues of Religious Freedom," *University of Chicago Law Review* 56 (1989): 17 ("The positive externalities arising from elementary and secondary education are created by a 'core curriculum' of training in basic skills plus education in the responsibilities of citizenship. These elements are required under state law as a condition for school certification whether the school is public or private, secular or parochial") (no citations omitted); Eric J. Segall, "Parochial School Aid Revisited: The Lemon Test, the Endorsement Test, and Religious Liberty," *San Diego Law Review* 28 (1991): 297–98. But see Eric A. Posner, "The Legal Regulation of Religious Groups," *Legal Theory*

2 (1996): 54 ("Religious organizations that fund private schools may absorb the subsidy without increasing the supply of education; and they may inculcate students with norms and skills that do not serve the state's interests").

29. Examples of this position among legal scholars include Marci Hamilton, "Power, the Establishment Clause, and Vouchers," *Connecticut Law Review* 31 (1999): 807, and Kathleen M. Sullivan, "Parades, Public Squares, and Voucher Payments: Problems of Government Neutrality," *Connecticut Law Review* 28 (1996): 258 (concluding solely from the fact that some observers might perceive vouchers as government endorsement of religion that vouchers must therefore be impermissible). Examples among public policy writers include Edd Doerr, Albert J. Menendez, and John Swormley, *The Case against School Vouchers* (Amherst, N.Y., 1996); Barry Lynn, "Religious School Vouchers Are the Wrong Answer," in *Democracy in America: Private Schools/Public Money*, CNN.com>in-depth specials, http://www.cnn.com (visited 9/19/2000); and numerous articles and press releases by Americans United For Separation of Church and State, available at http://www.au.org, and by People For the American Way, available at http://www.pfaw.org. Professor Hamilton in fact conceptualizes the voucher issue in terms of balancing the power of different segments of society. See Hamilton (arguing that Establishment Clause cases should be decided based on a pragmatic assessment of whether a particular measure will unduly tip the balance of power between state and religion, and contending that vouchers would unduly tip the balance of power in favor of religion).

30. See, e.g., Marci A. Hamilton, "Free? Exercise," *William and Mary Law Review* 42 (2001): 823–81; Jesse H. Choper, *Securing Religious Liberty: Principles for Judicial Interpretation of the Religion Clauses* (Chicago, 1995): 16–17; Lisa H. Thurau-Gray, "Trojan Ponies: Undermining the Establishment Clause in the Name of 'Child Benefit Theory,'" *Journal of Law and Education* 27 (1998): 435; Steven K. Green, "The Legal Argument against Private School Choice," *University of Cincinnati Law Review* 62 (1993): 44.

31. For a fuller description of this distinction between the roles of the religious clauses, see Ira C. Lupu, "Reconstructing the Establishment Clause: The Case against Discretionary Accommodation of Religion," *University of Pennsylvania Law Review* 140 (1991): 558–80.

32. 494 U.S. 872 (1990).

33. Indeed, at one time the courts wrestled with the question whether they should even confer standing on individuals to challenge in court violations of the Establishment Clause. The Supreme Court ultimately decided that it would, carving out an exception to the general rule that individuals have no standing qua taxpayer or citizen to challenge government spending contrary to constitutional limitations. See *Flast v. Cohen*, 392 U.S. 83 (1968).

Chapter 2. Education Reform and Adult-Centered Political Theory

1. See Will Kymlicka and Wayne Norman, "Return of the Citizen: A Survey of Recent Work on Citizenship Theory," *Ethics* 104 (1994): 352–81, 352.

2. Ibid., 352–53.

3. Eamonn Callan, *Creating Citizens: Political Education and Liberal Democracy* (Oxford, 1997), 9.

4. Amy Gutmann, *Democratic Education* (Princeton, 1989), 14.

5. Ibid., 13–14, 25–27, 38.

6. Ibid., 14. See also ibid., 26–27, 36–37, 38.

7. Ibid., 12 ("We can do better to try instead to find the fairest ways for reconciling our disagreements").

8. Ibid., 27.

9. Ibid.

10. Examples of recent work include Amy Gutmann, "Civic Minimalism, Cosmopolitanism, and Patriotism: Where Does Democratic Education Stand in Relation to Each?" in *NOMOS XLIII: Moral*

and Political Education, eds. Stephen Macedo and Yael Tamir (forthcoming); Gutmann's new epilogue in a new edition of *Democratic Education* (Princeton, 1999); Callan, *Creating Citizens,* and Stephen Macedo, *Diversity and Distrust: Civic Education in a Multicultural Democracy* (Cambridge, Mass., 2000).

11. Gutmann, "Civic Minimalism."

12. Gutmann, *Democratic Education* (1999), xii.

13. Gutmann "Civic Minimalism." See also Gutmann, *Democratic Education* (1999), xii.

14. Gutmann, "Civic Minimalism." Gutmann, *Democratic Education* (1999), 294.

15. Gutmann, *Democratic Education* (1999), 300.

16. I am not suggesting there is no child-centered argument for making some decisions and allocations of government benefits turn on parental choice. Often parental support is necessary for child welfare initiatives to benefit children. With respect to transfer of children to private schools, I suspect strong parental *opposition* would make transfer not conducive to a child's well-being. However, where a child's parents are simply indifferent, a transfer determined best for the child without regard to the parents' position would probably still be best for the child. My point here is that this is not the sort of reasoning taking place in Gutmann's musings about school vouchers.

17. Gutmann, *Democratic Education* (1999), 302.

18. Gutmann, "Civic Minimalism." Cf. Stephen Macedo, "Constituting Civil Society: School Vouchers, Religious Nonprofit Organizations, and Liberal Public Values," *Chicago-Kent Law Review* 75 (2000): 441 ("The recourse for religious and other private institutions that wish to resist public values is to not become conduits for public monies dedicated to public purposes").

19. For example, local majorities might be driven more by concern with reducing taxes, or with channeling tax revenues to projects other than schools, such as municipal golf courses, than by concern for children's welfare. Or they might be more concerned to make parents happy or to avoid parental complaints, and for that reason water down or abandon the requirements they would otherwise impose on schools.

20. See, e.g., Callan, *Creating Citizens,* 135 ("The case for schools that adhere closely throughout to the familial primary culture is typically presented as a matter of parents' rights. That is just the kind of argument we should expect if we are asking about possible moral limits on the coercive pursuit of politically desirable ends").

21. See, e.g., ibid., 146 ("parents have a right to make a choice that is bad for their children").

22. William Galston, "Two Concepts of Liberalism," *Ethics* 105 (1995): 516–34, 518.

23. Ibid., 521, 523, 524, 527.

24. William Galston, *Liberal Purposes* (Oxford, 1991), 252.

25. Ibid., 252–53. See also "Two Concepts of Liberalism," 528 n. 29 ("the scope of permissible diversity is constrained by the imperatives of citizenship").

26. Galston, *Liberal Purposes,* 254.

27. See, e.g., ibid., 255, Galston, "Two Concepts of Liberalism," 531–33.

28. The question whether to sterilize mentally disabled women is a case in point. The law today requires a court order to perform this procedure, and judges are to render such orders only after applying a best interest or substituted judgment test—asking what is best for the disabled woman or what she would likely decide for herself if able. In addition, the law precludes courts from considering the interests of parents or other guardians for the incompetent woman in deciding whether to authorize sterilization. See Elizabeth Scott, "Sterilization of Mentally Retarded Persons: Reproductive Rights and Family Privacy," *Duke University Law Journal* 1986 (1986): 817–22.

29. Callan, *Creating Citizens,* 144.

30. Ibid., 145–46, 143, 144, 144, 144 (quoting Robert Nozick, *The Examined Life* [1989], 28), 145. Callan defines a "zone of personal sovereignty" as "a sphere of conduct in which individuals are rightfully free to make *their own way* in the world" (emphasis added), states that personal sovereignty "is the social space where the traditional freedoms of liberal politics apply, such as freedom of conscience," and then proceeds to discuss child-rearing decisions as an aspect of personal sovereignty. Ibid., 145.

31. Loren Lomasky explicitly compares child rearing to other projects people pursue to give their lives value: "Few people can expect to produce a literary or artistic monument, redirect the life of a nation, garner honor and glory that lives after them. But it is open to almost everyone to stake a claim to long-term significance through having and raising children." Lomasky, *Persons, Rights, and the Moral Community* (New York, 1987), 167. The thinking seems to be that if we cannot have those other things—and most of us will not, because they are not things to which we are entitled—most of us can at least use our children as vehicles for expressing our vision, for satisfying our will to power, or for making ourselves important in others' eyes. And some theorists appear to infer simply from our having the opportunity to use our children in this way that we must have a moral right to do so.

32. See generally James G. Dwyer, "Parents' Religion and Children's Welfare: Debunking the Doctrine of Children's Rights," *California Law Review* 82 (1994): 1371–1447.

33. See ibid., 1416–20.

34. Callan, *Creating Citizens,* 138–40. In fact, Callan's argument could be made stronger, by taking into account children's interest in their parents' self-confidence and satisfaction as parents, and children's interest in a stable family life, both of which can be threatened by state intervention. These interests of children counsel in favor of granting parents somewhat greater discretion in child rearing than one might otherwise attribute to them. Callan commits a conceptual mistake, however, by characterizing the parental authority that children's interests support as a matter of parental right. If a certain rule of decision making regarding children's lives is predicated on the interests of children, it should be viewed as a right of the children, not of the decision makers. It is nonsensical to say that one person's interests generate rights in another person. Analogously, the law treats mentally incompetent adults as having a right that decisions be made according to certain procedures, and in some instances presumptively by an individual fiduciary (who is often a parent) rather than the state. The law does not attribute a decision-making *right* or *entitlement* to the fiduciary, but rather accords a revocable power, constrained by an obligation to make decisions in accordance with the ward's best interests and by a prohibition on self-dealing. See Dwyer, "Parents' Religion," 1416–20.

35. Some theorists actually acknowledge after the fact that they have done this, yet do not recognize how problematic this is. In Galston's *Liberal Purposes,* 254, for example, there is at the tail end of an analysis of parent-state conflicts over schooling the telling statement: "There are, after all, three parties to the educational transaction."

36. See, e.g., Stephen Macedo, "Liberal Civic Education and Religious Fundamentalism: The Case of God v. John Rawls?" *Ethics* 105 (1995): 485 (asking whether "families have a moral right to opt out of reasonable measures designed to educate children toward very basic liberal virtues").

37. See *Wisconsin v. Yoder,* 406 U.S. 205, 232 (1971) ("There is nothing . . . in the ordinary course of human experience to suggest that non-Amish parents generally consult with children of ages 14–16 if they are placed in a church school of the parents' faith").

38. Callan, *Creating Citizens,* 149.

39. Galston, *Liberal Purposes,* 254. Similarly, when Galston addresses the Amish question, he writes: "The issue is not simply the theological impulse to tyrannize over others. It is also the simple desire to be left alone." Galston, "Two Concepts of Liberalism," 520. The later Rawls speaks in a similar fashion about education: "Justice as fairness honors, as far as it can, the claims of those who wish to withdraw from the modern world in accordance with the injunctions of their religion." Rawls, *Political Liberalism* (Cambridge, Mass., 1993), 200. And Macedo writes that "we allow people to exclude themselves from public schooling and go to private schools, parochial and fundamentalist schools, and even school at home." Macedo, *Diversity and Distrust,* 202. The children whose education is at stake are not wishing to be left alone, are not wishing to withdraw from the modern world, and are not excluding themselves. In addition, the parents do not wish to be left *alone*—they want to be left with their children in their exclusive power. They are not excluding themselves from public schooling—they are seeking to exclude other selves, their children, from public schooling.

40. Galston, "Two Concepts of Liberalism," 530.

41. Peter de Marneffe, "Is It Fair to Adults to Make Children Moral? Response to Robert P. George," *Arizona State Law Review* 29 (1997): 581–84. De Marneffe would balance against this aim

the interests of parents and the need to protect children from known harms. Ibid., 583 ("This argument . . . *might* be trumped if we *knew* that children were likely to be *harmed*") (emphasis added).

42. See Dwyer, "Parents' Religion," 1405–23.

43. Alternatively, one could say that any theory of justice should give proper consideration to individuals' interests and rights over the course of complete lives, from birth to death. The Rawls of *A Theory of Justice* at times suggested such an approach, but the Rawls of *Political Liberalism* largely abandoned it. See James G. Dwyer, *Religious Schools v. Children's Rights* (Ithaca, 1998), chap. 6.

44. Parents' feelings might have greater indirect bearing, insofar as children's well-being is affected by parents' reaction to state-imposed restrictions on their child-rearing choices. This is a complex matter I address in *Religious Schools*, chap. 5. In addition, if parents believe a state policy threatens their children's temporal welfare, the state should seriously consider whether the parents are correct.

Chapter 3. A Utilitarian Assessment of Vouchers

1. For analysis of why the following requirements are essential aspects of a good liberal education, see generally Meira Levinson, *The Demands of Liberal Education* (Oxford, 1999), Harry Brighouse, *School Choice and Social Justice* (Oxford, 2000), and Michael S. Pritchard, *Reasonable Children: Moral Education and Moral Learning* (Lawrence, Kan., 1996). In chapters 7 to 9, I expand on certain of the aspects of liberal education that these requirements reflect.

2. As noted in Chapter 1, the voucher program in place in Milwaukee mandates that voucher schools give *parents* a choice to opt their children out of religious instruction and worship. An opt-out in schools is analogous to rules applicable to social service programs for adults; recipients of assistance must have a nonreligious option available to them in order for the government aid program to satisfy constitutional strictures. For example, section 104 of the Personal Responsibility and Work Opportunity Reconciliation Act of 1996, 42 U.S.C. sec. 604a (1996 Supp.), allows states to use federal funds to support private providers of welfare services, including religious providers, so long as the states ensure that beneficiaries are guaranteed access to a nonreligious provider if they want one. An opt-out *for students* might be required in voucher schools not simply because this is important for young people and afforded to students in other schools, but also because religious schools that accept vouchers become in some sense agents of the state. Again, the analogy to other government-funded private service providers is informative. Private medical clinics that receive state funding are viewed as agents of the state, and so their employees are forbidden, just like government employees, from coercing, or even influencing, private choice in matters of religion. See Michael McConnell, "The Selective Funding Problem: Abortions and Religious Schools," *Harvard Law Review* 104 (1991): 1023–24 (explaining that it is legitimate for the state to prohibit publicly financed family-planning counselors from encouraging or counseling a woman to have an abortion, because the funding makes the counselors agents of the state).

Arguably students in a religious school could never be free in a practical sense to opt out of religious services, prayer, and instruction, because school administrators, parents, and peers would impose great pressure to participate, pressure that the courts have acknowledged in the context of prayer in public schools. I will assume here that school employees, at least, would not exert such pressure and in fact would emphasize the voluntariness of participation in religious services or classes.

3. Some might contend that the school just described can hardly be called a religious school, because it has largely been stripped of the univocal, indoctrinatory features that define a religious school, and has been infused with features—critical, open-ended inquiry and a focus on the free mind of the individual—that are in fact antithetical to religion. However, while it might be true that religions inherently claim ultimate, univocal authority with regard to morality and social value (see Isaac Kramnick and R. Laurence Moore, *The Godless Constitution: The Case Against Religious Correctness* [New York, 1996], 23–43, 137–57), not all religions disapprove of critical and independent thinking, and many ostensibly embrace it as a prerequisite to authentic religious commitment. In any event, the school described could be termed a religious school even if it is not pervasively sectarian, not a

"total institution" (see Alan Peshkin, *God's Choice: The Total World of a Fundamentalist Christian School* [Chicago, 1986]), simply because it sponsors religious activities during part of the day, in contrast to public schools. The Catholic schools I attended for grades K through 12 actually had less religious observance than the school described above; there was little prayer and few masses, so the overt religious dimension was largely confined to a few (albeit mandatory) classes in religious education each week. On the other hand, critical and independent thinking was discouraged. The school I have described actually resembles many universities operated by independent religious orders, such as the Jesuit order. Religious services are offered for students who wish to participate and many of the administrators and faculty members are clergy, but the teaching of secular subjects in them is indistinguishable from that in state universities.

4. The financial effects of a program like Cleveland's that has a tuition cap are complicated. The program likely does increase the resources of private schools to some degree. Parents previously receiving tuition assistance from the school would require less or none once they have vouchers. Schools might ask parents to pay for supplies or equipment. And schools could take in students transferring from public schools until they reach a financially optimal student population. But parents previously paying full tuition would likely realize all or most of the benefit themselves. There is a case to be made, though, that even sparing parents from tuition costs, without increasing a school's total resources, serves the purpose of advancing children's educational interests. Many parents who send their children to private school can barely afford to do so, and sacrifice a large share of family resources to do so. Their children might now miss out on many nonschool learning opportunities for this reason. Vouchers would allow those families to devote more of their resources to learning activities for their children outside of school. And if the parents value secular educational experiences, we might assume that most would seek out such experiences for their children.

A study of the Milwaukee voucher program, which does not impose such a cap, found that "the voucher program helped to improve the financial status of several of the participating schools." Cecilia Elena Rouse, "Private School Vouchers and Student Achievement: An Evaluation of the Milwaukee Parental Choice Program," *Quarterly Journal of Economics* 113 (1998): 556. Some recent voucher bills would have mandated that, as in Cleveland, participating schools not charge any tuition above and beyond the voucher amount. Others, though, would have permitted private schools to charge parents an additional amount above the voucher amount. Simply having more money does not necessarily make a school better, of course; the additional money must be used efficiently for the purpose of enhancing the quality of education. I will assume that recipient schools would use any additional money effectively to improve the secular education they provide, by, for example, raising teacher salaries and thereby attracting more qualified teachers, and improving other classroom resources.

5. These two approaches are generally assumed to be conflicting theoretical alternatives. See Jeremy Waldron, "Rights and Majorities," in *Nomos XXXII: Majorities and Minorities* (1990): 45. Some theorists have attempted to reconcile the two, by arguing that some forms of utilitarianism would support conferral of rights or that a utilitarian approach to law and policy would protect the same things that rights protect. For my purposes, I will treat them as simply different approaches, the one taking into account all interests affected and balancing them and the other giving trumping power to claims grounded in particularly important interests. For a general description of the distinction between consequentialist, or "goal-based," theories and rights-based theories, see Jeremy Waldron, "Introduction," in *Theories of Rights*, ed. Jeremy Waldron (Oxford, 1984): 12–14. These two approaches to questions of justice do not, of course, exhaust the possibilities. But the utilitarian and rights-based approaches are closest to the modes of policy making and legal reasoning that prevail in our society, and therefore arguably present the best means of assessing the specific conclusions that policy makers and the legal system have arrived at regarding vouchers.

6. See, e.g., Joseph Claude Harris, "The Funding Dilemma Facing Catholic Elementary and Secondary Schools," in *Catholic Schools at the Crossroads: Survival and Transformation* (New York, 2000), 55–71.

7. Amy Gutmann and Dennis Thompson, *Democracy and Disagreement* (Cambridge, Mass., 1996), 165.

8. See Gerald Dworkin, ed., *Mill's On Liberty* (1997), xi ("Utilitarianism is a familiar framework even to those who are not philosophically sophisticated. Whenever we try to decide what to do by tallying up the benefits of a proposed course of action and weighing them against the costs, we are engaged in a kind of utilitarian reasoning"); Ronald Dworkin, "What Is Equality? Part 3: The Place of Liberty," *Iowa Law Review* 73 (1987): 7 ("we are now united in accepting the abstract egalitarian principle: government must act to make the lives of those it governs better lives, and it must show equal concern for the life of each").

9. See John Rawls, *A Theory of Justice* (Cambridge, Mass., 1971), 90: "[T]he principle of utility requires us to maximize the algebraic sum of expectations taken over all relevant positions. . . . utilitarianism assumes some fairly accurate measure of those expectations. Not only is it necessary to have a cardinal measure for each representative individual but these measures must make sense in interpersonal comparisons. Some method of correlating the scales of different persons is presupposed if we are to say that the gains of some are to outweigh the losses of others. It is unreasonable to demand great precision, yet these estimates cannot be left to our unguided intuition. For judgments of a greater balance of interests leave too much room for conflicting claims. . . . [Thus, f]or questions of social justice we should try to find some objective grounds for these comparisons, ones that men can recognize and agree to."

10. See Joel Feinberg, *The Moral Limits of the Criminal Law*, Vol. 1: *Harm to Others* (New York, 1984), 37.

11. Ibid., 37–38.

12. Rawls, *Theory of Justice*, 22. Rawls did not himself advance a utilitarian theory; he explicitly disavowed a utilitarian approach to questions of justice, in favor of an innovative social contract approach.

13. Ibid., 92, 62, 92, 95, 95.

14. Ibid., 62, 440, 440, 440.

15. For discussion of the connection between the Establishment Clause and the ideal of a secular state, see David A. J. Richards, "Religion, Public Morality, and Constitutional Law," in J. Roland Pennock and John W. Chapman, eds., *NOMOS XXX: Religion, Morality, and the Law* (New York, 1988): 153–59.

16. See *McGowan v. Maryland*, 366 U.S. 420, 465–66 (1961) (Frankfurter, J., concurring) ("The Establishment Clause withdrew from the sphere of legitimate legislative concern and competence a specific, but comprehensive, area of human conduct: man's belief or disbelief in the verity of some transcendental idea and man's expression in action of that belief or disbelief. Congress may not make these matters, as such, the subject of legislation, nor, now, may any legislature in this country"); Kathleen M. Sullivan, "Parades, Public Squares, and Voucher Payments: Problems of Government Neutrality," *Connecticut Law Review* 28 (1996): 258. Under a certain set of factual assumptions, it might be the case that children's temporal interests are advanced by receiving religious training— for example, if it were the case that only through religious training (of any sort? of a particular sort?) could children learn self-discipline—and in that case the state might (I will not attempt to decide the matter here) permissibly assume that religious training is of instrumental value to all children, and act on the basis of that assumption. But I am unaware that anyone has established the truth of any such set of factual assumptions.

Recognizing this limitation on state decision making sometimes leads people to assert that the state ought not to make decisions about children's education but should instead let parents decide, since parents *may* take their children's religious interests into account. This response ignores the fact that state action is inevitable in this context. That is obvious in the case of state financial support for education; the state has to act to direct aid to religious schools. It is also true in the case of state regulation of religious schools; if the state chooses *not* to regulate, then it is at the same time expanding parental legal authority. Any of these actions by the state must be justified, by reference to reasons the state can appropriately hold.

17. See Catherine Barnett Alexander, "Private School Daze: Privatization Comes to the Classroom As School Vouchers Drain Students—and Jobs—from Public Schools," *Public Employee*

63, no. 1 (1998): 18. Some voucher bills acknowledge this likelihood. A bill to create a pilot scholarship program in Missouri authorized participating school districts to offer severance pay or early retirement incentives to teachers should their enrollment decrease as a result of student transfers to private schools. Mo. H.B. 937, sec. 2.7 (February 18, 1999). The 1995 Ohio legislation creating the Cleveland voucher program provided for severance packages and early retirement incentives to ameliorate that problem. Oh. H.B. 117 (1995), codified as Ohio R.C. 3313.975(D).

18. Alan Brownstein points out that if teachers were laid off and if their only employment opportunity after losing a job at a public school were at a religious school whose ideology they did not share, then they might also experience a loss of ideological freedom. He also notes that some teachers might be unable to secure a position in a private school because of their religious beliefs. Alan Brownstein, "Interpreting the Religion Clauses in Terms of Liberty, Equality, and Free Speech Values—A Critical Analysis of 'Neutrality Theory' and Charitable Choice," *Notre Dame Journal of Law, Ethics, and Public Policy* 13 (1999): 255.

19. See Joel Feinberg, "The Child's Right to an Open Future," in *Whose Child? Children's Rights, Parental Authority, and State Power*, ed. William Aiken and Hugh LaFollette (Totowa, N.J., 1980), 124–53. As noted above, both Feinberg and Rawls include intellectual development among the most important human interests.

20. Joseph P. Viteritti, *Choosing Equality: School Choice, the Constitution, and Civil Society* (Washington, D.C., 1999), 9.

21. Dave Weber, "Educators Plot How to Help at Rimes: The School Can Improve its F Grade from the State, Educators Say, but Many Students Must Learn without Parents' Help," *Orlando Sentinel, August 4, 1999.*

22. In Cleveland, the public school system did lose funding following implementation of the voucher program, and as a result had to cut programs. See Alexander, "Private School Daze," 18.

23. See Viteritti, *Choosing Equality,* 38.

24. See ibid., 10 (noting belief that "[t]he loss of a middle-class constituency to nonpublic institutions would motivate political leaders to further divest funds from public schools").

25. Even if there is some connection between a poorer student's ability to learn and the presence of brighter students in the classroom, a concern arises about taking into account the interest one group of children might have in preventing another group of students from going to a better school. Satisfying that interest would entail treating the latter group of children instrumentally, as mere means to the fulfillment of others' ends. On some variations of utilitarianism, this interest might be ruled out. I try to avoid, however, any "idealization" (see Amartya Sen and Bernard Williams, eds., *Utilitarianism and Beyond* [New York, 1982], 9)—that is, any screening out of interests as morally inappropriate. This concern would certainly be relevant to a moral rights analysis, though; children left behind could not properly be said to have a right that other children not leave for their own betterment.

26. See Catherine Ross, "An Emerging Right for Mature Minors to Receive Information," *University of Pennsylvania Journal of Constitutional Law* 2 (1999): 223–75 (analyzing rights of public school students, under the First Amendment, to receive information, noting "the potential for harm posed by exaggerated public deference to parents who fear that a free flow of ideas to their youngsters outside of the home will undermine family values and authority," and asserting that "[t]he right to receive information is integrally related to any effort to achieve the individual self-realization that is essential to the structure of the First Amendment").

27. But see *Allen v. Wright,* 468 U.S. 737(1984) (holding that stigmatization felt by African American parents as a result of the federal government's granting tax-exempt status to racially exclusionary private schools was not a sufficiently substantial injury to support standing to challenge the grant of exempt status).

28. The best studies to date compare students whose parents applied for vouchers but did not receive them or declined to use them, and who remained in the public school, with students whose parents applied for vouchers, received them, and used them. This helps to reduce the effect of parental involvement or interest. One recent study of private voucher programs showed a small gain for African American children in some grade levels in some places, out of all the children of various

races in several grade levels studied. Even that small gain for one group must be questioned, because the study excluded the large number of students who initially used the vouchers but then, for whatever reason, left the private school. Those students are likely the worst-performing students among those who received vouchers. The authors of the study also excluded from consideration children whose parents did not receive the vouchers but who left the public school anyway, to go either to a public school elsewhere or to a private school without a state-provided voucher. Those students are likely to be the better-performing students among those who did not receive vouchers. See Jeffrey R. Henig, "School Choice Outcomes," in *School Choice and Social Controversy: Politics, Policy, and Law,* ed. Stephen D. Sugarman and Frank R. Kemerer (Washington, D.C., 1999), 96. For discussion of the studies of voucher student test scores and the heated debate surrounding those studies, see ibid., 89–97.

29. See Marci A. Hamilton, "Power, the Establishment Clause, and Vouchers," *Connecticut Law Review* 31 (1999): 837 (pointing out the great political clout religious groups have in our society today and adopting the position that "aid to nonsectarian students only—is likely constitutional on grounds that the exclusion of religious schools is necessary to avoid serious establishment difficulties," unless religious groups can demonstrate that the actual reason for their exclusion was animus toward religion).

30. See, e.g., Carl H. Esbeck, "A Constitutional Case for Governmental Cooperation with Faith-Based Social Service Providers," *Emory Law Journal* 46 (1997): 19 (and other sources cites therein); Sullivan, "Parades, Public Squares and Voucher Payments," 257–58.

31. See, e.g., Molly Townes O'Brien, "Private School Tuition Vouchers and the Realities of Racial Politics," *Tennessee Law Review* 64 (1997): 359. See also Douglas Laycock, "The Underlying Unity of Separation and Neutrality," *Emory Law Journal* 46 (1997): 61 (discussing fears expressed during the throes of desegregation in the 1960s and 1970s that subsidies for private schools would exacerbate white flight from public schools, and the factual basis for those fears).

32. See, e.g., Nicole Stelle Garnett and Richard W. Garnett, "School Choice, the First Amendment, and Social Justice," *Texas Review of Law and Politics* 4 (2000): 352–55.

33. Many confuse figures for minority percentage of religious school attendance nationwide with figures for minority percentage of attendance in individual schools. The reality seems to be that while a substantial percentage of minority students nationwide attend Catholic schools, they primarily attend Catholic schools that are almost entirely made up of minority students. In other words, there are white Catholic schools and nonwhite Catholic schools, and not a great number of integrated Catholic schools. See Joseph M. O'Keefe and Jessica Murphy, "Ethnically Diverse Catholic Schools: School Structure, Students, Staffing, and Finance," in *Catholic Schools at the Crossroads: Survival and Transformation,* ed. James Youniss and John J. Convey (New York, 2000), 132.

34. Esbeck, "Constitutional Case for Governmental Cooperation," 19–20.

35. William Galston, *Liberal Purposes* (Oxford, 1991), 256.

36. See *Employment Division v. Smith,* 494 U.S. 872 (1990) (holding that there is no right to a religious exemption to laws prohibiting drug use, or to other generally applicable laws regarding non-child-rearing conduct). Drug use by one person can affect others, of course, but part of the justification for drug laws is paternalistic, and there is no hint in *Smith* that a state must demonstrate that prohibiting use of the drug in question—there peyote—is necessary, or even likely, to prevent harm to others.

37. See National Center for Education Statistics, *1993–94 Schools and Staffing Survey: Data File User's Manual,* Vol. 1: *Survey Documentation* (1996), E-67.

38. See ibid., E-52.

Chapter 4. A Moral Rights–Based Assessment

1. For an explication of the notion of rights as trumps, see Ronald Dworkin, "Rights as Trumps," in *Theories of Rights,* ed. Jeremy Waldron (Oxford, 1984), 153–67.

2. See Ruth Jonathan, *Illusory Freedoms: Liberalism, Education, and the Market* (1997), 98 ("invoking rights in moral or political argument . . . implies that whatever liberty or entitlement is so labeled should not be denied or overridden by the usual pragmatic considerations of the incidental effects of removing the restriction"); Jeremy Waldron, "Rights and Majorities," in *Nomos XXXII: Majorities and Minorities* (1990): 52 ("Rights imply limits on the harms and losses that any individual or group may reasonably be expected to put up with; they indicate that certain losses and harms are simply not to be imposed on any individual or group for any reason. These are harms and losses that may not be traded off against a larger mass of lesser considerations in the way the utilitarian calculus allows").

3. See Waldron, "Rights and Majorities," 52 ("A theory of rights will identify certain human interests—some related to freedom, others perhaps to other aspects of well-being—and show the moral importance of those interests in receiving a guaranteed level of protection and satisfaction"); Joseph Raz, *The Morality of Freedom* (Oxford, 1986), 166.

As with my use of a utilitarian approach to decision making, it is not my intention in using a rights-based approach to resolve any foundational philosophical debates. I am simply offering an application of one rights-based approach, in the hope that it might shed some light on a real world issue. That said, I will offer some justification for adopting an interest-based conception of rights. One competing theory argues that rights protect choices rather than interests. In my view, a child-centered approach to child-rearing policy makes clear the superiority of a view that rights protect both choices and interests. Rights protect interests ultimately and protect choices derivatively, because protecting choices furthers a subset of important human interests—for example, interests in having one's choices be effective, in living a life best suited to one's own values and abilities, in learning from one's mistakes, etc. If choice-protecting rights did *not* serve any interests, it would be difficult to justify giving them to people, particularly since they often conflict with interests of other people. On the other hand, we also have many rights that do not appear to protect choices, and there is no reason why we should not have such rights. I have rights that prevent people from doing things to me and to my property even though I have never thought about or made a decision about whether I want people to do those things. This is even clearer in the case of persons incapable of making choices, such as newborn babies, senile elderly persons, and severely mentally retarded persons; they certainly have legal rights protecting things as to which they make no choices, such as their physical integrity and their property, and common intuitions are that they have a moral right to that protection. Philosophers who believe rights are grounded in autonomy, and therefore protect only choices, can accommodate these facts about the world only by the most contorted of reasoning, and it is not clear why anyone should hold so tenaciously to an autonomy-based conception of rights and engage in these intellectual gymnastics. It may be simply that as a historical matter rights were originally justified as protections of autonomy, which in turn can be explained by the facts that the only humans of concern to political theorists then were autonomous (propertied, white, male) adults, and that emphasizing autonomy as a basis for rights provided a means of limiting them to only that class of persons. Cf. Cynthia Ward, "On Difference and Equality," *Legal Theory* 3 (1997): 73–76, 83–91 (describing and responding to critiques of the autonomy-based conception of rights). As Tom Campbell aptly puts it, however,

> it is arguably a serious defect in a theory of rights that it cannot readily make room for the reality and distinctiveness of children's rights . . . . It may be that there is something very wrong with a theory which makes it impossible to say, for instance, that, in the fullest and most literal sense of the expression, a child has the same right to life as an adult, or, again, that a child [has] distinctive rights, such as the right to receive primary education.

Tom D. Campbell, "The Rights of the Minor: As Person, as Child, as Juvenile, as Future Adult," in *Children, Rights, and the Law*, ed. Philip Alston et al. (Oxford, 1992), 4. In other words, a theory of rights that cannot straightforwardly explain why a newborn baby has a right not to be kicked is a theory that should be scrapped. It is with good reason, then, that the choice theory of rights has been out of favor for some time. See Jeremy Waldron, "Introduction," in Waldron, *Theories of Rights*, 11–12.

4. In the schooling area, for example, the Supreme Court has held that children do not have a fundamental constitutional right to a good education (*San Antonio Independent School District v. Rodriguez,* 411 U.S. 1 [1973]), but some parents have a fundamental constitutional right to deprive their children of an education beyond the eighth grade (*Wisconsin v. Yoder,* 406 U.S. 205 [1972]). I cannot imagine a justification for those two decisions based upon the respective interests that children and parents have at stake in connection with children's schooling. A justification grounded in a distinction between positive and negative rights has some superficial appeal if one believes there is a principled reason for according people only negative legal rights, but loses appeal when one realizes that the children in *Yoder* had negative rights at stake. They had at stake a right (or to put it in more precise Hohfeldian terms, an immunity) against the state's giving someone authority to waive their statutory entitlement to an education. And they had an equal protection right (i.e., a right against state discrimination) to the same guarantee of an education that the state conferred on non-Amish children. The Supreme Court's decision in *Yoder* violated both of these "rights" of Amish children. In addition, one could characterize the claim of the parents in *Yoder* as a positive right claim—namely, a demand that the state confer on them legal custody and control of children and a special exemption from the schooling requirement that the state imposes on other parents as a condition for enjoying custody and control.

5. For critiques of natural rights theory, see Jeremy Waldron, ed., *Nonsense upon Stilts: Bentham, Burke, and Marx on the Rights of Man* (New York, 1987).

6. See Susan H. Bitensky, "Theoretical Foundations for a Right to Education under the U.S. Constitution: A Beginning to the End of the National Education Crisis," *Northwestern University Law Review* 86 (1992): 587. It does not appear that anyone has tried to force the voucher issue in court by asserting these state constitutional rights of children. Education is also a fundamental right under the constitutions of many countries and under several international human rights laws. See Cheryl D. Block, "Truth and Probability—Ironies in the Evolution of Social Choice Theory," *Washington University Law Quarterly* 76 (1998): 975.

7. I rely throughout this chapter on a distinction between infringing and violating a right. Rights entail duties on the part of others to perform or not perform some action. A right is infringed when others who owe this duty to the right-holder fail to fulfill the duty. However, some infringements are justified—for example, by the incapacity of the person owing the duty or by competing duties owed to other right-holders. A right is violated only when an infringement of the right is not justified. Judith Jarvis Thomson, *The Realm of Rights* (Cambridge, Mass., 1990), 122.

8. Of course, teachers might have contract rights that prevent termination in circumstances like those vouchers might create. But in that case they would also have a contract remedy.

9. See James G. Dwyer, *Religious Schools v. Children's Rights* (Ithaca, 1998), chap. 4.

10. See ibid., 73–79.

11. See ibid., 67–71.

12. Ibid., 71–79.

13. See Barbara Bennett Woodhouse, "Who Owns the Child? *Meyer* and *Pierce* and the Child as Property," *William and Mary Law Review* 33 (1992): 995.

14. In the legal world, this is reflected in the fact that the "unconstitutional conditions" doctrine the Supreme Court endorsed on a few occasions in the relatively distant past has received little support on the Court in recent decades. See Brooks R. Fudenberg, "Unconstitutional Conditions and Greater Powers: A Separability Approach," *University of California at Los Angeles Law Review* 43 (1995): 375–76.

15. See *Employment Division v. Smith,* 494 U.S. 872 (1990) (upholding state law prohibiting use of peyote, a drug used in sacred ceremonies by certain Native American groups). The Supreme Court in *Smith* did in dicta suggest that parental free exercise rights are stronger than self-determining free exercise rights, because the former are a "hybrid" kind of rights. Many commentators have contended that the hybrid rights notion is incoherent and not to be taken too seriously. In addition, the particular instance of parental free exercise rights is clearly paradoxical; it would give parents stronger rights in governing their children's lives than they have in governing their own. In any event, parental free

exercise rights would still be overridden by a compelling state interest, which the Court has said protection of children's educational interests is, and would be infringed only by a prohibition of conduct, not by a refusal to subsidize conduct.

16. 468 U.S. 737 (1984).

17. See Carl Esbeck, "Myths, Miscues, and Misconceptions: No-Aid Separationism and the Establishment Clause," *Notre Dame Journal of Law, Ethics, and Public Policy* 13 (1999): 312–13 (describing cases rejecting claims of religious coercion by secularist plaintiffs in Establishment Clause cases).

18. See, e.g., *Hernandez v. Commissioner,* 490 U.S. 680, 699 (1989) ("The free exercise inquiry asks whether government has placed a substantial burden on the observation of a central religious belief or practice"); *Buckley v. American Constitutional Law Foundation,* 525 U.S. 182, 119 S.Ct. 636, 654 (free speech).

Chapter 5. Making Sense of Antiestablishment Principles

1. *Employment Division v. Smith,* 494 U.S. 872, 885 (1990) (citation omitted).

2. See Frederick Mark Gedicks, "The Improbability of Religion Clause Theory," *Seton Hall Law Review* 27 (1997): 1233.

3. 413 U.S. 756 (1973).

4. 463 U.S. 388 (1983).

5. 521 U.S. 203 (1997).

6. 120 S.Ct. 2530 (2000).

7. See, e.g., *Agostini v. Felton,* 521 U.S. 203 (1997) (remedial teachers); *Board of Education v. Allen,* 392 U.S. 236 (1968) (secular textbooks); *Everson v. Board of Education,* 330 U.S. 1 (1947) (bus transportation). At one point in its opinion, the *Nyquist* Court suggested that bus transportation and textbooks are distinguishable on the basis that the benefit they provide to religious institutions is both indirect and "incidental," without explaining what it meant by "incidental."

8. See, e.g., *Campbell v. Manchester Board of School Directors,* 641 A.2d 352, 357 (Vt. 1994); *Simmons-Harris v. Goff,* 711 N.E.2d 203, 208 (Ohio 1999).

9. See, e.g., *Simmons-Harris v. Zelman,* 234 F.3d 945, 955 (2000); *Miller v. Benson,* 878 F.Supp. 1209, 1214–15 (E.D. Wis., 1995).

10. The Court also noted that the tax deduction component of the New York program reviewed in *Nyquist* was not a true deduction, insofar as all parents were permitted to deduct the same statutorily defined amount from their income regardless of what expenses they actually incurred for their children's education. Because the deduction was not tied to actual expenses, as the Minnesota deduction was, the New York tax provision did not "encourage[] desirable expenditures for educational purposes."

11. In a recent case involving aid to college student journalism groups, the Court expressed great concern about the state's making similar judgments about what print content was religious and which not. See *Rosenberger v. Rectors and Visitors of the University of Virginia,* 515 U.S. 819 (1995). The Court could easily distinguish that case, though, on the ground that such scrutinizing of content in that case would have interfered with free speech by adults to the general public rather than with instruction of schoolchildren.

12. *Jackson v. Benson,* 578 N.W.2d 602, 614–15 (Wis. 1998).

13. *Aguilar v. Felton,* 473 U.S. 402 (1985).

14. The only hint is the Court's mention, in relating the history of the case, that in *Aguilar* it had determined that the presence of public teachers in religious schools "created a 'graphic symbol of the "concert or union or dependency" of church and state' especially when perceived by 'children in their formative years.'" The dissenting justices in *Agostini* indicated a concern for the message that might be sent to the religious schools themselves by a symbolic union; they might perceive aid as endorsement of their religion, and this could amount to state influencing of religious belief.

15. 120 S.Ct. at 2541.

16. For evidence of the justices' views, see James G. Dwyer, "School Vouchers: Inviting the Public into the Religious Square," *William and Mary Law Review* 42 (2001): 985.

17. 473 U.S. 373 (1985).

18. The neutrality at times embraced by some Supreme Court justices, and the neutrality I endorse in this chapter, is a limited sort of neutrality. It calls for treating organizations evenhandedly, without regard to religious affiliation, when it comes to financial support of activities that further the state's secular ends. It is not neutrality as among religions, or between religion and nonreligion, in determining the aims of the state, a kind of neutrality that is impossible. See Steven D. Smith, *Foreordained Failure: The Quest for a Constitutional Principle of Religious Freedom* (New York, 1995), chap. 7. I take as a given here, as the Supreme Court generally does, that the state in this nation may pursue only secular ends, and may pursue secular ends even when they are inconsistent with some religious beliefs.

19. Even the Court's strongest statement of a strict separationist principle appeared in a decision that permitted an indirect form of aid—state provision of transportation to school for parochial school students. See *Everson v. Board of Education of Ewing*, 330 U.S. 1, 16 (1947) ("No tax in any amount, large or small, can be levied to support any religious activities or institutions"). Neutrality has always been the rule in nonschool contexts—for example, state and federal governments have provided financial aid to hospitals, colleges, and private social service providers for decades without being deemed to have violated the Establishment Clause. See, e.g., *Bowen v. Kendrick*, 487 U.S. 589 (1988) (federal grants for sex counseling of teens); *Roemer v. Board of Public Works*, 426 U.S. 736 (1976) (colleges).

20. See Michael W. McConnell, "The Selective Funding Problem: Abortions and Religious Schools," *Harvard Law Review* 104 (1991): 1018 ("no one disputes that it is just and proper for the government to refuse to pay the incremental cost of religious components of the education, in light of the conscientious objection many taxpayers have toward mandatory support for religious instruction"); Carl Esbeck, "Myths, Miscues, and Misconceptions: No-Aid Separationism and the Establishment Clause," *Notre Dame Journal of Law, Ethics, and Public Policy* 13 (1999): 288–89 ("in neutrality theory . . . monies are to be spent only for the purposes set out in the service contract or grant. These purposes . . . necessarily exclude use of the monies for inherently religious programming").

21. See Michael W. McConnell and Richard A. Posner, "An Economic Approach to Issues of Religious Freedom," *University of Chicago Law Review* 56 (1989): 1; McConnell, "Selective Funding Problem," 1020.

22. See, e.g., *Bagley v. Raymond Schl. Dist.*, 728 A.2d 127, 146 (Me., 1999) (calculating that the state aid would amount to roughly 70 percent of the school's per pupil cost of operation, while also finding no guarantee aid would be used only for secular purposes). The one exception was the Vermont Supreme Court's decision in *Chittenden*, which suggested that the kind of safeguards necessary to avoid state support for religious worship include segregating state and private funds and limiting the amount of the per pupil payment to reflect the portion of a school's curriculum that is secular. See *Chittenden Town School District v. Department of Education*, 738 A.2d 539, 541–42 (1999).

23. Alan Brownstein argues that excluding religious entities from programs of state aid to private service providers may serve to protect from coercive effects on religious belief those religious groups that are too small to provide the targeted services. Alan Brownstein, "Interpreting the Religion Clauses in Terms of Liberty, Equality, and Free Speech Values—A Critical Analysis of 'Neutrality Theory' and Charitable Choice," *Notre Dame Journal of Law, Ethics, and Public Policy* 13 (1999): 256. This is a valid point, but does not obviate the fact that excluding all religious providers from state aid does disfavor religious entities in general relative to secular organizations, and so creates a coercive effect that operates against all religious groups with an interest in receiving aid to provide the targeted services.

24. Carl H. Esbeck, "A Constitutional Case for Governmental Cooperation with Faith-Based Social Service Providers," *Emory Law Journal* 46 (1997): 21, 37.

25. Because of this coercive effect, the no impact position puts the Free Exercise Clause in conflict with the Establishment Clause, since the latter prohibits favoritism for religion, and Esbeck himself believes that any interpretation of the religion clauses that puts them in conflict with each other is presumptively incorrect. See Esbeck, "Myths, Miscues, and Misconceptions," 300–304. In a more recent iteration of the argument for exemptions, Esbeck contends that by creating exemptions for religious entities, the government exerts no influence on religious belief, because the effect is simply to "leave religion 'where it found it,' " which cannot amount to favoritism for religion. Ibid., 315. That contention is implausible, in part because it overlooks the fact that government does not leave nonreligious organizations as it finds them when it decides to impose regulations, and in part because it rests on an untenable distinction between benefits and relief from burdens. Clearly the government can greatly influence religious belief by use of exemptions, by imposing substantial burdens on people who do not hold certain religious beliefs, while exempting from those burdens people who hold the right beliefs.

26. 426 U.S. 736, 747 (1976). See also *Bowen*, 487 U.S. 589 (1988) (holding that state support for teen counseling programs run by religious organizations was permissible so long as the state ensured that the money was used for secular counseling services); ibid., 623–24 (O'Connor, J., concurring) (emphasizing that only where aid is clearly directed toward satisfaction of temporal needs, such as shelter for the homeless or medical treatment for the infirm, is it permissible for aid to go to religious organizations for their efforts directed toward that same secular end); ibid., 624–25 (Kennedy, J., concurring, joined by Scalia, J.) (indicating that aid is permissible so long as it is actually used by religious organizations for the designated *public* purpose).

27. Nevertheless at least one prominent voice in the voucher debate has advanced this view. See Joseph P. Viteritti, "Choosing Equality: Religious Freedom and Educational Opportunity under Constitutional Federalism," *Yale Law and Policy Review* 15 (1996): 138 (suggesting neutrality requires including religious schools in any voucher program even if there is no clear secular aspect to the religious school curriculum).

28. See, e.g., Stephen V. Monsma and J. Christopher Soper, "The Implications of Equal Treatment," in *Equal Treatment of Religion in a Pluralistic Society,* ed. Monsma and Soper (Grand Rapids, Mich., 1998), 208–9 (arguing that equal treatment should be the rule only for state-conferred benefits in Establishment Clause cases, and not for state-imposed burdens in free exercise cases); Frederick Mark Gedicks, "An Uniform Foundation: The Regrettable Indefensibility of Religious Exemptions," *University of Arkansas Little Rock Law Journal* 20 (1998): 555 (stating that free exercise exemptions are justifiable where "necessary to give religious institutions the freedom to promote their unique spiritual perspectives, as a kind of ideological compensation for the fact that they are constitutionally prohibited from competing for government endorsement in the way that secular philosophies may"); Michael W. McConnell, "A Response to Professor Marshall," *University of Chicago Law Review* 58 (1991): 329 (explicitly advancing a quid pro quo argument for exemptions).

29. See, e.g., Arlin M. Adams and Charles J. Emmerich, *A Nation Dedicated to Religious Liberty: The Constitutional Heritage of the Religion Clauses* (Philadelphia, 1990): 43 ("history supports the view that the nonestablishment and free exercise guarantees play different, although mutually supportive, roles in protecting religious liberty"); Michael A. Paulsen, "Religion, Equality, and the Constitution: An Equal Protection Approach to Establishment Clause Adjudication," *Notre Dame Law Review* (1986): 313 ("the establishment clause protects religious liberty"); Eric J. Segall, "Parochial School Aid Revisited: The Lemon Test, the Endorsement Test, and Religious Liberty," *San Diego Law Review* 28 (1991): 284–85.

30. This is true whether or not the choosing is a matter of constitutional right. People have a constitutional right to choose their church, but that does not strengthen the case for state financing of church construction.

The situation in *Witters v. Washington Dept. of Services for the Blind,* 474 U.S. 481 (1986), in which the Supreme Court approved a form of monetary aid—a tuition grant for a blind student to use at a religious seminary—was significantly different from that being addressed here. The aid in *Witters,* which was part of a larger program to promote independent living for persons with disabilities, could be justified by the purpose of equalizing the opportunity that persons with serious disabilities have for a fulfilling life of their own choosing. The aid in that case therefore should not be viewed as aid for choice in the abstract, or as aid for religious instruction per se. While the substantive choice made—attending a religious seminary—is not one the state can intend to promote, there was value for the individual and the state inherent in the choosing itself, or in having the choice be effective. That value was of a secular nature and of sufficient magnitude to constitute an adequate and secular state purpose. The *Witters* Court also emphasized that it was unlikely the program would ever result in a large amount of money going to religious institutions.

31. *Nyquist,* 413 U.S. at 774, 780. In emphasizing that there was no means of "guaranteeing that the state aid derived from public funds will be used *exclusively* for secular, neutral, and nonideological purposes" (id. at 780 [emphasis added]), the Court implicitly indicated that even a program ensuring that only a small portion of aid would be used for religious activities would fail the primary effect test. If that is so, then the Court must be saying that the primary effect is to aid religion if any portion of aid provides any support for religious activities.

32. *Mueller,* 463 U.S. at 406 (Marshall, J., dissenting) ("Moreover, even if *one* ' "primary effect" [is] to promote some legitimate end under the State's police power,' the legislation is not 'immune from further examination to ascertain whether it also has the direct and immediate effect of advancing religion.' ") (quoting *Nyquist,* 413 U.S. at 783–84, n. 39).

33. See Agostini, 521 U.S. at 221 (describing *Aguilar* reasoning).

34. 521 U.S. at 223. See also ibid., 230 ("placing full-time employees on parochial school campuses does not as a matter of law have the impermissible effect of advancing religion through indoctrination"), 234 ("To summarize, New York City's Title I program does not run afoul of any of three primary criteria we currently use to evaluate whether government aid has the effect of advancing religion").

35. Laura S. Underkuffler, "Vouchers and Beyond: The Individual as Causative Agent in Establishment Clause Jurisprudence," *Indiana Law Journal* 75 (2000): 167.

36. See, e.g., *Bagley,* 146; *Simmons-Harris v. Zelman,* 54 F.Supp.2d 725, 741 (1999).

37. See, e.g., *Jackson v. Benson,* 618.

38. See, e.g., *School Dist. of Grand Rapids v. Ball,* 473 U.S. 373, 390 (1985) ("The symbolism of a union between church and state . . . is most likely to influence children of tender years, whose experience is limited and whose beliefs consequently are the function of environment as much as of free and voluntary choice").

39. See, e.g., *Lynch v. Donnelly,* 465 U.S. 668, 688 (O'Connor, J., concurring).

40. See Esbeck, "Myths, Miscues, and Misconceptions," 299 n. 42 (citing cases).

41. Douglas Laycock opines that the Supreme Court's explanation of what it means by "pervasively sectarian" has been "inconsistent and incoherent," and that the Court seems simply always to deem religious elementary and secondary schools pervasively sectarian and usually to deem religious colleges and universities not pervasively sectarian. See Douglas Laycock, "The Underlying Unity of Separation and Neutrality," *Emory Law Journal* 46 (1997): 55.

42. Ibid.; *Bagley,* 131 ("There is no dispute that Cheverus High School is a . . . 'pervasively sectarian school,' educating its students in both secular and religious subjects"). Interestingly, litigants who support aid to religious schools appear never to argue against the assumption. This might be for public relations reasons, given that they typically advertise in broad (and, in my experience, more aspirational than accurately descriptive) terms that they create a learning environment that reflects religious creed throughout.

43. In *Ball,* the Court noted approvingly that the trial court had found that forty of the forty-one private schools eligible to participate in the aid program at issue were pervasively sectarian, meaning that " 'the purposes of these schools is to advance their particular religions,' " and that "a substantial portion of their functions are subsumed in the religious mission" (473 U.S. at 379). The evidence upon which the district court relied included a "Parent Handbook" articulating "the goals of Catholic education as '[a] God oriented environment which permeates the total educational program,' '[a] Christian atmosphere which guides and encourages participation in the church's commitment to social justice,'

and '[a] continuous development of knowledge of the Catholic faith, its traditions, teachings and theology' "; a policy statement by certain Christian schools that "proclaims that 'it is not sufficient that the teachings of Christianity be a separate subject in the curriculum, but the Word of God must be an all-pervading force in the educational program.' "; and the fact that Christian schools required "all parents seeking to enroll their children either to subscribe to a particular doctrinal statement or to agree to have their children taught according to the doctrinal statement." Ibid., 379.

44. See, e.g., *Roemer; Tilton v. Richardson,* 403 U.S. 672, 680–82 (1971).

45. Cf. McConnell, "Selective Funding Problem," 1012 (distinguishing between religious groups that "do not consider the teaching of secular subjects in a secular way morally or religiously objectionable" and religious groups that do).

46. 521 U.S. at 233–34. The Court noted that "in *Lemon* itself, the entanglement that the Court found 'independently' to necessitate the program's invalidation also was found to have the effect of inhibiting religion." Ibid., 233 (citing *Lemon,* 403 U.S. at 620). The Court also indicated that two additional considerations added to the finding of excessive entanglement in *Aguilar*—the administrative cooperation between the school board and the schools that the program would require and the dangers of political divisiveness. But the Court stated that under its current understanding of the Establishment Clause, those two considerations "are insufficient by themselves to create an 'excessive' entanglement." Ibid., 233–34.

47. *Lemon,* 403 U.S. at 619.

48. *Meek v. Pittenger,* 421 U.S. 349, 370 (1975).

49. *Aguilar,* 473 U.S. at 412.

50. It is uncertain whether the sort of regulations attached to the voucher program I have outlined, or the supervision that might be needed to enforce it, would constitute an excessive entanglement in the view of the Supreme Court. The Court's discussion of entanglement in a few cases suggests what sort of regulation is not excessive. For example, in *Bowen v. Kendrick,* 487 U.S. 589, 615–17 (1988), the Court found that government review of private adolescent sex counseling programs, including review of the literature they used and periodic visits to the counseling centers, did not amount to excessive entanglement. In *Roemer,* 426 U.S. 736, the Court determined that annual audits to ensure that colleges were not using grants to teach religion did not create excessive entanglement. And in *Agostini,* 521 U.S. at 234, the Court opined that "unannounced monthly visits of public supervisors" to religious schools where Title I teachers were placed, and even "far more onerous burdens" than that, would not run afoul of the excessive entanglement proscription.

51. 472 U.S. 38, 91 (1985). The full Court acknowledged it in *Bowen v. Kendrick. Bowen,* 616. This might help explain the Court's demotion of entanglement in *Agostini.*

52. *Wallace,* 472 U.S. at 109–110.

53. See Adams and Emmerich, *Nation Dedicated to Religious Liberty,* 37 (indicating that the drafters of the First Amendment "intended the establishment and free exercise clauses to be [freedom of religion's] complementary co-guarantors," with the Establishment Clause preventing Congress from prescribing religion and the Free Exercise Clause preventing Congress from proscribing); ibid., 43 ("[H]istory supports the view that the nonestablishment and free exercise guarantees, play different although mutually supportive, roles in protecting religious liberty"). See also Paulsen, "Religion, Equality, and the Constitution," 313 ("The two [religion] clauses, naturally enough, address a single, central value from two different angles: The free exercise clause forbids government proscription; the establishment clause forbids government prescription").

54. 494 U.S. 872 (1990).

55. For example, Native American tribes that historically have used peyote would be able to challenge criminal prohibitions on its use, under the Establishment Clause, simply by alleging that the monitoring necessary to ensure that they do not use peyote creates an excessive entanglement. It is unclear after *Agostini* whether a finding of excessive entanglement would itself require holding an aid program unconstitutional. The Court's demotion of entanglement in *Agostini* from an independent prong to a factor presumably means it is just one consideration among several in deciding whether a program survives the effect prong of the test. The Court has not yet decided a case under

this revised test in which it found excessive entanglement, though, so it has not had to state what should happen in such a case—that is, whether a court must then go on to consider whether other factors count in favor of upholding the program and outweigh the excessive entanglement. It is conceivable that the Court demoted entanglement to a factor precisely because of fears that it could be used to produce the sort of perverse results I have hypothesized.

56. The dissenters in *Agostini,* for example, expressed reservations about aid to religious schools that comes with regulatory strings attached, because of the coercive effect this could have on religious belief: " 'even the favored religion may fear being "taint[ed] . . . with a corrosive secularism." The favored religion may be compromised as political figures reshape the religion's beliefs for their own purposes; it may be reformed as government largess brings government regulation.' " 521 U.S. at 243.

Chapter 6. The Equal Protection Strategy for Compelling Aid to Religious Schools

1. See, e.g., *Committee for Public Education v. Nyquist,* 413 U.S. 756, 93 S.Ct. at 2970, n.38 (1973) (cautioning against providing "a basis for approving through tuition grants the complete subsidization of all religious schools on the ground that such action is necessary if the State is fully to *equalize the position of parents* who elect such schools").

2. See, e.g., *Strout v. Commissioner, Maine Department of Education,* 13 F.Supp.2d 112, 114 (D.Me. 1998) ("The plaintiffs certainly are free to send their children to a sectarian school. That is a right protected by the Constitution. The law is clear, however, that they do not have the right to require taxpayers to subsidize that choice") (citations omitted). In the Maine state court litigation, one dissenting judge would have upheld the equal protection claim on behalf of parents. See *Bagley v. Raymond School Dept.,* 728 A.2d 127, 147 (Me. 1999).

3. See Stanley I. Benn, "Egalitarianism and the Equal Consideration of Interests," in *Equality: Selected Readings,* ed. Louis P. Pojman and Robert Westmoreland (New York, 1997), 112; Ronald Dworkin, *A Matter of Principle* (Cambridge, Mass., 1985), 191 ("there is broad agreement within modern politics that the government must treat all its citizens with equal concern and respect").

4. See, e.g., *Califano v. Westcott,* 443 U.S. 76, 85 (1979) (welfare benefits); *Maher v. Roe,* 432 U.S. 464, 468–70 (1977) (medical care); *United States Dep't of Agric. v. Moreno,* 413 U.S. 528, 537 (1973) (food stamps); *Weber v. Aetna Casualty & Sur. Co.,* 406 U.S. 164, 168 (1972) (workmen's compensation benefits); *Levy v. Louisiana,* 391 U.S. 68, 72 (1968) (right of action for wrongful death of parent); *Brown v. Board of Education,* 347 U.S. 483, 493 (1954) ("Such an opportunity [for an education], where the state has undertaken to provide it, is a right which must be made available to all on equal terms").

5. Michael W. McConnell, "The Selective Funding Problem: Abortions and Religious Schools," *Harvard Law Review* 104 (1991): 1017.

6. See James G. Dwyer, "The Children We Abandon: Religious Exemptions to Child Welfare and Education Laws as Denials of Equal Protection to Children of Religious Objectors," *North Carolina Law Review* 74 (1996): 1321–1478, 1394–96.

7. Indeed there is a logical symmetry between saying, as many supporters of vouchers do in discussing the "primary effect" prong of the Establishment Clause analysis, that the state is not responsible for the effects of vouchers on religious schools because parents' choice of schools shifts the locus of responsibility to parents, and saying in considering fairness to parents that the state is not responsible for the effects on parents' pocketbook that its declining to provide vouchers has. Parents' choice of schools shifts the locus of responsibility to parents in the latter context as well.

8. Libertarians might retort that the government ought not to operate any programs for which there can be private analogues, because government should be limited to pursuing aims that cannot be accomplished by private endeavor. This is not the prevailing view of government in this nation; most people want the government to provide health insurance for the poor and elderly, police protection, workers' compensation, and common schooling. My point is that the government would not

be able to do these and numerous other things that most people want it to do if it also had to finance private alternatives in every religious community that asserted a religious basis for opting out of the government program. The libertarian objection provides no support for the position that when government *does* undertake to advance certain secular aims through its own programs (even though private enterprises could also advance these aims), then it must also fund private alternatives.

9. Commentators find little support on the Supreme Court today for the "unconstitutional conditions" doctrine, which says that in some circumstances it is impermissible for the state to condition receipt of public benefits on a willingness to forgo exercise of one's constitutional rights. See, e.g., Alan Brownstein, "Evaluating School Voucher Programs through a Liberty, Equality, and Free Speech Matrix," *Connecticut Law Review* 31 (1999): 897–98 ("While parents and schools may argue that some of the regulations imposed on schools receiving vouchers constitute unconstitutional conditions, the utility of this contention under recent authority is limited at best. Within the confines of a funded program, government appears to have substantial discretion to control the activities of the project receiving a subsidy. It is not clear why vouchers should operate any differently than direct grants in this regard"); Brooks R. Fudenberg, "Unconstitutional Conditions and Greater Powers: A Separability Approach," *University of California at Los Angeles Law Review* 43 (1995): 375–76. However, this perception might simply reflect the type of case the Court sees, which is far different from that hypothesized here, typically involving conditions clearly tied to the legitimate state objectives underlying the program of aid. In those more ordinary cases, the Court is generally unwilling to compel exemptions. For further discussion of this doctrine in the voucher context, see James G. Dwyer, "School Vouchers: Inviting the Public into the Religious Square," *William and Mary Law Review* 42 (2001): 1002–4.

10. Of course, it might well be that the state is not giving enough money to the public schools and that with greater funding the public schools would provide a good education. But this possibility does not undermine the parents' objection that the state is giving some money to schools that are currently inadequate. The parents might argue that the state should either spend enough on the public schools to make them good or help parents afford a good private school.

11. However, the areas in which the public schools are worst are the areas in which the government takes the smallest amount of money from parents, because they are areas where parents have the least to give—namely, the poorest urban and rural areas. See Jonathan Kozol, *Savage Inequalities* (New York, 1991).

12. See *Church of Lukumi Babalu Aye, Inc. v. Hialeah*, 508 U.S. 520, 531–34 (1993).

13. For discussion of the Supreme Court's criteria for identifying suspect classifications, see Dwyer, "Children We Abandon," 1393–96. The Supreme Court's decision in *Lukumi Babalu* suggests that strict scrutiny would be in order under the Free Exercise Clause if the government imposed regulatory *burdens* only on religious organizations, at least if the government's intent was to suppress religious practice per se. 508 U.S. at 533. It is not clear that the Court would say the same of excluding religious groups from benefits, or whether the Court would say a government motive of avoiding Establishment Clause problems either obviates concerns about seeking to suppress religion or provides a compelling justification for infringing free exercise rights. Certainly the Court's own decisions disallowing state support for religious instruction and worship per se suggest that it does not view all targeting of religious practice for special treatment as illicit.

14. See, e.g., Stephen L. Carter, "Parents, Religion, and Schools: Reflections on *Pierce*, Seventy Years Later," *Seton Hall Law Review* 27 (1997): 1204–5 (voicing an objection to regulation of religious schools based on a supposed First Amendment right to the survival of existing religions).

15. See, e.g., Michael Stokes Paulsen, "A Funny Thing Happened on the Way to the Limited Public Forum: Unconstitutional Conditions on 'Equal Access' for Religious Speakers and Groups," *University of California at Davis Law Review* 29 (1996): 714–15.

16. See Dwyer, "Children We Abandon," 1347–48.

17. For a different and more philosophically developed approach to establishing a right of children to educational equality in the context of school choice, see Harry Brighouse, *School Choice and Social Justice* (New York, 2000), chaps. 6 and 7. Michael McConnell also suggests a kind of unfair-

ness argument on behalf of children when he asserts that, in the absence of vouchers, "religious schoolchildren are required to pay twice." McConnell, "Selective Funding Problem," 1019. What he means is that these children must pay now for religious school (indirectly, through their parents), and then will also have to pay taxes for public schooling throughout adulthood even though they did not receive a public education themselves. I view the unfairness in terms of not so much money paid as developmental interests sacrificed, as a result of either inferior schooling or lack of family resources for extracurricular learning activities. This loss is a much greater harm and therefore a much stronger basis for a claim of unfairness on behalf of children.

18. 347 U.S. 483, 493 (1954).

19. See, e.g., *Clark v. Jeter*, 486 U.S. 456 (1988) (invalidating on equal protection grounds a state statute that imposed a limitation period on the ability of children born out of wedlock to establish paternity); *Trimble v. Gordon*, 430 U.S. 762 (1977) (holding that a state statute entitling legitimate children, but not illegitimate children, to a distribution of intestate property violated the Equal Protection Clause); *Weber v. Aetna Casualty and Surety Co.*, 406 U.S. 164 (1972) (holding unconstitutional a state statute precluding illegitimate children from bringing workers' compensation claims on behalf of a deceased father).

20. 406 U.S. 164 (1972).

21. 411 U.S. 1 (1973).

22. See Karen Swenson, "School Finance Reform Litigation: Why Are Some State Supreme Courts Activist and Others Restrained?" *Albany Law Review* 63 (2000): 1147–82.

23. See Dwyer, "Children We Abandon," 1465–76.

24. See *Ohio Association of Independent Schools v. Goff*, 92 F.3d 419, 421–22 (6th Cir. 1996) (citing cases).

25. See *Rodriguez*, 411 U.S. 1, 27–28 (1973).

26. See Dwyer, "Children We Abandon," 1390–91. I argued in that article, however, that children of "religious objectors" to mainstream child-rearing norms should be treated as a quasi-suspect class, in light of a history of disregard for the distinct interests of those children, as well as their political powerlessness. Ibid., 1393–1412. Children in type B schools would be included in that class. It is less clear, though, that any children in type A schools would fit into that category.

27. Ibid., 1391–93.

28. Cases involving education-related benefits in which the Court has declined to provide heightened scrutiny are distinguishable either on the basis of the relative insignificance of the benefit in question in those cases (e.g., a $93 transportation fee) or on the basis of how classifications were drawn (e.g., by political units rather than by groups of schools within a political unit). For a full discussion of precedent on this issue, see Dwyer, "Children We Abandon," 1414–22.

29. 457 U.S. 202, 223–24 (1982).

30. 347 U.S. 483, 493 (1954).

Chapter 7. An Introduction to the Real World

1. See Lisa Kelly, "Yearning for Lake Wobegon: The Quest for the Best Test at the Expense of the Best Education," *Southern California Interdisciplinary Law Journal* (1998): 41–79; Linda Darling-Hammond and Beverly Falk, "Using Standards and Assessments to Support Student Learning," *Phi Delta Kappan* (November 1997): 190–99; Frank Smith, *Insult to Intelligence: The Bureaucratic Invasion of Our Classrooms* (Portsmouth, N.H., 1986), 129–68.

2. For a fuller general description of these and other Fundamentalist Christian schools, as well as Catholic schools, see James G. Dwyer, *Religious Schools v. Children's Rights* (Ithaca, 1998), chap. 1, 13–44. Primary sources for the description here of Fundamentalist schools include Edward T. Babinsky, *Leaving the Fold: Testimonies of Former Fundamentalists* (Amherst, N.Y., 1995); David C. Berliner, "Educational Psychology Meets the Christian Right: Differing Views of Children, Schooling, Teaching, and Learning," *Teachers College Record* 98, no. 3 (1997): 381–416; Alfred

Darnell and Darren E. Sherkat, "The Impact of Protestant Fundamentalism on Educational Attainment," *American Sociological Review* 62 (1997): 306–15; Peter P. Deboer, *The Wisdom of Practice: Studies of Teaching in Christian Elementary and Middle Schools* (Lanham, Md., 1989); Ed Doerr and Albert J. Menendez, "Should Dollars Subsidize Bigotry?" *Phi Delta Kappan* (October 1992): 165–67; Mary Beth Gehrman, "Reading, Writing, and Religion," *Free Inquiry* (fall 1987): 12–18; Paul F. Parsons, *Inside America's Christian Schools* (Macon, Ga., 1987); Alan Peshkin, "Fundamentalist Christian Schools: Should They Be Regulated?" *Education Policy* 3 (1989): 45–56; Alan Peshkin, *God's Choice: The Total World of a Fundamentalist Christian School* (Chicago, 1986); Susan D. Rose, *Keeping Them Out of the Hands of Satan: Evangelical Schooling in America* (London, 1988); Melinda Ballar Wagner, *God's Schools: Choice and Compromise in American Society* (New Brunswick, N.J., 1990); and Marlene Winell, *Leaving the Fold: A Guide for Former Fundamentalist Christians and Others Leaving Their Religion* (Oakland, Calif., 1993).

3. The U.S. Department of Education regularly collects and publishes data on private schools and breaks down aggregate figures for number of schools and students into religious and nonreligious categories and into broad denominational classes within the religious school category. It recently calculated that roughly 700,000 students, or 14 percent of all private school pupils and 16 percent of all pupils in religious schools, are in "Conservative Christian" schools, which is the department's term for Fundamentalist Christian schools. Another 450,000 students, or 9 percent of all private school pupils and 11 percent of all students in religious schools, are in "unaffiliated" religious schools, a large but uncertain percentage of which are also Fundamentalist Christian. See National Center for Education Statistics (NCES), *Private School Universe, 1995–96* (Washington, D.C., 1998), 5. I thus assume here that a total of 1 million students, or 20 percent of all private school pupils and nearly 25 percent of all religious school pupils, are in Fundamentalist Christian schools. The department does not identify which Christian schools are self-paced curriculum schools. I assume here that one-third of Fundamentalist Christian schools are self-paced curriculum schools, which one author believed to be the case fifteen years ago. See Paul F. Parsons, *Inside America's Christian Schools* (Macon, Ga., 1987), 41. Other Fundamentalist Christian schools operate formally like the typical public or private school, in the sense that students are separated by grade level and given instruction by a teacher. Catholic schools enroll roughly half of all pupils who attend religious schools. See NCES, *Private School Universe*, 5.

4. In Fundamentalist schools that do have teachers, the teachers generally have little or no formal training in teaching, no preservice or inservice training, no staff development programs, and no continuing teacher education. Thus, even if they wished to instill higher-order thinking skills in their students, which they do not, they likely would not be capable of doing so. See Linda Darling-Hammond, "Educating Teachers for the Next Century: Rethinking Practice and Policy," in *The Education of Teachers*, ed. Gary A. Griffin (Chicago, 1999), 221 ("The kind of pedagogy needed to help students to think critically, create, and solve complex problems as well as to master ambitious subject matter content is much more demanding than that needed to impart routine skills. . . . Only very knowledgeable and skillful teachers who are able to respond differentially and appropriately to students' needs can enable diverse learners to succeed at these much more challenging learning goals"). In addition, numerous Christian schools have only one teacher, and these teachers will also lack the benefits that can be derived from teacher interaction—collaborative curriculum development, observation and critique of teaching, and exchange of information.

5. Sources for the following composite description of curricular materials used in Fundamentalist Christian schools, include Frances R. A. Paterson, "Teaching Intolerance: Anti-Catholic Bias in Voucher-Supported Schools," *The Educational Forum* 64 (winter 2000): 139–49; Frances R. A. Paterson, "Building a Conservative Base: Teaching History and Civics in Voucher-Supported Schools," *Phi Delta Kappan* 82 (2000): 150–55; Frances R. A. Paterson, " 'Supreme Court: Enemy of Freedom?': Constitutional Law in Christian School Textbooks," *Journal of Law and Education* 29 (2000): 405–31; Albert J. Menendez, *Visions of Reality: What Fundamentalist Schools Teach* (New York, 1993) Cathy Speck and David Prideaux, "Fundamentalist Education and Creation Science," *Australian Journal of Education* 37 (1993): 279–95; Dan B. Fleming and Thomas C. Hunt, "The

World as Seen by Students in Accelerated Christian Education Schools," *Phi Delta Kappan* 66 (March 1987): 518–23; Bette J. Krenzke et al., "Curriculum Materials: An Evaluation," *Lutheran Education* 121 (March / April 1986): 196–203.

6. Meira Levinson, *The Demands of Liberal Education* (Oxford, 1999), 60.

7. Harry Brighouse, *School Choice and Social Justice* (Oxford, 2000), 75.

8. Michael S. Pritchard, *Reasonable Children: Moral Education and Moral Learning* (Lawrence, Kan., 1996), 58 (quoting Peter Facione, ed., "Report on Critical Thinking," American Philosophical Association Subcommittee on Pre-College Philosophy, University of Delaware [1989], 3). On the importance of critical thinking skills, see also Elliot W. Eisner, "The Uses and Limits of Performance Assessment," *Phi Delta Kappan* (May 1999), and Linda Darling-Hammond, *The Right to Learn: A Blueprint for School Reform* (San Francisco, 1997).

9. See Fleming and Hunt, "The World as Seen by Students in Accelerated Christian Education Schools," *Phi Delta Kappan* (March 1987): 523 ("If parents want their children to obtain a very limited and sometimes inaccurate view of the world—one that ignores thinking above the level of rote recall—then the ACE materials do the job very well. The world of the ACE materials is quite a different one from that of scholarship and critical thinking"); Krenzke et al., "Curriculum Materials," 196 ("Instructional strategies do not accurately reflect current child development theories"), 203 ("The aim of these materials seems to be to the Bible . . . ; to indoctrination, not education; to transmission, not inquiry"). In fact, a representative for the company that produces Accelerated Christian Education workbooks even stated that "ACE does not necessarily embrace philosophical beliefs compatible with those of most contemporary secular writers of curriculum," and that the ACE "curriculum provides what we believe to be adequate opinion-forming rhetoric." Ronald E. Johnson, "ACE Responds," *Phi Delta Kappan* (March 1987): 520. See also Darnell and Sherkat, "Impact of Protestant Fundamentalism," 313 ("fundamentalist orientations significantly retard educational attainment").

10. Regarding the substantive content of a good education, see generally E. D. Hirsch, *The Schools We Need and Why We Don't Have Them* (New York, 1996).

11. Some supporters of religious schooling contend that religious schools better instill a sense of responsibility in youth, which is important to their success in life. This may be true to some degree, but it is unlikely to be so for schools that promote dogmatism and unthinking compliance with norms, because these are incompatible with responsibility, properly understood. Responsibility means "high-quality compliance with norms—thoughtful compliance oriented toward achieving the objective of the norm or meeting one's obligations to others rather than toward avoidance of blame or superficial conformity" and entails "flexible adjustment to changing conditions." Carol A. Heimer and Lisa R. Staffen, *For the Sake of the Children: The Social Organization of Responsibility in the Hospital and the Home* (Chicago, 1998), 6–7. See also Michael Pritchard's discussion of reasonableness, in *Reasonable Children*, chap. 1.

12. For references to evidence that these harms do occur and discussion of their likely long-term consequences, see Dwyer, *Religious Schools*, 20–44.

13. For a summary of the regulatory environment in which public schools in this country operate, see James G. Dwyer, "The Children We Abandon: Religious Exemptions to Child Welfare and Education Laws as Denials of Equal Protection to Children of Religious Objectors," *North Carolina Law Review* 74 (1996): 1329–38.

14. See Christian Smith, *American Evangelicalism: Embattled and Thriving* (Chicago, 1998), 139 (reporting results of study showing that a majority of Evangelicals and Fundamentalists view public schools as hostile to their values).

15. See Dwyer, *Religious Schools*, 22–44.

16. Authority for the description of private school regulation that follows can be found in Dwyer, "Children We Abandon," 1338–43.

17. See Neal Devins, "Fundamentalist Christian Educators v. State: An Inevitable Compromise," *George Washington Law Review* 60 (1992): 822, 833–34.

18. W.S.A. 118.165(1)(d) (2001).

19. Ibid.

20. See W.S.A. 119.23 (2001).

21. 42 U.S.C. § 2000d (2000) provides: "No person in the United States shall, on the ground of race, color, or national origin, be excluded from participation in, be denied the benefits of, or be subjected to discrimination under any program or activity receiving Federal financial assistance."

22. W.S.A. 119.23(7)(c) (2001) provides: "A private school may not require a pupil attending the private school under this section to participate in any religious activity if the pupil's parent or guardian submits to the pupil's teacher or the private school's principal a written request that the pupil be exempt from such activities."

23. W.S.A. 119.23(7)(a) (2001).

24. See Wis. Admin. Code chap. PI 35 (2001).

25. See Catherine Barnett Alexander, "Private School Daze: Privatization Comes to the Classroom As School Vouchers Drain Students—and Jobs—from Public Schools," *Public Employee* 63, no. 1 (1998): 18–20.

26. State Superintendent of Wisconsin Department of Public Instruction to the Governor, Members of the Wisconsin Senate, and Members of the Wisconsin Assembly, memorandum, February 14, 2001, "DPI Responsibilities in the Administration of the Milwaukee Parental Choice Program," available at http://www.dpi.state.wi.us/dpi/dfm/sms/pdf/mpcpaper.pdf.

27. Ohio R.C. 3301.14, 3301.16, 3321.07; Ohio Admin. Code 3301–35–08.

28. Ohio R.C. 3313.976(A)(3) (2001).

29. See Scott Stephens and Mark Vosburgh, "Murderer on Staff of State-Funded Private School: Building's Windows Broken, Lead Paint Flakes Off Wall," *Cleveland Plain Dealer,* July 1, 1999, 1A.

30. Ohio R.C. 3313.976, 3313.977 (2000).

31. See Susan T. Zelman, Editorial: "A Plan to Make Schools Safe, Accountable," *Cleveland Plain Dealer,* July 13, 1999, 9B.

32. See Ohio Admin. Code §§ 3301–35–01 to 07 and 3301–35–11 to 12 (2001).

33. See Ohio Admin. Code § 3301–35–12(A).

34. See Ohio R.C. §§ 3301.16, 3301.0710(B), and 3313.612; Ohio Admin Code § 3301–13–01(A)(27).

35. Fla. Stat. §§ 232.0315 (health examinations), 232.032 (immunizations), 229.808, 232.021; Fla. Admin. Code Ann. R. 6A-1.09512 (2001).

36. See Fla. Stat. §§ 229.0537(4), (5), 229.57(3), 229.591 (2001).

37. The one requirement that might appear to impose significant constraints on how participating schools operate—conformity with the standards of an accrediting body—is an empty requirement. Any private entity, including the publishers of the Fundamentalist self-paced curriculum kit, can call itself an accrediting body and accredit on whatever basis it chooses.

38. See Fla. State § 229.57 (2001).

39. The testing requirement would have an indirect effect if test results were published and if parents' choice of schools were affected by the test results. However, where parents share the school's aim of thwarting rather than fostering higher-order cognitive skills as a means of ensuring that offspring remain believers (and one would expect that they generally do), poor results on such tests might actually encourage parents to continue sending their children to the school.

40. See, e.g., Arkansas HB 2275, Sec. 12(b) (1999); Georgia HB 195 (1999); Kansas HB 2462 (1999); Louisiana SB 1115 (1999); Missouri HB 937 (1999).

Chapter 8. A Moral Assessment of Existing Voucher Programs

1. The Florida program restricts participation to students who would leave the worst public schools in the state, so it presumably would not be true in Florida that vouchers would result in transplanting children from public schools that succeed substantially in providing a good secular education. However, children in Florida might still be transplanted to private schools that do not even aim to provide a good secular education. The Milwaukee and Cleveland programs do not require that

voucher students be leaving a failing public school. They respond to aggregate data about public schools in an entire school district, and the data suggest widespread failure, but the aggregate data do not demonstrate that every public school in the district is doing poorly; some might be doing quite well.

2. See Dwyer, *Religious Schools v. Children's Rights* (Ithaca, 1998), chap. 1.

3. 413 U.S. 465 (1973).

4. See James G. Dwyer, "The Children We Abandon: Religious Exemptions to Child Welfare and Education Laws as Denials of Equal Protection to Children of Religious Objectors," *North Carolina Law Review* 74 (1996): 1335–38 (citing studies), and Yisrael Rich and Roni Golan, "Career Plans for Male-Dominated Occupations among Female Seniors in Religious and Secular High Schools," *Adolescence* 27 (1992): 73.

5. I elaborate on the grounds for and proper limitations on children's intellectual rights in Dwyer, *Religious Schools*, chap. 6.

6. *Norwood v. Harrison*, 413 U.S. 455, 465 (1973).

7. On the importance, nature, and preconditions for reasonableness, see generally Michael S. Pritchard, *Reasonable Children: Moral Education and Moral Learning* (Lawrence, Kan., 1996). Pritchard characterizes reasonableness as a social disposition that entails, among other things, respect for others, preparedness to take into account the interests and views of others and have one's own views be influenced by them, and an inclination to think critically about one's own views and others' and to deliberate rationally and objectively with others about matters of importance. Ibid., 3–7.

8. See Ibid., 3–14. It is readily apparent that the school described in Chapter 7 does not do these things, and that it in fact does the opposite. This is true of some other types of religious schools as well.

Chapter 9. Applying Constitutional Principles to Vouchers in the Real World

1. See *Capitol Square Review and Advisory Board v. Pinette*, 515 U.S. 753, 777 (O'Connor, J., concurring) ("the Establishment Clause forbids a State to hide behind the application of formally neutral criteria and remain studiously oblivious to the effects of its actions. . . . [N]ot all State policies are permissible under the Religion Clauses simply because they are neutral in form") (quoted with favor by Souter, Stevens, Ginsburg, and Breyer, JJ., dissenting in *Rosenberger v. Rectors and Visitors of the University of Virginia*, 515 U.S. 819, 878 (1995).

2. Michael W. McConnell, "The Selective Funding Problem: Abortions and Religious Schools," *Harvard Law Review* 104 (1991): 1020.

3. Indeed, one could argue that even public school teachers should be able occasionally to use examples from religious traditions in a literature class or a math class, so long as this did not have the purpose or effect of promoting religious belief. One might think any education impoverished if it ignores religious tradition and texts entirely, since these are so large a part of our culture. If public school teachers were doing this, and their doing so were deemed acceptable, then it would be harder to justify nonsupport for instruction in secular subjects in religious schools simply because they also incorporate references to religious tradition and use of religious texts. However, to avoid a proselytizing effect, public school teachers would probably have to draw from a variety of religious traditions, and one could argue that religious school teachers should likewise be required to give substantial and unbiased treatment to religious traditions other than their own, since otherwise they would be providing a culturally impoverished education.

4. For information on better performance assessment tools, see, e.g., Elliot W. Eisner, "The Uses and Limits of Performance Assessment," *Phi Delta Kappan* (May 1999): 658–60 (and articles by others that follow in the same issue); Sandra Schnitzer, "Designing an Authentic Assessment," *Educational Leadership* 50, no. 7 (1993): 32–35 (discussing McREL assessment model).

5. Alternatively, a state might establish different criteria for different levels of funding. For example, the state could offer vouchers in amounts equal to 50 percent of the per pupil cost of operation, 70 percent, and 90 percent, and establish criteria for each level designed to ensure that the

secular portion of a school's activities is at least equal to the percentage of costs financed. To qualify for receiving 60 percent vouchers, a school would have to present evidence that secular education is 60 sixty percent of all that they do, and so on.

6. See Alan Peshkin, *God's Choice: The Total World of a Fundamentalist Christian School* (Chicago, 1986), 137. Supporters of other types of religious schools, such as Catholic schools, might claim that sexist attitudes and practices of the past have been eliminated from their schools or that they are working on eradicating them. If that is the case, then they should have no objection to a regulation that requires them to do so and compliance with which is a condition of voucher participation.

7. This suggests that the religious exemption contained in Title IX, the federal statute prohibiting gender discrimination in schools receiving federal aid, is unconstitutional, and an offense to the equal personhood of girls in religious schools. See 20 U.S.C. sec. 1681(a)(3) (2000).

Conclusion

1. See, e.g., Luis A. Huerta, "Losing Public Accountability: A Home Schooling Charter," in *Inside Charter Schools: The Paradox of Radical Decentralization,* ed. Bruce Fuller (Cambridge, Mass., 2000), 177–202 (describing clandestine use of charter systems in California to subsidize home schooling); Jay Matthews and Valerie Strauss, "Problems Vex Two Charter Schools: Repairs Eat Funds; Trustees Squabble," *Washington Post,* November 19, 1998, B1; Lynn Schnaiberg, "Charter Schools Struggle with Accountability," *Education Week on the Web* (June 10, 1998), http://www.edweek.org (visited 10/8/2000); Eric Premack, "Charter Schools: A Status Report," *School Business Affairs* (December 1996): 10–15; Finn, Manno, and Beirlein, "Charter Schools in Action: What Have We Learned?)" Center for Education Reform Website, http//www.edreform.com/pubs/hudson1.html (July 1996) (visited 10/8/2000)

2. See Frank R. Kemerer, "School Choice Accountability," in *School Choice and Social Controversy: Politics, Policy, and Law,* eds. Stephen D. Sugarman and Frank R. Kemerer (Washington, D.C., 1999), 187 (reporting "relatively high failure rate" of schools and fraud in the Milwaukee program, and mismanagement of funds in the Cleveland program).

3. Joseph P. Viteritti, *Choosing Equality: School Choice, the Constitution, and Civil Society* (Washington, D.C., 1999), 60.

4. See Neal Devins, "Fundamentalist Christian Educators v. State: An Inevitable Compromise," *George Washington Law Review* 60 (1992): 825–34 (describing states' inability or unwillingness to overcome Fundamentalist Christians' defiance of court decisions upholding state regulation of their schools).

Index